For Jacqueline

Contents

PART IV
Mobile convergences

List of illustrations

Acknowledgements

I wish to thank Professor Graeme Turner at the Centre for Critical and Cultural Studies, University of Queensland, for his generous and, as always, critically astute, shaping role in this project. I also owe a debt of gratitude to my colleague Andrea Mitchell for her support and keen eye for things mobile.

This book was written while I was the recipient of an Australian Research Fellowship, and I gratefully acknowledge the Australian Research Council for its support.

My ideas about and experience of mobile telecommunications have come from over a decade of direct involvement in policy and regulation. In recent times I have learnt a great deal from various members of the mobiles industry while serving as a public member of the Telephone Information Services Standard Council.

Many of the ideas contained here had their first outing in various academic colloquies, and so my thanks to my esteemed colleagues and hosts at Lingnan University, City University of Hong Kong, Griffith University, the University of New South Wales, and the University of Western Sydney.

I put the finishing touches to this book as I took up a new appointment in the Department of Media and Communications, University of Sydney, and I have appreciated the assistance and goodwill of my colleagues during this transitional period.

At Routledge, Rebecca Barden not only gave this book a gracious welcome but her early feedback was invaluable in the shape it took. I am grateful also to her successor Natalie Foster and other staff for their careful attention.

Most of all I wish to thank my wife Jacqueline Clark, for her unstinting support, proffering of countless items on mobiles, many stimulating and amusing conversations, as well as her invaluable assistance with preparing the text, that have all made this book not only possible but great fun too. Finally I am grateful to our young son Liam, whose acute phenomenology of telephony evokes the sense of wonder this technology and its cultural possibilities still elicit.

Gerard Goggin

The University of Sydney, January 2006

List of abbreviations

AMPS	advanced mobile phone service
AT & T	American Telegraph and Telephone Company
CB	citizens band (radio)
CDMA	code division multiple access (digital transmission system)
CMT	car mobile telephone (Finland network)
DVB	digital video broadcasting
DVB-H	digital video broadcasting – handheld
DVB-T	digital video broadcasting – terrestrial
EDGE	enhanced data rates for GSM evolution
FCC	Federal Communications Commission
FM	frequency modulation (radio)
1G	first generation (analogue mobile system)
2G	second generation (digital cellular mobile system)
2.5G	second and a half generation (digital cellular mobile system)
3G	third generation (digital cellular mobile system)
4G	fourth generation (digital cellular mobile system)
GPRS	general packet radio service
GSM	global system for mobiles (originally Groupe Spécial Mobile)
HTML	hypertext markup language
IP	Internet protocol
MMS	multimedia message service
NMT	Nordic mobile telephone
PDA	portable digital assistant
PSTN	public switched telecommunications network
RFID	radio frequency identification
SIM	subscriber information module (card)
SMS	short message service
TDMA	time division multiple access (digital transmission system)
TACS	total access communication systems
UMTS	universal mobile telecommunications service

VoIP   voice over Internet protocol
WAP   wireless access protocol
W-CDMA   wideband code division multiple access
XML   extensible markup language

1 Introduction: what do you mean 'cell phone *culture*'?!

Since its invention in the second half of the nineteenth century, the telephone has become part of the everyday lives of billions of people around the world. By the middle of the twentieth century, talking to other people over telephone lines was a well-established way to keep in touch with friends and family, engage in social activities and organisations, and conduct business – at least in richer countries. At the opening of the twentieth-first century, the fixed telephone had been officially eclipsed – by its mobile counterpart.

Known as the cell phone, especially in the Americas, or the mobile phone, in Europe, Asia, Australasia, Africa and elsewhere, and by many other words in other languages, in roughly two and a half decades of commercial availability this technology has enjoyed a staggering rate of adoption. In 2004 there were an estimated 1,752 billion cell phone subscribers worldwide (up from approximately 91 million in 1995, and 1.158 billion in 2002): that is, 58.5 per cent of total telephone subscribers were using cell phones (ITU 2005a). As you might expect, rates of ownership and use of cell phones vary quite widely. In broad terms, the historically wealthy and powerful countries predominate. The fifty-eight countries in the world classed as low-income account for only a little over 98 million cell phone subscribers (a little over 4 per 100 subscribers). In comparison cell connections number over 775 million for fifty-four high-income countries (approximately 77 per 100 subscribers); some 606 million for fifty-three lower middle-income countries (about 25 per 100 subscribers); and roughly 276 million for thirty-eight upper middle-income countries (or 48 per 100 subscribers) (ITU 2005a).

The so-called emerging markets in Asia are seen as the new locales of the cell phone. Take, for instance, the top ten mobile operators in the world in 2004. A sign of the times was that China Mobile now ranked as the world's biggest operator, followed in descending order by Vodafone, China Unicom, Deutsche Telekom, America Movil, France Télécom, Telefonica (Spain), NTT DoComo (Japan), Verizon (USA), and finally TeliaSonera, the dominant, merged, Finnish and Swedish telecommunications company (ITU 2005b). Asia hosts 709 million of the world's cell phone subscribers, compared to 573 million in Europe, 373 million in the Americas, 77 million in Africa, and only 20 million in Oceania (of which Australia and New Zealand would account for the lion's share). On 2004 figures, China, classed as a lower middle-income country, had 335 million subscribers, at a rate of a little over 25 per 100 potential subscribers. Also acclaimed for its rapidly growing cell phone market is the other current darling of the bourses, India, which has 47 million cell phone subscribers (but only a shade over 4 per 100 subscribers, and so classed as low income for these ITU statistical purposes) (ITU 2005a).

While these numbers on the distribution of cell phones reveal much variation and concentration, nonetheless it is safe to observe that in the mere two and a half decades since it was first marketed commercially, the cell phone has become much more than a device for voice calls – it has become a central cultural technology in its own right. Telecommunications has undergone a radical shift from being about voice (or fax) communications to becoming: mobile; flexible and customisable; associated with a person rather than a household (at least in some societies and situations); and a communications and services hub. Cell phones, mobile technologies, and wireless networks play an indispensable role in the everyday lives of consumers. A bewildering and proliferating range of cultural activities revolve around cell phones: staying in constant contact, text messaging, fashion, identity-construction, music, mundane daily work routines, remote parenting, interacting with television programs, watching video, surfing the Internet, meeting new people, dating, flirting, loving, bullying, mobile commerce, and locating people. Cell phones have come to be associated with qualities of mobility, portability, and customisation. They fit into new ways of being oneself (or constructing identity and belonging to a group); new ways of organising and conducting one's life; new ways of keeping in touch with friends, romantic intimates, and family; new ways of conducting business; new ways of accessing services or education.

At the same time, mobile devices are of intense economic and political interest because they are at the centre of the vast transformation in communication and media summed up by the rubric of 'convergence', or 'digital technology' or 'new media'. Cell phones are being integrated into television – in voting on programs like *Big Brother* or *Idol*, as well as picture and video downloads, as well as directly into digital broadcasting systems themselves. Wireless Internet has wide-reaching implications. Mobiles have become hybrid devices that articulate with other new technologies such as digital cameras, portable digital assistants, or location technologies. Third-generation (3G) and fourth-generation (4G) cell phones promise finally to realise ubiquitous and personal video communications.

Telephones have had something of an invisible presence in society and culture, but with the advent of cell phones the role of telecommunications has become much more central and harder to ignore. In this book, I explore the *cultural* dimension of cell phones and mobile telecommunication technologies generally.

Cultural treatments of telecommunications are still comparatively rare, but in the case of the cell phone such an investigation is essential. Not only have cell phones developed their own 'little' cultures of consumption and use that – though sometimes disparaged – merit and indeed require reflection; we need to grasp and debate the place of cell phones and mobile technologies in our larger cultural settings, interpreting what they signify, what people are doing with and around these devices, and what the implications of all this are for understanding culture at the most general level. Before we turn to considering how to approach cell phone culture, I would like to review briefly the main traditions of studying telecommunications in the humanities and social sciences.

Phone studies

Surprisingly, the telephone has been neglected by scholars of society and culture. Since Ithiel de Sola Pool lamented such inattention, in his pioneering 1977 collection on *The Social Impact of the Telephone* (de Sola Pool 1977), there has been some important work on the telephone from different perspectives and disciplines through the 1980s and 1990s. Leaving aside the vast number of technical and scientific studies, there has been an increasing amount of work on the economics of telecommunications as well as legal, policy, and regulatory aspects, especially with the transformations from the 1970s with new markets, forms of governance and regulation, and technological innovation. There have been important psychological and linguistic studies. The interest in the telephone and telecommunications among sociologists (and anthropologists) also grew. In the early 1990s a number of important studies of gender and telecommunications were published (Martin 1991; Moyal 1992; Rakow 1993). Studies have charted the development, history, and characteristics of the telephone and telecommunications in many countries (an exemplar being Fischer 1992). Study of the telephone and telecommunications has for some time been a respectable if speciality interest in disciplines such as communications (for instance, Katz 1999) and media studies, but little work has been undertaken by cultural theorists and scholars (one early exception being Ronel 1989).

With the liberalisation of telecommunications in the 1990s, and the growing centrality of telecommunications technologies and networks to other convergent media, social issues become of interest to policymakers internationally, with much debate and some research also. Important social and policy concepts in telecommunications had achieved acceptance with decades of monopoly delivery by unified state administrations (called PTTs, standing for posts, telegraph and telephone) around the world through the twentieth century. Taken-for-granted ideas such as universal service (or the notion that all citizens in a nation-state should have access to a telephone wherever they lived) were being challenged and transformed with the dismantling of monopolies, with privatisation of national telecommunications carriers, with so-called deregulation and the introduction of competition in equipment manufacture and network operation. Much research was commissioned and funded by government, regulators, industry, and funding bodies to provide knowledge about the use of telecommunications, especially evolving new services, as well as to inform or intervene in fierce debates about the reforms and new telecommunications regimes.

As well as a greater appreciation of the social centrality of telecommunications to communications and everyday life, what slowly emerged too through the 1990s was a realisation that telecommunications was becoming central to questions of culture. As telecommunications networks became more complex, not least with their symbiotic relationship with the Internet and other online communications, and the use of cell phones for voice communications rapidly grew during the 1990s, the relative 'invisibility' of the telephone as both social object and a cultural technology could no longer be ignored. While there were some important inquiries into cell phones in the early to mid-1990s, especially the co-ordinated work carried out in Europe (well summarised in Haddon 2004), it was not until Kopomaa's pioneering *The City in Your Pocket* (2000), and then in 2002 the appearance in the same year of Plant's *On the Mobile* (commissioned by Motorola), Katz and Aakhus's edited collection *Perpetual Contact*, and Brown, Green, and Harper's anthology *Wireless World*, that comprehensive systematic scholarly work on the cell phone started to become available.

One of the interesting things about this work on mobiles is the comparative, cross-cultural aspirations shown. In recognition, no doubt, of the near simultaneous appearance and rapid adoption of the cell phone in many different countries, studies of the cell phone (or mobile society studies) have tended to be mindful of the national and social contexts of use. Recently, there has been a torrent of work on the cell phone pouring forth. As well as countless journal articles, there have been a number of important books, though mainly, to date, edited collections (interestingly enough), as an international epistemic community of engaged mobiles scholars has emerged. A central focus, still, has been the social dimensions of the cell phone, represented best perhaps by Rich Ling's *The Mobile Connection* (2004). There has also been keen interest in the implications of cell phones for communication (Nyíri 2003a). An abiding concern for scholars has been how the cell phone is implicated in the redrawing of boundaries between the private and the public, the subject of many discussions (in which Erving Goffman's work often reappears) but especially Ling and Pedersen's 2005 collection *Mobile Communications*. Text messaging has been a fascination in its own right, with one book-length study (Kasesniemi 2003) and two dedicated collections (Glotz and Bertschi 2005; Harper, Palen, and Taylor 2005). Important studies of the cell phone and work have emerged from different places but especially the computer-supported co-operative work tradition (see contributions to Brown, Green and Harper 2002; and Ling and Pedersen 2005 in particular). The Hungarian philosopher Kristóf Nyíri has convened a series of symposia and subsequent collections on important political and social concepts and institutions, such as mobile democracy (2002), mobile learning (2003b), mobiles and place (2005). The relationships among social and cultural contexts, use and design have received some attention (for instance in a number of contributions to Harper, Palen, and Taylor 2005, Lindholm, Keinonen, and Kiljander 2003, Taylor and Harper 2003). Despite the great public concern over the psychological and linguistic aspects of mobiles, these have been two of 'several dimensions of the work on mobile telephony . . . not . . . as completely developed [as others]' (according to Ling and Pedersen, who include a section of useful studies on each of these; 2005: v). There has been significant work undertaken by anthropologists; two good examples are both concerned with text messaging, namely Bella Elwood-Clayton's 2003 and 2005 ethnographic work on SMS in the Philippines and Taylor and Harper's work on the gift and texting (Taylor and Harper 2002; Berg, Taylor, and Harper 2005).

As this selective and partial rendering of the exponentially growing literature on cell phones illustrates there is now a wealth of studies, analysis and debate in this area, though it is quite recent. Yet there is also much work to be done, and many conversations and debates to be had. My assessment of the work on cell phones is that we do have substantial discussions, if still largely fragmentary and incomplete, of how existing and new social structures, relationships, and behaviours have incorporated and been changed by cell phones. Thus far sociology has played an important role in studying cell phones. I also think there has been considerable study and debate on important aspects of communication and cell phones. There is recurrent public fascination and some scholarly work on how people communicate with cell phones, and to what extent – a recurring theme in new technologies and communicative practices – modes and patterns of communication have fundamentally shifted; or whether, in fact, the cell phone, like the Internet, has brought long-lived, fundamental aspects of human communication to the surface. It still remains very unclear – and is probably quite unlikely – that the nature of communication radically changed with the use of cell phones, and of course this is a large and philosophically testing question.

It seems to me that there are two important aspects of cell phones that merit sustained inquiry at this juncture. First, I think that *cultural* aspect of cell phones has been underexplored. While there have been quite some studies attentive to cross-cultural context, there has been little work that systematically explores local or international cell phone culture, and its implications for general accounts of culture. In particular, I think there has been a lack of recognition and analysis of how power relations and structures shape cell phone culture. Here international cultural studies have something to contribute with their historical and still current preoccupation with the inescapable constitution of culture through power. Secondly, an important way to approach inquiry into the nature of cell phone communication is to take the medium itself seriously. As Marshall McLuhan wittily pointed out, the message cannot so simply be extricated from the medium that bears it. Intimately related to the matter of the medium – or media – are questions of culture. Communication is embedded in media, and ultimately too in the elusive yet nurturing realm of culture. To date, cell phone and mobile technologies studies may have not needed to consider the media dimension of cell phones. However, as the cell phone moves centre stage as a device criss-crossed by media flows and cultural forms and content, borrowing and cross-fertilising from audio and radio cultures, television cultures, print cultures, Internet and other new media cultures, and is increasingly regarded as a mobile medium, media studies approaches are likely to be very helpful.

About cell phone culture

In approaching cell phone culture, I begin with the 'circuit of culture' framework devised to theorise another mobile cultural technology, the Sony Walkman (du Gay et al. 1997). The starting point for the 'circuit of culture' approach is the proposition that culture is not merely reflective or expressive of other processes, as though in reductive versions of the Marxist tradition of culture being part of the superstructure of society rather than the economic base. Rather 'culture is now regarded as being constitutive of the social world as economic or political processes' (1997: 2). The task of understanding culture is compelling not just as an exercise in its own right, but rather as a necessary undertaking for understanding social practices and processes:

> The production of social meanings is therefore a necessary precondition for the functioning of all social practices and an account of the cultural conditions of social practices must form part of the sociological explanation of how they work. Cultural description and analysis is therefore increasingly crucial to the production of sociological knowledge.
>
> (1997: 2)

To inquire into culture in late modernity, du Gay et al. take as their case study the Sony Walkman, as a 'typical cultural artefact and medium of modern culture' (2). Their 'biography' of the Walkman seeks to take account of culture's shaping by large, commercial, transnational enterprises. However, rather than just looking at the processes of production, the 'circuit of culture' model 'analyses the biography of a cultural artefact in terms of a theoretical model based on the *articulation* of a number of distinct processes whose interaction can and does lead to variable and contingent outcomes' (3). Following Stuart Hall's definition, an 'articulation' is the

form of the connection that can make a unity of two or more different or distinct elements, under certain conditions. It is a linkage which is not necessary, determined or absolute and essential for all time; rather it is a linkage whose conditions of existence or emergence need to be located in the contingencies of circumstance.

(Hall 1996: 3)

In seeking to explain a cultural artefact, du Gay et al. suggest, the analyst needs to study it through the five major interlinked processes they identify: representation, identity, production, consumption, and regulation: 'Taken together, they complete a sort of circuit . . . through which any analysis of a cultural text or artefact must pass if it is to be adequately studied' (1997: 3). As they note, such an approach has also been suggested by Richard Johnson (1986; cf. Johnson et al. 2004).

The 'circuit of culture' approach exemplified in the *Doing Cultural Studies* book and its accompanying volumes in the Open University series has been widely used for pedagogical purposes. The framework has also been taken up by a number of scholars to study media (Miller et al. 1998) and also new technology. In a rich paper in the *Wireless World* collection, Nicola Green invokes the 'circuit of culture' approach to understand the mobile. Drawing on an analysis of cell phone advertising and marketing, she considers some of the common narratives of use that have been represented. Then she attempts to contrast these with other narratives of use drawn from field-work and observation of mobile users (Green 2002). Green's use of the 'circuit of culture' approach indicates its usefulness, as does its use and critical evaluation in a recent study of the Napster peer-to-peer technology (Taylor et al. 2002).

In considering the 'circuit of culture' approach, we might start with the similarities between the Sony Walkman and the cell phone. Foremost are the novel possibilities for mobility associated with each. For du Gay et al. the 'Sony Walkman is not only part of our culture, it possesses a distinctive "culture" of its own. Around the Walkman there has developed a distinctive set of *meanings* and *practices*' (10). More than this, however, the Walkman:

connects with a distinct set of *social practices* (like listening to music while travelling on the train or the underground, for example) which are specific to our culture or way of life. It is cultural because it is associated with certain *kinds of people* (young people, for example, or music-lovers); with certain *places* (the city, the open air, walking around a museum) – because it has been given or acquired a social profile or *identity*. It is also cultural because it frequently appears in and is represented within our visual languages and media of communication. Indeed, the *image* of the Sony Walkman – sleek, high-tech, function in design, miniaturized – has become a sort of metaphor which stands for or represents a distinctively late-modern, technological culture or way of life. These meanings, practices, images and identities allow us to place, to situate, to decipher and to study the Walkman as a cultural artefact. To study the Sony Walkman 'culturally' is therefore, in part, to use it as a clue to the study of modern culture in general.

(du Gay et al. 1997: 11)

Such claims about the Walkman resonate with the cell phone too. In its turn, the cell phone has become a metaphor for a 'distinctively late-modern, technological culture or way of life' (11). And it is a metonym too, often used as a short-hand for this larger culture. It is fitting then that we study the cell phone to understand the modernities in which we are placed now.

There are resemblances between the Walkman and the cell phone, in thinking about how both are involved in the production of a cultural artefact. One of the important frames of reference for du Gay et al.'s biography of the Walkman is the cluster of meanings that gather around 'Japanese' and 'high technology' and 'modern'. An analogy could be drawn with the Sony Walkman and the Nokia cell phone. Although the US corporation Motorola played an important role in the development of the cellular cell phone in the 1930s through to the 1960s, it is the Finnish corporation Nokia that is most identified with the heyday of the 1990s and 2000s when the cell phone technology rapidly diffused and usage intensified. Nokia was a leader in designing cell phones to make them attractive and customisable. A number of meanings have become associated with Nokia such as cool design, the technical avant-garde reputation of the Nordic countries, and the technological, aesthetic and marketing savvy of a small, highly advanced European country. Nokia and its 'Finnishness' has also attracted much interest for its industrial and commercial success, in a manner reminiscent of the international discourse on Japanese companies, industrial and business culture, and technology from the 1970s onwards. Nokia fascinates business analysts because it is a case of a flagship company in a relatively small country competing worldwide.

However, while Nokia has played a leading role in cell phone culture, it is important to recognise the wider configuration of businesses, industries, communications platforms, services, and networks that have made the cell phone possible. Nokia, for instance, is a handset manufacturer, and it faces considerable competition from other handset manufacturers such as Siemens (Germany), Philips (Netherlands), Motorola (USA), Sony (Japan), Samsung (Korea), not to mention a number of newer, smaller handset developers around the world (often joint-ventures). These firms have also been responsible for many sociotechnical and technocultural innovations in cell phones. It is also important to note that mobile or cell phones are not a stand-alone technology in the way that the Walkman might appear to be. Rather, cell phones are a networked communication device. (In the same way, one of the successor technologies to the Walkman, namely the Apple iPod portable music player, is now reliant on ownership of a computer and, in most cases, Internet access for obtaining music tracks or information about the music) (Fig. 1.1).

In this sense, telecommunications carriers and service providers have very much shaped mobile culture. There are former national telecommunications carriers, such as AT & T, British Telecom, Deutsche Telekom, or France Télécom,

Figure 1.1 The Nokia 3230 – Serious Finds Fun.

which added mobile services to their existing telecommunications services during the 1980s. Then there are new international carriers specialising in cell phones, notably Vodafone (which rose to prominence with second-generation digital GSM cell phones), Hutchison (a pioneer in third-generation cell phones around the world), and emergent giants such as China Mobile. There are also companies which are specialising in mobile resale, or retail, such as Orange, as well as companies such as Virgin Mobile that offer other consumer services (travel and music, for instance), which now are prominent in selling mobile services in a number of countries (as a virtual mobile network operator).

Of course, the existence of the Sony Walkman too is only possible through complex corporate, technology, economic, and social networks – and the various portable music players that have now taken up its mantle (whether iPod, MP3 player, or cell phone with radio or digital music player) bear this out. However, the complexity of the commercial, technical (hardware and software), and regulatory characteristics of the cell phone are not brought together by one company, brand, or technology in the same way as the Walkman.

The cell phone as technology

The differences between the cell phone and the Walkman, and the things about the Walkman that the cell phone retroactively highlights, point to the need to draw upon another body of theory to extend and even reframe the 'circuit of culture' approach. To grasp cell phone culture, we need to understand not only the relationships between society and culture, as highlighted by du Gay et al., but also how these relate to another important concept, technology.

The cell phone is a technology, among the many other technologies that surround and constitute us. We often consider our society to be saturated by technologies of many sorts. Cell phones are often classed among information and communication technologies, and here we observe that, while communication has always been materially embedded and mediated, the importance of new forms of technologies is quite pronounced at the present time, as the use of the Internet, computers, and telecommunications demonstrates. Viewed from another angle, however, we might see cell phones as just one alongside many other technologies for living, whether these be commonly associated with the home (the microwave, vacuum cleaner, television, or baby monitor), transport (global positioning device, combustion or jet engine, railway track), workplace (elevator, computer, office equipment, video surveillance) or other public spaces (technologies to be found in the shopping centre, gymnasium, nightclub, bar, café, restaurant, place of worship, racetrack, and so on).

In the last two decades there has been a great deal of work on technology in the overlapping traditions often called the social studies of science and the social studies of technology. A shared idea in much of this writing has been the social and cultural shaping, or construction, of science and technology (most famously presented in MacKenzie and Wajcman 1985 and 1999). MacKenzie and Wajcman point to the need to investigate empirically how the social shaping of technology takes place:

> If the idea of the social shaping of technology has intellectual or political merit, this lies in the details: in the particular ways technology is socially shaped; in the light these throw on the nature both of 'society' and of 'technology'; in the particular outcomes that result; and in the opportunities for action to improve those outcomes.
>
> (1999: xvi)

In cultural and media studies in particular, one strand of the social studies of science tradition that has attracted considerable attention is actor-network theory. Associated most with the work of Bruno Latour, studies constellated by the rubric of actor-network theory have sought to rethink the binary opposition between machine and human. Latour, for instance, has pointed out that agency is not just exercised by human actors, it is also an attribute of the configurations of technology – and so one needs to consider the influence of non-human actors also. While actor-network theory has been critiqued, not least its account of gender and power (for instance, Wajcman 2004) for my purposes here, I want to highlight two aspects of actor-network theory.

First, actor-network theory characteristically refuses or reworks what it takes to be formulaic oppositions between technology and society, and rather directs our gaze to the manner in which both of these entities are created in tandem with each other. Just as it declines the lures of technological determinism, or the notion that technology exerts an inescapably powerful shaping force on society, so too does actor-network theory demur from the countervailing reaction that society determines technology. Neither technology nor society is taken to be pre-existing, nor is this couplet immutable, and so their mutual implication and creation, and ongoing reinvention and becoming, need to be carefully charted.

Leading on from this, secondly, actor-network theory has a strong anti- or de-essentialist tendency. It does not take a technology as a given, its history or future as stable. Instead, technology exists in networks of things, actors, actants, institutions, investments, and relationships. The fate of a technology – its 'success' or 'failure', or whether it is 'useful' or a 'waste', or a 'white elephant' or something one 'can't live without' – is contingent, depending on many factors that cannot be read off absent or present causes or forces such as 'capital' or 'government' or the inherent brilliance of the idea or invention. Rather a technology needs to be loved, nurtured, and, above all, materially fashioned and supported, as Latour bears out in his classic study *Aramis, or the Love of Technology*

(1996). That is, to be kept alive and working, a technology needs supporters and resources, and active efforts to be made. All of which, in their turn, modify the technology.

From an actor-network approach, we need to be mindful of the multifarious, specific, and ongoing accomplishment that is the cell phone, or, indeed, the various technologies that we group under that heading. Cell phones and other mobile communications devices are a work-in-progress, comprising dynamic networks or assemblages. In appreciating the development and histories of cell phones, we will need to attend to the many people and things these devices have enlisted and to follow these actors as these technologies unfold (as I seek to do in attending to the complexity of histories of text-messaging in chapter 4).

Social studies of technology traditions, such as actor-network theory, have already been usefully brought to bear on the study of cell phones (especially in various contributions represented in Brown, Green, and Harper 2002 and Hamill and Lasen 2005). Take, for instance, Steve Woolgar's provocative and helpful meditation on the relations between theory and technology. Woolgar is keen to decry the 'schematic assumption that we are applying a given theoretical perspective to a fixed, singular and knowable entity: the technology'. Rather he draws upon science and technology studies to emphasise the '*interpretative flexibility* of technology', proposing that:

> the particular form of a technology, its technical capacity and effects are historically and socially contingent. The form and capacity are not given, and, in particular, they cannot be straightforwardly extrapolated from preceding technologies. They are, instead, the upshot of processes of social construction. In short, the technology *could be otherwise*.
>
> (Woolgar 2005: 27)

Woolgar elaborates this 'interpretative flexibility' to forestall any reification of technology as a found, monadic object in the world, countering:

> the view that technology can (or should) be treated like any definite singular object, by stressing that interpretation, reading and making sense of technology are a constant feature of social life. Technologies are not given. They are instead discursive moves in a never ending cacophony of efforts at social ordering . . . [Technologies] are social arrangements rendered material. The social arrangements are thereby blackboxed, the inner workings of which are known only to technical experts, and which in virtue of their material construction attain an apparent robustness, resist deconstruction and endure.
>
> (2005: 29–30)

From Woolgar's formulation here, one can see clearly how such an account of the contingent, social (and cultural too) nature of technology complements (though not necessarily comfortably!) a modified 'circuit of culture' approach.

Technology and culture

To think about the pertinent relations between technology and culture, we might fruitfully compare work on mobiles with that in Internet studies. For instance, Woolgar proposes five rules of mobility, drawn from a similar set of propositions regarding Internet technologies. Among these are two worth mentioning here:

1. the uptake and use of the mobile technologies depend crucially on the local social context . . .
5. the more global the more local!

(2005: 39–40)

As Internet studies has consolidated as a field, and there has been a working through and critiquing of early notions of 'virtuality' and 'cyberspace', there has also been important work on information and communications technologies more broadly that resists both technological and social determinism, in favour of attending to the open-endedness of technology and its constitution in particular local social and cultural contexts. Much work already on mobiles, by comparison, has already incorporated such considerations of the interrelatedness of the global and the local, and the importance of attending to context and its constructions. It has become clear, though, that there needs to be much more documentation and discussion on this point, not least because of the growing cultural importance of mobile technologies.

To be more specific, it is fair to say that thus far scholarly study of cell phones has been dominated by a focus on European and North American examples and assumptions. Work on cell phones in other parts of the world – especially Asia – is now emerging, as it is, rather too slowly, in studies of Internet and other new media. Japan has been of particular interest, owing to the use of cell phones for accessing the Internet during the 1990s (Coates and Holroyd 2003; Funk 2001; Gottlieb and McLelland 2003). Ito, Okabe, and Matsuda's important 2005 collection is not only a rich and sophisticated set of studies for understanding mobiles in Japanese life, it is a model for systematic study of mobiles in general. Mobile use in other Asian countries is now becoming more widely appreciated, with a number of studies on China now published (Yu and Tng 2003). The mobile, as too the Internet, has been mutually implicated in cultural and social change in Asia (Berry, Martin, and Yue 2003). Just as the Internet is clearly internationalising – with the number of English-language speakers, and other European language groups and cultures, being overtaken by Spanish and Chinese, and other language groups – so too the sheer size, scale, and significance of mobile use in the most populous countries especially is difficult for the Anglophone academy and analysts to ignore any longer.

There is a more profound question at stake here also, of how far theories about cell phones developed largely in Europe, the UK and the USA, and with their theoretical and geopolitical bearings in these societies, are adequate for comprehending the take-up and use of these technologies in Asia, Africa, Latin America, and elsewhere; and of how well these grasp the deeper cultural dimensions of different societies. An important question concerns the overarching concept of modernity, and what its relationship is to the cell phone. If it is the case that, from the mid-1980s until the early 2000s, theories of cell phones have been shaped by Western concepts of modernities, how well do these encompass Asian modernities and communication practices, as a 2005 conference theme (Lin 2005b) proposed? How do the social and cultural appropriations in cell phones by different societies and traditions relate to questions of design and templates for use (Pertierra and Koskinen 2006)? If we understand that at various levels theories may be culturally specific, then we cannot assume our ideas about cell phones, conceived in a particular configuration, will travel across cultures without requiring translation, transformation, challenge, disavowal, or abandonment.

There is much scope for cross-referencing, borrowing, and dialogue between Internet studies and mobile studies, in regard to understanding the international character of these technologies and the cultural specificity of their construction and the theories developed to understand these. There is also much urgency in thinking from the point of view of cell phones and mobile technologies, at this historical moment of their framing, about some of the cultural concepts, attributes, and agency crystallised in important concepts in Internet and new media cultures and studies (Goggin 2004; Lovink 2002; Manovich 2001; Marshall 2004). I am thinking here about much meditated, and sometimes much maligned, ideas such as: interactivity, the creative commons; the politics of code; open platforms and software; the consumer-as-producer; peer-to-peer models of cultural exchange; any-to-any communication. With mobile telecommunications being positioned for even greater strategic influence subtending questions of communications, culture, and media, the resources of critical Internet and new media studies have much to offer inquiry into the cultural politics of mobile media.

Setting the scene

My discussion of cell phone culture in what follows is broadly set within the framework I have indicated above. I think it is worthwhile retaining the sense of multiple, connected perspectives in the 'circuit of culture' approach, as it reminds us of the inescapable articulations among spheres that jointly bring a cultural artefact to life. The 'circuit of culture' needs to be opened up, and combined with some important other approaches necessary to understand cell phone culture –

namely, social studies of technologies, Internet and new media studies, and non-Anglophone traditions of cultural and media studies.

Before I give an overview of the book, just two prefatory remarks on style. First, throughout this book I tend to use the term 'cell phone', but sometimes will instead use the description 'mobile phone'. For my purposes I regard these terms as interchangeable but it is important to note that both accent slightly different aspects of this technology (as do the many other terms for cell phones and mobiles in other languages, some of which, for instance, associate the technology with mobility while others associate it with its portability, convenience, or status as an extension of the hand). I will also speak of 'mobile' and 'wireless' 'technologies' and 'devices' to indicate the proliferating range of wireless connected telecommunications, Internet, and indeed media and communications devices that are now often articulated or affiliated with cell phones. Secondly, given the nature of the topic, I have thought it important to summarise key technical features of cell phone and mobile technologies as clearly and concisely as possible, in order that the reader will have the requisite basic information. Hopefully, the non-technically inclined reader will not find such overviews too daunting (or will skip through them), and the technically well-versed reader will forgive me for unavoidable simplifications.

That said, the book contains four main parts: part 1, 'Producing the cell phone'; part 2, 'Consuming the cell phone'; part 3, 'Representing and regulating the cell phone'; and part 4, 'Mobile convergences'.

In part 1, chapter 2 outlines the important features of the early history of the cell phone, and what was significant about making voice communications portable. It looks at the early, commercially oriented deployment of the cell phone in the 1980s, then explores the range of ways that cell phones are routinely used in everyday life now: how the mobile has moved from being the preserve of business people, realtors, builders, and tradesmen, to becoming the prized possession of teenage girls (and boys). Chapter 3 considers the role of image-creation, advertising, and design in creating mobile culture. Here I look at two key case studies that illustrate the cultural design and production of mobile telecommunications. First, I review the role of one of the most important cell phone handset manufacturers, the celebrated Finnish multinational firm Nokia, exemplary in its creation of the mobile as an object of desire. Second, I evaluate the development of mobile networks, their identities and those of their consumers around the world – focusing on the internationally active firm Vodafone.

Part 2 opens with chapter 4, and a discussion of the defining phase of cell phone culture. Text messaging was conceived as a minor aspect of the second-generation digital cellular system, but it was enthusiastically adopted, and created new cultures of use. This chapter provides an overview of text messaging and elucidates the role it plays in cell phone culture. In doing so, I explore text messaging as an intriguing case study in cultural consumption and user experimentation. Chapter 5 looks at how the needs, expectations, and desires of possible users are factored into the design of cell phone technology. It does so via the important case study of people with disabilities. Often overlooked as media users, people with disabilities number approximately half a billion people worldwide. Drawing on critical disability studies, this chapter looks at the consumption of cell phones by people with disabilities and the responses to this by technologists.

In part 3 of the book I turn to the representation and regulation of the cell phone, an important component of the development of cell phone culture. In chapter 6 I chart the various ways in which cell phones have been a subject of public fascination because of their perceived danger. My case studies here include panics around the effects of mobiles on health, cultural values, and literacy and grammar, as well as the 'happy slapping' panic in which deviant young people again figure. In chapter 7, I suggest that cell phones, like the telephone before them, have been associated in popular culture with new possibilities, licit and illicit, for making connections and expressing intimacy. I look at some celebrated instances where unintended effects of cell phones for celebrity romance have captured the popular imagination, such as the British cell phone tapping royal scandals of 'Dianagate' and 'Camillagate', footballer David Beckham's and cricketer Shane Warne's text message affair scandals, and the hacking of Paris Hilton's smart phone.

In the fourth part of the book I survey and interpret new developments in cell phone culture associated with the convergence of technologies. Mobile photography, camera phones, moblogging, and new visual cultures are the subject of chapter 8. Here I theorise this new, culturally significant technology and its appropriations, looking at how camera phones allow anyone to create photographs, edit them, and quickly and easily distribute them across communication networks. I look at how mobile photography is another step in a long, contradictory process of making technologies democratic, or at least demotic. In chapter 9 I chart the mobile's implication in new sites of cultural consumption and production, borrowing and reconfiguring features associated with television and Internet cultures. This is followed in chapter 10, with a discussion of the new area of the development, design, and deployment of 3G and 4G cell phones, and associated technologies, and what their implications are for mobile culture.

As the book documents, the cell phone has recast established communications technologies, but also holds the key to the future of network cultures. In the conclusion, I reflect upon the status that cell phones have as *mobile media*, discussing their centrality for media today and in the near future, and also considering what the implications of this shift are for cultural research and theory, as well as design, policy, and regulation.

Part I
Producing the cell phone

2 Making voice portable: the early history of the cell phone

New Take-Along Telephones Give You Pushbutton Calling to Any Phone Number
. . . Fishing offshore, driving home from work, or riding horse-back – this phone
user could place and receive calls anywhere . . .

(Motorola's DynaTAC gracing the cover of *Popular Science* magazine, quoted in
Murray 2001: 22)

Have we reached the day and age when a key accessory in every schoolkid's
pocket is a mobile phone?

(Gibson 1997)

While it took the domestic telephone approximately thirty years to migrate from
an instrument most often in the hallway of the home in the 1960s, to its ubiquitous position today in the living room, kitchen and bedroom, the mobile telephone
found it way into our pockets in less than half that time.

(Lacohée, Wakeford, and Pearson 2003: 203)

In the nineteenth century, the telegraph emerged as a communication technology
with pervasive implications for the spatial organisation of society, but also how
news, information, and entertainment were circulated (Blondheim 1994; Coe
1993; Hubbard 1965; Kieve 1973); in short an important predecessor to the cell
phone. There was a close relationship between the telegraph and the railways, both
important technologies and infrastructures for communication; one communicating signals, codes, and messages; the other communicating people, goods,
materials, and texts. With the first working mechanical telegraph created by the
Chappe brothers in the 1790s, and the first telegram sent in August 1794, by the
middle of the nineteenth century the telegraph had approximately 5000 km of line
with 354 stations across France (Solymar 1999: 22–31). The French's antagonists
in the Napoleonic wars, the British, responded with an extensive shutter telegraph
system by the time of the Treaty of Paris in 1814 (1999: 34–8). The first commercial electric telegraph, devised by Cooke and Wheatstone, was in operation by
1839, providing communications for railway operations (1999: 52–3; Hubbard

1965). From 1840 to the late 1860s, telegraphy expanded greatly, especially with the laying of submarine channels, pioneered, like commercial telegraphy, by Britain (Headrick 1991: 11–49). By the end of the nineteenth century the telegraphy had become a truly global communications network, intimately involved in the intricacies of global trade and war, colonialism and the intensification of imperialism (Headrick 1991: 50–72) no less than nationalist movements (Livingston 1996).

In the closing years of the century, a new communications technology was developed which displaced the telegraph, and gave today's modern industrialised cities their nervous systems – the telephone. The appearance and rise of the telephone is especially associated with the United States, the scene of Alexander Graham Bell's famous 1877 demonstration, involving songs and conversation between himself located in a Salem lecture hall and his assistant Watson in nearby Boston: 'As I placed my mouth to the instrument it seemed as if an electric thrill went through the audience, and that they recognized for the first time what was meant by the telephone' (Bell quoted in Bruce 1973: 217). The dominant telegraph company Western Union was initially not interested in the new invention, but then did enter the telephone business until their 1879 loss to Bell in a protracted patent case. Bell and his partners continued to defend vigorously its patent rights as well as to consolidate its business, founding American Telephone and Telegraph Company (AT & T) in 1885 (Bruce 1973: 258–87; Garnet 1985; Smith 1985). Eventually, after a period of widespread competition from 1884 to 1912, AT & T was able to achieve legitimacy for its eventual regulated monopoly status under the catch-cry of its president Theodore Vail of 'one system, one policy, universal service' (Mueller 1997).

Though the invention of the telephone was famously credited to Alexander Graham Bell, a number of other individuals and companies around the globe also developed important innovations in this technology. The telephone was an instrument that allowed sound to travel along wires, and so people to use telephones to speak to each other. Telephones were installed in a home or office, and connected by lines – copper wires – to the telephone system. The phone system connected individual subscriber telephones through switches. Initially one picked up the phone, and an operator answered and made the connection with the desired number, opening a circuit between the two telephones for voice communication. Eventually the switching process was automated, electromagnetically, and then become digitalised (that is, through digital technologies and computer software). The term 'telecommunications' was coined in 1932 to designate voice telephony, but also referred to other sorts of communications at a distance over networks. Connected by wires to their networks, telephones were inset in their places in houses, offices, or public payphones. However, the dream of ease of communication in different places, or while on the move, was long nourished. After all, new sorts of mobility had emerged in the late nineteenth and early twentieth centuries, as represented by conveyances such as the automobile.

By 1914, the number of telephone subscribers in the USA had reached 1 per cent of the population, well outstripping most European countries in this period except Sweden and Denmark (Solymar 1999: 111–13). The first reliable figures show that there were 10 million telephones in use worldwide in 1910, with the USA accounting for almost 70 per cent of these: 'The worldwide number of telephones reached the 20 million mark in 1922, the year that Alexander Graham Bell died, the 50 million mark in 1939, and 75 million in 1950' (Huurdeman 2003: 228–9; citing AT & T's *Telephone Statistics of the World*).

There is much to say about the development of the telephone, how communicative and cultural practices and norms emerged, and how voice communication at a distance became an important part of daily life. What I wish to reflect upon briefly are the imagined and actual uses of this novel instrument. It is worth noting that there was a multitude of emotions, affects, and ideas about the telephone, and telephonic communication, both hundreds and thousands of years before its materialisation, but also in the early years before its now customary identity reached a stable form.

Claude S. Fischer's social history of the telephone in the United States bears out that in 'several ways, the telephone industry descended directly from the telegraph industry' (Fischer 1992: 81); for example, key figures in the development, building, and marketing of the telephone industry were formed in the telegraph industry, and many companies involved also shared this lineage. The importance of this lay in the early uses those championing and financing the telephone imagined for this instrument. According to Fischer, the uses conceived by marketers very much revolved around the business uses, modelled on the example of the telegraph: 'the uses for the telephone these men first proposed and then repeated for decades largely replicated those of a printing telegraph: business communiqués, orders, alarms, and calls for services' (1992: 81). Businessmen were the first target of the marketers, as in its 'earliest years the industry paid only secondary attention to marketing residential service' (1992: 67). When the industry did seek to persuade households of the benefits of telephones, it 'emphasized the "business" of the household, the ways in which the telephone could help the affluent household manager accomplish her tasks' (1992: 67).

In contrast the telephone industry did not in general, in the USA at least, envisage or encourage what became one of the most important uses of the telephone: namely, its use for sociability. Early on, for instance, the telephone was used for social and familial contact, and relationships, for 'visiting'. Fischer suggests that:

> Industry leaders long ignored or repressed telephone sociability . . . because social conversations did not fit their understanding of the technology. Feeding these attitudes, no doubt, was the common perception that women made most social calls and their conversations were not serious. That view, in

turn, may have reflected a general close-mindedness towards people different from themselves. Many early telephony company officers, in correspondence or other comments, dismissed immigrants, blacks, and farmers as people who could not use or perhaps could not comprehend the telephone. The dissidents were the ones who suggested that such people . . . were plausible customers.

(1992: 81)

It was not until the 1920s that the use of the telephone for sociality, and its place as in the private, domestic sphere of the household, become an important, accepted focus. The history of the uses of the telephone discerned by Fischer offers instructive lessons for thinking about its mobile successor:

the promoters of a technology do not necessarily know or decide its final uses; that they seek problems or needs for which their technology is the answer, but that consumers themselves develop new uses and ultimately decide what will predominate . . . vendors are constrained not only by its technical and economic attributes but also by an interpretation of its uses that is shaped by its and their histories, a cultural constraint that can persist over many years.

(1992: 85)

There are other forces at work, of course, in the social and cultural shaping of the telephone, as with other technologies. An important dynamic which I touch upon in later chapters is the relationship between representations of technology (not least images, dreams, and fantasies), and embodied practices and uses. Carolyn Marvin provides an important account of discourse about the telegraph, telephone, and electric lamp in Anglo-American culture in the late nineteenth century, and how these new communicative devices and the imagining of their possibilities function as 'vehicles for navigating social territory in the late nineteenth century' (Marvin 1988: 8). For Marvin, this is evidence of the 'process of social adjustment around new technology' (233) and the 'history of continuous concern about how new media rearrange and imperil social relationships' (235).

There is a great deal more to be said about how the telephone developed its cultural and social arrangements, and vitally important rituals, practices, vocabularies, and meanings. What I wish to end this passage of the argument with here, however, is a famous instance of the use of the telephone for broadcasting in the early period before it had been enshrined as a voice communication medium (first with party-lines on which conversations could be easily overheard, then ultimately with secure two-way, dyadic conversations). Pioneering attempts to use the telephone for broadcasting entertainment in Britain and the USA were not profitable, but a viable and relatively popular enterprise that did offer such a service was the

Telefon Hirmondó in Budapest (Hirmondó being a Magyar word for the medieval town crier). Established in 1893, Telefon Hirmondó involved the transmission of daily programming of various sorts of news and announcements as well as concerts, attracting sizable audiences of telephone subscribers over the next two or more decades (Marvin 1988: 222–31). Compared to other telephonic experiments in broadcasting events or entertainments (what Marvin terms 'occasions'):

> The Telefon Hirmondó was a hybrid of newspaper practices, conventional modes of oral address, and telephone capabilities that anticipated twentieth-century radio . . . In its time it was seen as a novel newspaper form, but it was radically forward-looking in its continuous and regularly scheduled programming, the origination of some programs from its own studios, and the combination of news and entertainments in the same service.
>
> (1988: 231)

Such alternative histories and uses of the telephone not only have important resonances and resemblances for thinking about later developments in broadcasting such as cable or pay television, as Marvin reminds, but also prefigure possibilities of the cell phone beyond a portable device for voice telephone conversations.

Making voice communications portable

If histories of media have their difficulties, there are peculiar challenges and characteristics in seeking to formulate histories of the newer media (Flichy 2002). This is certainly the case with doing the histories of the cell phone. Despite its relatively recent commercial availability and consumer adoption from the early 1980s onwards, the cell phone has been in development for at least fifty years. It also recursively adopts and reconfigures habits, expectations, and cultural forms from the telegraph and the telephone, these two other technologies central to modernity I have just briefly reviewed.

One particular difficulty in writing histories of telecommunications is that, while there have been many institutional, technical, or national histories of telecommunications, studies that take the social and cultural dimensions of telecommunications are relatively scarce compared to a wealth of literature on other media (notable exceptions include Fischer 1992; Marvin 1988; Sconce 2000; the history of telecommunications also features in Winston's important 1998 history of media technology). As for work on cell phone and mobile technology history, this is very much in its infancy. There is one lively and accessible book devoted to the subject (Agar 2003), coverage of the subject in a number of other books (for example, Steinbock 2003), an evolving website on the topic (Farley 2005), special issues of journals devoted to the history of the technical and standards development of mobiles (such as Lehne 2004; Lyytinen and King 2002), and the histories and politics of mobiles (Goggin and Thomas 2006), as well as suggestive treatments in various articles and collections on social aspects of the mobiles (Goggin 2006; Hamill and Lasen 2005; Ito, Okabe and Matsuda, 2005; Katz 2002 and 2003; Lacohée, Wakeford and Pearson 2003; Ling 2004). Given this relative dearth of material, I will discuss some of the features I think are important for understanding cell phone culture.

As a form of radiocommunications, the beginnings of the cell phone are found in the extraordinary career of Guglielmo Marchese Marconi, who dominated the early development of radio. The young Italian brought his wireless telegraphy instrument to England in 1896, patenting his invention and founding his own company the next year (Baker 1970; Huurdeman 2003: 207ff). Marconi also developed the use of wireless telegraphy in maritime communications, with clever, if anti-competitive tactics, to ensure ships adopted Marconi sets and operators (by requiring operators not to communicate with wireless operators of other companies) until this policy was countermanded by a resolution of countries participating in the new International Radiotelegraph Conference (Huurdeman 2003: 232; 357–8; Solymar 1999: 134–6). The sinking of the Titanic on 14 April 1912 underscored the importance of wireless telegraphy at sea, and it led to the next Conference where sweeping regulations were put in place because of failures to heed radio warnings (Huurdeman 2003: 282–3). In 1919–22 there was a trial of radiotelephony to ships as an extension to the existing Bell Telephone System, followed by the commencement of public telephone service to ships on the Atlantic Ocean in 1929 (Huurdeman 2003: 284).

Portable and transportable telephones had already been developed on land in the late 1890s. They were used by telephone companies to test lines, as well as by armies in battle (in the Boer War, for instance) (Attman et al. 1977; Steinbock 2003: 73). Marconi is credited with the first mobile car radio: 'A steam-driven wagon was equipped with a transmitter, a receiver, and a cylindrical antenna about 5 m high mounted on the roof' (Huurdeman 2003: 285, 287; Michaelis 1965: 133). In 1909 the US Army Signal corps experimented with radio equipment mounted on horse carriages, and '[m]ilitary mobile and transportable radiotelegraph equipment was used widely during World War I' (Huurdeman 2003: 286). In 1911, Lars Magnus Ericsson, eponymous founder of the famous Swedish telecommunications equipment manufacturer, and his wife Hilda, tried to develop a car phone: 'Hilda used two long sticks, like fishing rods to hook them over a pair of telephone wires. Lars Magnus cranked the dynamo handle of the telephone, which produced a signal to an operator in the nearest exchange' (Steinbock 2003: 73). As Agar remarks:

> When Lars Magnus Ericsson was driving through the Swedish countryside, he
> still had to stop his car and wire his car-bound telephone to the overhead

lines. If he had pressed his foot on the accelerator, the wire would have whipped out, wrecking the apparatus.

(Agar 2003: 16)

The first radio telephone was that used by Bell Laboratories in 1924 (Steinbock 2003: 73). Land mobile use, however, was not pioneered by the American telephone company AT & T; rather it was the Detroit Police Department that did so in 1921, for police car despatch. Patrolmen would be paged, and once alerted they would need to find a wireline telephone to call back (Steinbock 2003). By the early 1930s in Detroit, New York, and elsewhere, police cars were regularly using one-way mobile radio communication. A leader in car radio communications was Galvin Manufacturing Corporation in Chicago, which designed a less bulky two-way radio for the mass market in 1931. Galvin called the radio 'Motorola', and this was how the company was renamed also in 1947 (Huurdeman 2003: 286). In 1933, the first two-way radio communications were established in New Jersey. This was at a time when radios in automobiles were becoming popular and the Frequency Modulation (FM) band was devised. Motorola officially entered into police radio communications in 1937, quickly becoming the market leader, with emergency services, government agencies, and essential services using two-way land–mobile radio (Noble 1962; Steinbock 2003: 78–9).

New technical advances in wireless communications came during World War II, with the design and manufacturing of two-way radio sets for the American forces by General Electric and Motorola, in particular the latter's 'Handie Talkie' (or Walkie-Talkie), the first portable radiotelephone launched in 1943 (Huurdeman 2003: 286). After the war, civilian organisations took up the new radio technology, especially taxi cabs for despatch, and by 1952, 350,000 two-way private mobile radios were in use, usually for brief calls or communication (Steinbock 2003: 82–3). The first commercial mobile radiotelephone service in the USA was offered in 1946 in St Louis, Missouri, by AT & T and Southwestern Bell, allowing calls from fixed phones to mobile users. Even in its improved version, the service had relatively poor voice quality and was quite inefficient in its use of radio spectrum. Another system was introduced in 1956, which had almost 1.5 million users by 1964, when AT & T introduced an 'Improved Mobile Telephone System':

> Operation was in a manual mode; an operator could establish a call between two mobile subscribers or between a mobile subscriber and a subscriber on the PSTN. The mobile terminals equipped with electronic vacuum tubes were large, heavy, had high power consumption, needed shock-protected mountings, and were expensive.
>
> (Huurdeman 2003: 519)

Making more productive use of mobile radiocommunications by dividing spectrum into cells, what was to prove a vastly more efficient and reliable method of mobile communications, was an idea first devised in the Bell Laboratories in 1947 (Farley 2005; Lucent Bell Labs 2004).[1] Transmission of signals was organised around a grid of interlocking, polygonal cells, rather like the honeycomb of bees. A phone would send and receive signals via the transmitter tower that provided dedicated service to the cell in which it was located. When the user moved location and passed from one cell to another, the responsibility for maintaining the reception of the phone would be passed from one cell base station to another. Radio spectrum could be shared far more efficiently, with greater overall capacity.

The Bell Laboratories were renowned for many scientific achievements and innovations, not least in 1948 Shannon and Weaver's famous theorem central to modern communication theory. Bell Labs developed a number of other technologies that also made the cell phone possible, such as important work on computers, computer languages, and software in the aftermath of World War II, 'programming them to switch telephone calls, turn radios on and off, change radio frequencies and automatically connect radios to the telephone system. These applications were the building blocks for what would ultimately become a network of mobile telephones' (Murray 2001: 18; cf. Bernstein 1984). Bell Labs scientists were responsible for pivotal research that went to the heart of the portability of cell phones, namely the replacement of bulky, unwieldy vacuum tubes with the transistor through the 1970s, making the mobile phone much easier to use (Brock 2003). Bell Labs scientists tried to address the issue of limited radio channels, such as finding ways to improve non-cellular mobiles by allowing phones automatically to find an open channel without the caller having to search manually for one (Murray 2001: 19). With improvements and the opening up of additional frequency bands (Brock 2003), subscriber numbers worldwide were estimated at 600,000 by 1985, but at the cost of severe network congestion (Huurdeman 2003: 519). In the late 1970s, trunking, or the organised sharing of channels by professional mobile users (such as taxi drivers, trucks, emergency services), was introduced, something which has survived into the present day (Huurdeman 2003: 519–20). Other countries developed their own versions of radio mobile telephones, but the prices of terminal equipment remained relatively high.

For all Bell Labs' technical innovations, however, AT & T for various reasons did not have the prescience, motivation, or conditions to capitalise on the beginnings of commercial cellular telephony, when it finally eventuated. AT & T had been enduring anti-trust investigations by the Justice Department, stretching over many years that culminated with Judge Harold Greene's famous consent decree that dictated the break-up of the monopoly. By January 1984 AT & T was forced to divest itself of its local telephone service, and created seven independent regional Bell Operating Companies (RBOCs; also known as Baby Bells). AT & T retained long-distance service and also its equipment manufacturing concern Western Electric (now Lucent Technologies, housing Bell Labs as its 'corporate research' laboratories). The thorough and turbulent transformation AT & T was experiencing in the 1980s is one important factor in explaining why the company failed to position itself adequately in the new wireless services market. AT & T dramatically underestimated the future demand for cellular (cf. Murray 2001: 26), though it certainly would not be the first corporation to have difficulty forecasting the future (definitely captured at this time in de Sola Pool's striking 1983 study of earlier forecasts for telephony). Famously, AT & T's chairman Charles Brown indicated that the company would pass on offering cellular services, saying in a television discussion in January 1982 that AT & T would not compete for the custom of local businesses: 'all we'll do is to make the technology available' (quoted in Murray 2001: 27). The irony was palpable: 'The company that invented cellular telephony would have no part in the industry it spawned . . . until it would buy its way back into the industry a decade later, at a staggering price' (Murray 2001: 27).

While cellular telephony continued to be developed, and telecommunications policy and regulation moved towards market liberalisation, other mobile communications technologies became popular. In the mid-1970s, the Citizens' Band radio become popular, as a form of communications in trucks but also cars, immortalised in the movie *Smokey and the Bandit* (featuring Burt Reynolds) and its theme song, C.W. McCall's 'Convoy':

> Simple push-to-talk radios that allowed users to talk on a kind of party line system (no private conversations and no telephone connections were possible) . . . They were relatively cheap to buy and easy to use; they had no per-minute charges; they came with their own catchy jargon; and they were embraced by Hollywood and the music industry.
>
> (Murray 2001: 23)

As Murray notes, CB radios were made possible by integrated circuits, now also incorporated in other consumer goods: 'This new wave of microtechnology included smaller transistor radios, clocks, calculators and, eventually, two-way radios' (2001: 23). At the height of the CB craze, there were an estimated 50 million users in the USA, with as many as one in seven cars equipped with the technology (2001: 23). Murray interestingly suggests, however, that the enthusiasm for CB was seen as a popular culture fad and not worthy of serious recognition despite its extraordinary takeup (cf. Owen 1999 on the CB fad as a cautionary tale): 'the FCC [Federal Communications Commission] and most communications executives saw it as no more than a blue-collar fad; no one really recognized it as a clear indicator that Americans were clamouring to drive and talk on the phone' (Murray 2001: 24). Interestingly, we see the conventions of CB radio use, including the possibility of communicating with a wide group of listeners overhearing conversations – reminiscent of telephony party-line culture that survived in rural areas until the 1990s – being reactivated in the push-to-talk mobiles of the late 1990s and early 2000s.

Paging services also attracted millions of users in the 1980s and early 1990s. The first telephone pager-like device was patented in 1949 by Alfred J. Gross, the Canadian also credited with inventing the first walkie-talkie, CB radio, and cordless telephone. Gross's devices were used in the Jewish Hospital in New York City (FCC 2004). The FCC approved the spectrum for public use in 1958 (FCC 2004), but it was Motorola that coined the term a year later when they made a small receiver to which radio messages could be transmitted. In 1974 Motorola introduced its Pagebay 1, the first successful pager for the consumer market (FCC 2004). As it achieved a stable definition as a technology, the pager was a form of messaging. It allowed a person to phone an operator and request a text message be sent to another person. The receipt of the message was announced with a sound (characteristically a 'beep', so pagers became called 'beepers'), and the person could then read the message. However, they needed to find a phone to call the originator of the message, or someone else, or to page someone else, until the development of two-way pagers.

The pager became widely used in business and industrial contexts. Pagers became, and still remain, part of the communicative and management practices and identities of some professions. Most notable, even iconic, is the use of pagers by doctors and other medical personnel in hospitals. Because doctors are engaged in various tasks away from their fixed phones (or not wishing to use their cell phones, and so be engaged in conversation), in meetings, or consultations, or treating patients on their rounds, they are contactable by pager (often needing to be so for reasons of emergency). In the 1970s, especially, with improvements in technologies, there was a growth in both pager demand and supply. According to the FCC, there were 3.2 million pagers worldwide in 1980, rising to 61 million by 1994 (after wide-area paging was invented in 1990) (FCC 2004). In the USA, for instance, in the lead-up to the Federal Communications Commission's auction of spectrum in the early 1980s, a number of aspirant wireless carriers applying for licences established or acquired paging businesses.

There was also some use of paging by residential customers, for personal and social reasons without the ostensible rationale of business or professional needs. A leading instance of this was in Japan, where paging culture was especially important for teenage girls and young women in the 1990s, co-existing with the emerging text message culture (as discussed in chapter 4). Thus, as a set of communicative and cultural practices, paging not only prefigured the potential mobility of cell phone devices; it also anticipated, and shaped, narratives and meanings that began to appear with text messaging.

Mobiles to market in the 1980s

In 1978, the US FCC called for industry proposals for a better land and mobile telephone system. AT & T's proposal was called the Advanced Mobile Phone System (AMPS), and was based on the cellular idea first conceived some decades before (Young 1979). In 1978, the first commercial cellular telephone systems were trialled, in Bahrain, and then in the USA, with Bell and AT & T piloting services in Newark, New Jersey and Chicago, and car-mounted telephones following within six months (Steinbock 2003: 97). In 1981, the US regulator awarded licences to service different areas. Ameritech, one of the 'Baby Bells' formed from the break-up of AT & T, offered the first commercial cellular service in Chicago.

The Japanese, however, had already begun what has been seen as the world's first cellular radio service in December 1979, with the Mobile Control Station system. Radio paging had been introduced in Japan in 1968 but the country had not otherwise had a public mobile radiotelephone system (Huurdeman 2003: 520; Steinbock 2003: 143–51). NTT's Electrical Communications Laboratories had been researching land–mobile systems since 1953, and in 1967 a technical paper was published proposing a nationwide cellular system (Araki 1968; Pempel 1978). This indigenous cellular system was piloted in 1975, leading to the 1979 launch.

Analogue cellular radio systems were introduced in other countries. The Nordic Mobile Telephone (NMT) was introduced in 1981, but was used in over forty countries (including those in Asia, Russia, and Eastern Europe); Total Access Communication Systems (TACS), a British version of AMPS, was first used in the UK in 1985, and then taken up around the world; various proprietary systems were mainly used in the countries that devised them, especially in France (Radio-Com 2000), Germany (C 450), and Italy (RTMS) (Huurdeman 2003: 521–4; Steinbock 2003). These systems were incompatible with each other, but played an important function in international competition as well as the buttressing of patriotic industrial pride (Funk 1998, 2002). The neat boundaries of national innovation systems started to blur considerably in response to forces of globalisation (Nelson and Rosenberg 1993; Niosi and Bellon 1994) and also to initiatives to learn the lessons of first-generation cell phones and devise common standards (Fig. 2.1).

Indeed other countries quickly outstripped the USA in cell phone subscription. Although from the 'pre-cellular era to the end of the analog era, US leadership in mobile communications paralleled the monopoly era in telecommunications' (Steinbock 2003: 111) by the early 1990s, there was a widespread perception that an opportunity had been squandered. One of the companies most associated with mobile phones in the 1970s and 1980s, and with first-generation cellular telephony, was the American firm Motorola. It was a Motorola chief executive, Martin Cooper, who in 1973 made the 'world's first' call on a portable, hand-held cell

Figure 2.1 Mobile telephone user on Westminster Bridge, London, c. 1986.

phone. This was the DynaTAC, a nearly two-and-a-half pound object, which soon received the moniker of the 'Brick'. Motorola promised that the DynaTAC system 'will ultimately permit personal radiotelephone service to be offered to hundreds of thousands of individuals in a given city' (quoted in Steinbock 2003: 223).

The importance of the portable device to subsequent cell phone culture cannot be overstated. However, it took some time for the portable cell phone to become widely adopted by companies and network operators. Even until the mid-1980s, there was a strong assumption among engineers, marketers, and managers shaping second-generation digital systems that cell phones would continue to be installed and used in cars, and that portables were not viable.[2] Motorola did establish the portable cell phone as the dominant design (see Steinbock 2005: 43–4), and so became the market leader in first-generation systems. In 1989 Motorola followed up with the MicroTAC personal cellular phone, 'the smallest and lightest portable on the market . . . the size of a wallet and weighed less than eleven ounces', and then in 1996 the first wearable cell phone, the 3.1 ounce StarTAC (Steinbock 2003: 228–9). Despite these achievements, as Steinbock convincingly argues, Motorola was not well placed to move with the intense competition and globalisation of second-generation cell phones, finding it difficult to slough off its pre-occupation with the USA, despite its presence in a number of jurisdictions as well as pioneering the Chinese market (2003: 213–41).

Digital cell

Broadly, the features of first-generation cell phones revolved around voice communications. A limitation of first-generation cell phones was not only the relatively low functionality, large size, and quality of handsets and the stage of evolution of mobile networks, but also the capabilities of the rest of the telecommunications network (known as the public switched telecommunications network or PSTN).

The telecommunications network had been engineered over a century for voice communication over circuits. From the 1960s onwards, data communications via the telecommunications network emerged as increasingly important, whether by telex, fax, computers, or modems. Decisive changes were transpiring because of a combination of technical, industrial, economic, and social factors. Telecommunications had become central to how people communicated with each other for friendship, family, civil society, government, or business purposes. Digitisation of networks in the 1980s and 1990s allowed their architecture to be changed, with fewer switching centres and hubs, greater use of computing and software, more network functions, and automated and remote maintenance. There also emerged new possibilities for information storage, and voice and data communications, and new forms of control (Mansell 1993). For instance, 'intelligent' network software allowed features such as calling number display, where the number of the calling party could be displayed or captured in a computer.

The processes of digitisation also involved cell phones. The second generation of cell phones was predicated upon digital technologies. Sound from a cell phone receiver was digitally coded, compressed, and transmitted via radio waves, then received and decoded, and could be heard by the receiver. Sharing of the radio spectrum could also be more efficiently managed through precise allocation of channels and transmission of data. The process of digital encoding and encrypting of the signal made it a more secure form of communication than its first-generation analogue predecessors, far more difficult to be intercepted (certainly by amateurs).

Various standards for second-generation cell phones were implemented, including the widely used Global System for Mobiles (GSM) standard (developed in Europe but deployed worldwide), the Code Division Multiple Access standard (CDMA; used in the USA but also in Latin America and elsewhere), and the Time Division Multiple Access standard (TDMA; also used in the USA and a number of other countries). Each standard represents different ways to deal with key problems of sharing spectrum and ensuring good connectivity. The new digital cell phone technology was accompanied with promises of better reception and voice quality, but brought problems too. For instance, the European GSM standard was designed to provide reception for the relatively densely populated countries of its region, and so the effective range of reception from base stations was approximately 30 kilometres. By contrast, analogue cell phones were designed for a range of reception of 50 kilometres, but often had an effective range of 70 or even 100 kilometres in some instances. Whereas the digital signal tends to break up altogether and reception becomes very difficult at 30 kilometres, an analogue signal 'fades' slowly rather than abruptly, a substantial problem for countries with many remote, sparsely populated areas.

The new standards for mobile telecommunications networks and the technical innovations they represented, not least with digital technologies, were closely related to new possibilities in the handsets. The cell phones themselves offered a much greater range of features. Most obvious was the address book, allowing phone numbers but also other details of contacts to be stored in the phone. Phone numbers could be stored in the subscriber identity module (SIM) card too, allowing the data to be easily transferred from one phone to another (Dietze 2005).[3] The capabilities of the cell phone were integrated with those of the network, so a person was now able to call up a friend's stored number and dial it, but also to store the details of a received phone number. Other features of digital cell phones included the clock, alarm function, calendar, calculator, and games. With greater sophistication in their displays, interfaces, and menus, digital cell phones, combined with the possibilities of intelligent telecommunications networks, were replete with new modes for controlling telephonic interactions. Key attributes of calls could be tracked, and data collated, such as calls sent and received, and the numbers associated with these; missed calls; the duration of calls. Voice messages (or 'voicemail') functions were integrated into the phone and network.

The cell phone in the 1990s, then, extended its range of features, and the repertoire of voice telephony it supported and shaped (Lindholm, Keinonen, and Kiljander 2003). Digital technology in cell phones also made possible something much talked about with respect to new media more generally: multimedia, or communication and cultural exchange through text, image, sound, and touch, as well as voice. In the immense activity and din around communications, culture, and media – whether under the banner of 'being digital', 'Information superhighways', 'the Internet revolution', the 'new economy', or the 'dot.com' boom

– the social and technical system of the telephone had become absolutely pivotal by the close of the twentieth century.

One of the most prominent of these new dimensions of digital mobile communications is text messaging. Text messaging allows phone users to key-in characters via the alphanumeric keyboard of their device, compose short messages, and send these to other phone users. The widespread adoption of text messaging from the early 1990s onwards was roughly contemporaneous with the explosion in another form of writing and text, namely electronic mail over the Internet (see chapter 4 for a discussion of mobile messaging cultures). As the capabilities of digital cell phones were steadily augmented and elaborated, a new term was developed to describe them – 2.5 (or second and a half) generation cell phones. 2.5G services especially feature multimedia applications, such as the ability to receive and send images or short videos, as well as audio capabilities (the most popular of which is probably downloading music to customise the ringtone of a phone). From the late 1990s to 2003–4 mobile messaging and other mobile data services became a lucrative segment of the industry. The narrative of an upward march through progressively advanced 'generations' of the cellphone was interrupted here. The 3G of mobile networks and phones was premised on technical systems and standards that finally made 'picture' phones a commercial reality (a long-cherished dream since their first appearance in the late 1960s). 3G phones offered the possibility of interactive video communications wherever the user happened to be located. As I discuss in chapter 10, the promoters of 3G have faced a number of challenges, not least the cost of licences and relatively slow take-up of video and valued-added rich data services.

Before closing this brief history of the development of the cell phone, it is worth noting that there are many other mobile communication devices that are articulated with or overlap with cell phones. Walkie-talkies and pagers, as I have already noted, but also portable digital assistants (PDAs), Blackberries, computers with wireless access, and digital cameras. Especially in the realm of digital technologies, there are many devices that have multiple functions and distinctive cultures of use – and there is much debate about whether these devices will converge into hybrid equipment or keep a separate function, or how such 'convergence culture' will be navigated by consumers (Jenkins 2005).

Imagining users

I have covered much ground in giving a potted history of the cell phone's development. What I would like to do now is to draw upon some vignettes of how cell phones were received, especially in the late 1980s through to the mid-1990s when they became much more commonplace and so came to public notice and prominence. For this purpose I often draw on examples from Australia, a country neither an early nor a late adopter of cell phones – but I am certainly aware of and am keenly interested in the differences in how cell phones were received and imagined across different countries, a worthy project still to be undertaken.

Reminiscent of the telephone before it, the attention of those involved in marketing cell phones was first on the business user. As Lacohée, Wakeford, and Pearson observe, in its early days the 'mobile telephone was an elitist device mainly used for business by middle and upper class males' (2003: 205). In 1965 in the UK,

> an exclusive (and expensive) service called System 1 was launched in West London that was used primarily by the chauffeurs of diplomats and company chairmen. By 1967, use had trickled down to 14,000 privileged and wealthy users of the System 4 mobile telephone.
>
> (Lacohée, Wakeford, and Pearson 2003: 205)

When cell phones arrived on the scene, and started to become more visible in the mid to late 1980s, they quickly became tagged as a 'yuppie' status symbol:

> The yuppie age reached its zenith on the morning of October 18 last year. Standing among the rubble of San Francisco's earthquake was a posse of stockbrokers doing deals on portable phones. Undeterred by the restriction order that had been slammed on the San Francisco Stock Exchange until construction engineers could assess the extent of the earthquake damage, these young bloods were making the most of the available technology to carry on business as usual.
>
> (Head 1990)[4]

A 1987 survey of US cell phone users by the Cellular Telephone Industry Association found that 'fully 70 percent of cell phone users made more than $50,000 per year – well above the national average of $18,426' (cited in Murray 2001). The role of the cell phone as status symbol, and the mere fact of its possession as evidence of conspicuous consumption, took some years to shake off. In Australian debates on the reform of telecommunications, one consumer lobby group depicted mobile phone users as the very epitome of the new rich, winning at the expense of low-income and older people:

> The winners will be the yuppies and forex dealers and the broader business sectors. They are the principal user of long-distance and international services, and the owners, or rather the taxpayer-subsidised lessees, of all manner of mobile services . . . Prominent among [the losers] will be the low-income and housebound older people of Australia, who use the phone as a lifeline, rather than a business or recreational tool.
>
> (Barber 1990)

Yet at this time the cellular mobile was already starting to move beyond the circle of wealthy business users, executives, and the reviled figure of the merchant banker, to be avidly used by tradespeople: 'Yuppies, beware. Those carphone-toting merchant bankers are actually carrying a tradesperson's tool . . . the bulk of Australia's 80,000 mobile phone subscribers are sales staff, carpenters, plumbers and technicians' (*Business Review Weekly* 1989). With falling prices of phones, small-business and blue-collar workers started to use cell phones heavily. *New York Times* reporter Calvin Sims summarised the trend: 'When cellular mobile telephones were introduced four years ago, they were gadgets only of the rich and powerful. Now everyone from drug dealers in Miami to the taco vendor in Rockefeller Plaza has one' (cited in Murray 2001: 211).

If a technology is to become a 'black box', rather than a relatively unstable and unfinished project (Latour 1996), it needs to enrol supporters, especially users, who are completely taken with it: 'From the BMW-driving yuppie showing his latest status symbol on the freeway to the tradesman taking calls out on the job, we have fallen in love with cellular phones' (Kavanagh 1989). Telephones had become unremarkable by the 1980s, and their reconfiguration and expansion could pivot on this achieved domestication (Haddon 2003): 'Today's lifestyle revolves around the phone and there are few homes in Australia which can function comfortably without one' (Gibbs 1990). The discourse on the mobile phone quite quickly shifted to emphasising its usefulness, indeed that this technology was essential. This is clearly observable in the articles by specialist technology writers, reliant on industry marketing information: 'mobile phones have become a permanent part of life. They have been essential for business and even social communication, with users ranging from corporate executives to the one person company, from tradespeople to husbands and wives' (Cantlon 1992).

Writers sought to address the perception of the technology as a species of conspicuous consumption: 'The age of mobile communications is, however, not solely the preserve of the yuppie. Small business people are finding the ability to communicate with their office or customers at any time is not a luxury but a necessity' (Head 1990). Testimonials were offered to underline the point. Cell phones were a must not only for builders, for instance, but also for their wives, as this risible account of gender and the phone reveals:

> Mr Hamilton, a builder, finds it handy to have one phone in the car and one he can take up ladders, Mrs Hamilton said. She has just begun working again, now that her two children are at school, and she has found she needs a phone.
>
> 'I'm running around and visiting people for my mother-in-law, and I've found I need to be in contact', she said. 'I need one of my own. Jim's is so bulky and it won't fit in my handbag without bending the aerial . . . I like to know I can be contacted anywhere', she said.
>
> (Powell 1992)

As cell phones diffused through different demographic groups, there was a shift in how the device was perceived and represented. Reviewing media coverage of cell phones in the late 1980s and early 1990s, for instance, it is hard not to be struck by the many articles that report and turn upon the novelty of the technology, such as this representative item:

> On Thursday afternoon, as he was being wheeled in a humicrib from a delivery room at Royal North Shore [hospital] three minutes after birth, Kai McConnell was howling into a phone held by his grandmother and listened to by his great-great-aunt.
>
> (Column 8 1992b)

Stories began to be told about the ways that mobiles reconfigured place. A real estate agent could not find the builder he had arranged to meet – only to discover eventually he was in Richmond, New South Wales, rather than the town by the same name in another state entirely (Column 8 1992a). The posturing of the mobile phone user became a commonplace for social satire: 'About 300 people turned up for lunch, bringing their mobile phones for company. It was rumoured that . . . they had instructed their office to phone them every 15 minutes' (Robertson 1991). Later a discourse was commenced on the ubiquity of mobile phones in everyday life, but disquiet was voiced too: 'Portable telephones have come a long way – but now they're trying to take over our whole lives' (Jones 1998). Mobiles were seen as a symbol, or indeed a cause, of the changing boundaries between work and leisure, public and private spheres. For some they offered new possibilities for flexible working. For others they signalled problems with paid work increasing and invading the domestic sphere: 'Busy schedules, mobile phones, laptop computers and job insecurity have also made us reluctant to take holidays' (*Daily Telegraph* 1997). New groups, not culturally coded as technologically adept, were newsworthy for their enlistment into mobile practices:

> Elderly people of the 90s have embraced the electronic age with gusto and marketers are hot on their heels. In the build-up to Christmas, the elderly have been targeted as a group who prefer gifts such as mobile phones and Internet link-ups instead of comfy cardigans or bath salts.
>
> (*Daily Telegraph* 1996)

Even the poor might be a possibility, with a Telecom marketing manager citing the 'example of the British television programme called Bread where the Boswell family of Social Security dependants rely on the mobile phone for almost all their communications' (Head 1990). Nonetheless, the whiff of fatuity or uselessness did persist, after the yuppie label became less common, and sometimes applied to specific groups whose behaviour deviated from the norm: 'Childless couples will make up almost 30 per cent of the population by 1999 and are splurging on toys such as mobile phones, new research shows' (Bye 1997).

As the cell phone began to become popular in the early to mid-1990s, for young people it became an object of considerable commercial desire: 'Mobile phones are no longer exclusive to the business community and Yuppies, with young people representing the market's highest growth segment . . . [Telstra's] new commercial speaks to young people in their own language, using big, bright and bold images' (Hornery 1995). This raised mixed feelings, however, among the wider community. In Australia, as elsewhere, the use of mobiles in schools, for instance, became the 'great mobile debate' (Wood 1997), with phone companies targeting teens and pre-teens (though not necessarily being keen to acknowledge this): 'Newington College [a private school in Sydney] is gearing up for a bunch of 10-year-olds who want to keep in touch with the Jones boy. That's Todd Jones, 10, who never leaves home without his mobile' (Wood 1997). One columnist reproved dominant provider Telstra for its juvenile marketing, when it offered a NEC 'Sportz Digital' as a special back-to-school deal: 'I'd have thought Telstra could sell enough mobile phones to adults in this country, without homing in on the school kids' (Gibson 1997). What especially raised the hackles of the scribe were early intimations of girl-power:

> But there's no prize for guessing why Telstra used a young lady in their advertisement. It's because young ladies spend most of their waking lives on the phone. Young ladies pick up the telephone when they turn 11, and don't put it down again until they're 18. Giving a young lady her own personal digital mobile is like giving Saddam Hussein a scud missile. Someone is going to get hurt.
>
> (Gibson 1997)

As cell phones became widely used by young people, the financial consequences of heavy use became apparent – not least because this is often one of the first contracts into which young people enter. Spending on cell phones appeared in omnibus national surveys as a significant area of expenditure (Eastway 1997), and credit management problems began to raise concerns (Cox 1999; Funston and MacNeill 1999), but by this time cell phones were an integral part of youth culture – and subject to frequent moral panics because of it (as I shall discuss later in the book).

Cellular uses

I have only been able to offer a few impressions of the ways that the cell phone was discussed and represented as it became incorporated into everyday life and popular life. I will take up this aspect of cell phone culture later on, especially in chapters 6 and 7 (not least concerning representations of cell phones and young people). To draw to a close this account of the early diffusion of the cell phone, I would like to consider how too often we narrowly define what we mean by such a technology, and what tends to lie outside conventional histories.

Much research and public discourse on cell phones has been entranced by the novelty of the device. It is not saying anything new to observe that there are real problems with this approach, of course. We need to be attentive to the career of a technology as we write its biography. The settled, more-or-less agreed upon (or still disputed) form of a technology takes some time to emerge, and is historically, socially, and culturally very specific. In considering how researchers establish the limits of the cell phone as an object of study, Leslie Haddon asks: 'what might be the boundaries of what we consider to be a communication practice within this repertoire? . . . how broad a vision should we have of what elements count as communication?' (Haddon 2005: 8). Haddon argues that 'we should always try to imagine what could count as communications-related practices that go beyond, but help to make sense of the more detailed patterns of communi-cation' (2005: 8). Reflecting on the history of computing, and how researchers grappled to understand popular computing as it emerged in the mid-1980s especially, Haddon makes the point that computing is not just what happens in a narrow dyad between the computer screen and the user. Rather it was important to 'consider all the acts related to "computing" ' (2005: 8). As a number of studies of computing and the Internet bear out (Hine 2000; Lally 2002; Miller and Slater 2000), especially those influenced by anthropological and ethno-graphical approaches, we need to think more broadly about communication. Haddon suggests that:

> Thinking of the mobile phone more generally, we might include the way in which we control mobile use, such as controlling who the mobile number is given out to, switching it off and switching it to voice mail. These can all either shape 'use' or may be considered to be a part of an expanded definition of 'use'. We might also include how people talk about communications, such as the way they exchange information about how best to exploit mobile tariff structures. Then there are practices such as changing SIM cards or else people borrowing someone else's mobile phone if the mobile phone network of the person being called means this is cheaper or effectively 'free'.
>
> (2005: 8–9)

We will consider a multitude of such practices in relation to texting in chapter 3, but for the present it is worth considering such a broader conception of com-munication and use. Haddon counsels researchers to look at how such broader sets of actions can 'modify the communication act' (2005: 8). In tandem with this approach, we might care also to bring culture to the fore as a key concept. Some of the practices Haddon indicates here, and others I will proceed to mention, can also be seen as cultural practices, associated as they are with matters of articulation, expression, identity, and meaning. Cultural studies practitioners have been especially interested in the practices of everyday life and the constitution of popular culture, and so I would like to reframe Haddon's useful account from this standpoint. Accordingly, a history of the development of cellular voice telephony needs to bring together a number of prosaic yet important things.

First there is the dialectic between adoption (whether of the avid, uncaring, or reluctant variety) versus resistance to cell phones. Foreswearing technology of different sorts, but especially in recent times of computers, the Internet, and phones, has been a recurrent motif of discourses, shaping meanings and uses of cell phones. Such a discourse has been especially acute with the cell phone, as we noted from the conversations and even clamour accompanying its appearance on the scene, and is still continuing. Perhaps this is due to its potential greater ubiquity than some other information and communication technologies; but especially because the cell phone represents a challenge to and transformation of the accepted cultural place and social relations of voice telephony and telecommunications.

Second there is the relationship between 'use' and 'non-use'. When is it appropriate to switch a cell phone on or turn or leave it off? Or under which circumstances do users choose not to receive calls? What do such acts or omissions signify? And when did they develop?

Third, what of the many uses designed, devised, or arising unexpectedly, during the domestication of the cell phone? During the 1980s and 1990s, for example, telephone answering machines were introduced as an adjunct to the telephone instrument and telecommunications network. The machine could receive a call automatically, and record a message for the subscriber to play back at leisure. The introduction and diffusion of telephone answering machines occasioned a debate in its own right, now perhaps forgotten for the most part. Many people took great offence at being asked by a machine to leave a message, rather than being able to speak to their intended interlocutor. Others welcomed the facility for its ability to relieve them from staying at home or in their office waiting for the phone to ring. Or for the possibility simply to record or overhear who was calling, or even to dodge unwanted calls, rather than to need to be a slave to the telephone and always answer. Answering machines were incorporated into the cell phone via a network answering and recording device that became widely known as 'voicemail'. Given it resided in the network, voicemail could also be used in conjunction with wireline phones, and grew in popularity. It is arguable that voicemail has been much more closely affiliated with the cell phone, not least, latterly, because of the possibilities for alerts (beeps, tones) to indicate when a message has been received.

In carefully observing the cultural practices that are associated with the cell phone, we find that the boundaries around what counts as a cell phone, or is constellated by such a technology, can look quite different depending on where these are drawn. For instance, the customisation of cell phones is a vital part of cultural practice, representation, and identity, as the work of Larissa Hjorth and others have shown (Hjorth 2005 and 2006), yet is still not often taken seriously. Similarly the framing of the cell phone as a part of the codes of dress and cultural field of fashion became extremely significant from the mid-1990s, as I discuss in chapter 3. For the most part, detailed cultural histories of the early uses and representations of cell phones have yet to be undertaken, yet how such uses were imagined, and what cultures of use did actually emerge, exert much influence upon the production of such culture – even in the realm of the production of commodities and consumer and brand identities to which we now turn.

3   Cool phone: Nokia, networks, and identity

. . . a little Le Corbusier, a little Matrix . . .

(Vogue on the Nokia 8860, Sullivan 2000)

Just as Marimekko had rethought the idea of the dress, Nokia rethought the idea of the telephone.

(Steinbock 2001b: 272)

The name rings a bell but can't say why? Maybe, because one has been glued to the box watching the test match at Old Trafford . . . Off the field it's the largest mobile telecommunications network company in the world with interests in mobile networks in 29 countries across five continents. Vodafone has just signed a three-year sponsorship deal with Ferrari Formula One to adorn the team's cars with its quote mark logo . . .

(Pandya 2001)

Culture is something that is actively produced and consumed. In contemporary capitalism this production of culture involves large-scale, systematic relations of the creation of image, significance, sensuousness, and tactility, with many actors involved. For producers of the sorts of commodities that communications technologies have become, this involves intense, creative labour and capital around the discourses and practices of advertising (Frith and Mueller 2003); identities of things and the corporations that marshall their production and circulation; branding; imagining audiences, users, and consumers (Cronin 2004); and the reflexive and recursive recuperation of knowledge about consumption in the production of culture. Such an enterprise was demonstrated in *Doing Cultural Studies*, through du Gay et al.'s analysis of the different sorts of corporate myths, brands, and advertising that were devised and deployed to make the Sony Walkman attractive for prospective buyers.

The roles of image-creation, advertising, and design have been fundamental in the production of cell phone culture. To open up this topic, this chapter looks at two key case studies that illustrate the cultural design and production of mobile telecommunications. First, I review the role of one of the most important mobile phone handset manufacturers, the celebrated Finnish multinational firm Nokia, and show how Nokia made an important contribution to shaping the mobile phone as cultural object. With chic design values, customisation (interchangeable faces), availability of accessories and different models, portability, and minaturisation, Nokia was exemplary in its creation of the mobile as an object of desire. Secondly, I look at how network brand identities for both producers and consumers have developed, discussing the case of the multinational network operator Vodafone. In both cases, the corporations investigated – handset manufacturers (Nokia) and mobile network providers (Vodafone) – operate in a range of countries, including developing countries. This provides an opportunity, in the third and concluding part of the chapter, to consider briefly how cell phone culture has become an important part of how nations, regions, and communities negotiate the larger cultural forces in the contemporary world, not least globalisation.

Nokia: 'Connecting people'™

In 1865 Fredrik Idestam, a young Finnish mining engineer, received a licence to operate a stone groundwood plant, an innovative new process for manufacturing paper. Though he built his plant first at Tampere, Finland, he soon built a larger mill some kilometres west along the River Nokia (Häikö 2002; Steinbock 2001b).[1] He successfully exported his product to St Petersburg, Warsaw, Riga, and London, and by the early 1890s the firm owned a much larger mill as well as a pulp factory and a paper factory (Steinbock 2001b). The roots of the firm that came to define mobile phone culture, then, were firmly tied to the great artefact of print culture: paper. From there Nokia diversified into an important new industry that came to underlie modern media and communications, namely electricity. Another new Nokia venture was the founding of Finnish Rubber Works in 1898, which grew to feature the manufacture of tyres for cars (its Hakkapeliitta snow tyre was especially popular). Finally Nokia moved into the steadily profitable area of cables with the establishment of Finnish Cable Works in 1912. The three independent companies of Nokia Forest and Power, Finnish Cable Works, and Finnish Rubber Works became a cohesive, de facto group owned by the latter in the 1918–22 period (Häikö 2002: 49–51). The official merger of the three companies did not occur, however, until 1966–7.

In the late 1950s and early 1960s Nokia developed its expertise in electronics, and importing English and German computers and designing and producing equipment for industry (especially the military). In 1971 Nokia began to develop its own computers, and soon after began to produce digital telephone exchanges. At this time, as Häikö notes, telephone networks were integrating exchange and transmission facilities, and equipment was becoming computerised and fully electronic (2002: 57–8). Nokia formed a joint telephone exchange venture with the other significant domestic manufacturer, the state-owned Televa Oy, in 1978, which it took over nine years later. Nokia's court historian emphasises the pedigree of the company in explaining how it came to focus upon mobiles:

> the roots of Nokia's telecommunications strengths of the 1990s are in electronics and cables, an area in which Nokia had accumulated extensive experience since the beginning of the century. The groundwork for digitalization, the foundation for Nokia's modern-day success, was laid as early as the 1960s.
>
> (2002: 54)

In the 1980s Nokia invested heavily in an ill-fated bid to become a competitive force in television, 'the most costly odyssey ever' (2002: 54). There was not the growth or sales in television, despite Nokia's excessive capacity fuelled from massive acquisitions. Furthermore Nokia experienced a bewildering diversification during the 1980s, under its charismatic CEO Kari Kairamo. Pursuing growth and profitability above all, and focused on projecting Nokia beyond its Finnish co-ordinates to realise itself as a truly *European* firm, Kairamo overreached – ending in his tragic suicide in 1988. A long-overdue reorganisation of the corporation ensued. Its forestry business was divested, its rubber enterprises were sold down, and ultimately, in 1994–6, the company shed cables, tires, power, and industrial and consumer electronics arms. This dismantling and reorganisation served new CEO Jorma Ollila's desire to refocus the corporation on the Telecommunications and Mobile Phones divisions.

Finland's national carrier had first offered services on its car mobile telephone network (CMT) in the early 1970s, after the government had authorised its construction in 1968. As well as national initiatives and policies, co-operation among the Nordic countries was pivotal in the development of mobile networks. In 1969 Finland joined Sweden, Norway, and Denmark to form the Nordic Mobile Telephone (NMT) Group. The aim was to develop a new mobile telephone system, with fully automatic operation, handset compatibility, full 'roaming' capability (that is, a customer could receive and make calls in other countries than her own), secure conversations, high reliability, and good future capacity (Garrand 1998; Steinbock 2001b: 96). Sweden launched its NMT system first in late 1981, with Finland doing so the following year. In this collaboration among neighbouring competitors, there was also a fascinating tension to be observed:

> From the very beginning, mobile communications was promoted in the Nordic regions as a working tool rather than as a status symbol . . . Paradoxically, it was the egalitarianism inherent in the public policies of Nordic countries that prepared the pioneering companies of the region for mass-market competition in the 1990s. Because consumer needs, such as

availability, price, and usability, had been considered during the initial planning of the network, mobile phones moved quickly from business-to-business
to consumer markets.

(Steinbock 2001b: 96–97)

The company Mobira, which Nokia started as a joint venture with Salora, then
took over in 1983, incorporating its Telenokia radiophone unit, was the vehicle
for Nokia's push into mobiles selling the NMT system in the Scandavian and
Western Europe markets during the 1980s. As Steinbock notes, Mobira and Nokia
executives had grand visions for the technology:

> NMT represents a critically important development phase in worldwide scale
> . . . It has already changed the general thinking and views on radiophones . . .
> The ultimate objective must be a worldwide system that permits the indefin-
> ite communication of mobile people with each other, irrespective of the
> location.

(Koivusalo 1995:55, cited in Steinbock 2001b: 98)

One difficulty was the hope of a common European system, dashed in 1983 by
other influential nations such as UK, France, Germany, and Italy introducing
different standards, as we saw in chapter 2.

The first cellular phone made by Mobira was the Senator, launched in 1982,
which suffered from lack of time to ensure ease of use. At only 5 kilos, its
successor, the Mobira Talkman, was the firm's first transportable phone: ' "The
new Talkman does not bind your calls into the car", promised the advertisements.
"You can take the phone wherever you go." ' (Steinbock 2001b: 99).[2] In 1986,
Mobira was renamed Nokia-Mobira Oy, and Nokia's first handset, the Cityman,
was launched. By the following year the rebadged entity was the top-selling
mobiles company in the world, grossing $269 million with 13.5 per cent of
market share (2001b: 104). For the next few years, into the early 1990s, Nokia
struggled with price pressures and competition (not least in its maladroit entry
into the US markets), its competitive position, and those of other European
companies – a task which was not made any the easier with the babel of different
first-generation mobile standards. Focusing on the development of the next-
generation digital standard, Telenokia Oy was renamed Nokia Telecommunications Oy in 1988, and managed eventually to prosper through difficult internal
reorganisation and external challenges.

In Nokia's favour were contemporaneous moves towards European economic
and political integration. This changed environment was one factor in the European adoption of the new GSM standard (Steinbock 2001b: 107–10). The first
GSM call was made on 1 July 1991 when Finnish prime minister Harri Holkeri,
using a Nokia phone on a Radiolinja network (equipped by Nokia), reportedly

calling the mayor of Helsinki to discuss the price of Baltic herring. (This was also the year, of course, that fellow Finn Linus Torvalds released the first version of the open source computer operating system Linux.) Exactly ten years later, when Holkeri served as President of the United Nations General Assembly, he starred in the staging of the world's first 3G call. Nokia played a crucial role in the widespread adoption of GSM in Europe, and then around the world, especially the Asia-Pacific region (Martikainen and Palmberg 2005). It also ensured its phones could be used on rival standards, launching a series for all major digital standards in 1994 (Steinbock 2001b: 111) as well as maintaining phones for still-used analogue standards. In 1998, Nokia accounted for approximately 30 per cent of market shape, outstripping its competitor Motorola (2001b: 157). Nokia's rise to prominence to become the pre-eminent mobile phone company has been a source of fascination, and there is extensive discussion of its 'success' in the management and innovation literatures (Ali-Yrkkö and Hermans 2004; Ali-Yrkkö et al. 2000, 2004; Leinbach and Brunn 2002; Palmberg 2002; Roper and Grimes 2005; Sadowski et al. 2003) Nokia's distinctive corporate culture ('the Nokia Way') has been much promoted by the company, and praised by business journalists and management scholars (Roberts 2004: 173–4; cf. Merriden 2001's breathless compendium).[3] Worthy of further discussion though this is, my interest lies in the way Nokia decisively contributed to the emergence of cell phone culture.

Nokia's prizing of research and development led it to develop a great many innovations in cell phones that were valued by users and subsequently adopted by other mobile phone manufacturers: 'Many of the standard features that are now considered generic were originally developed by Nokia, including large graphics displays, signal and battery indicators, coloured covers, and ringing tones' (Steinbock 2001b: 157). Enormously important to the reception of such innovations was Nokia's emphasis on design. Dan Steinbock has written persuasively on the importance of design to Nokia's influence on the cell phone, arguing that design's 'significance in the mobile cellular businesses has coincided with the transition from the institutional and business markets to consumer markets' (2001b: 271). Steinbock points to the reputation for design the Finns have enjoyed, represented notably perhaps by the Marimekko company, famous for fashionable clothes. He characterises Finnish design as a species of minimalism, but also partaking of the Nordic countries' reputation for being design leaders for 'their functionality, esthetics, and environmental consciousness' (2001b: 272). Significantly Steinbock singles out Sony as an important exemplar: 'For years, Nokia's senior managers have been ardent admirers of Sony, the Japanese consumer electronics giant' (2001b: 271). Steinbock identifies a number of parallels between Sony and Nokia:

> Like Sony's founders, Morita and Ibuka, the Nokians concentrated on innovation, doing what has not been done before. Second, they wanted to lead, not

follow. Like Sony's Design Centre, they were willing to make bold moves, pursue markets with products that no one else had, invent rules rather than follow them, and develop management structures and processes that nurtured talent and initiative. Similarly, Sony's 'Sunrise/Sunset' strategy, which guided the design and development of virtually all of its products, had something of a parallel in Nokia's combination of branding, design, and technology-adoption life cycles.

(2001b: 271–2)

I agree with Steinbock about the importance of design as a unifying and integrating force in Nokia, but I think also that design has achieved something of a mythical place in the story of the corporation's rise to success.

If there was a pivotal moment in the mass consumer diffusion of the mobile phone, 1994 would certainly be a candidate. This was a key year in the popular knowledge and take-up of the Internet also, but at Nokia it was the year of consolidation of the cell phone as cultural artefact: 'At Nokia, the breakthrough design was the classic 2100 cell phone . . . The phone's size was actually increased to give it an elliptically shaped top and a rounded keypad' (Steinbock 2001b: 272). One of the Nokians lionised for this achievement was 'vice president of design' Franck, who explained his aim that the 2100 phone 'would be friendly, like a companion, not a little, square, hard box . . . Putting a brick up to your face was not something I thought would be very good' (cited in Steinbock 2001b: 272). While Nokia 2100 was an everyman or -woman's phone, four years later Nokia's cell phones were being positioned for other, more elite taste cultures. In particular Nokia made decisive contributions to the emerging sense of the cell phone as an important part of fashion, something that has been the subject of a number of studies (notably those collected in Fortunati, Katz, and Riccini 2003). So, the sleek 8860 phone was acclaimed by the fashionistas, and Frank Nuovo was adulated by no less than *Vogue* as the 'designer who made wireless technology a fashion statement':

Nuovo's newest phone is the big hit in the world of wireless communication, the hottest cell phone on the charts. It is the sleek, streamlined, and aerodynamic phone that's a little Le Corbusier, a little Matrix – the first fashion phone.

(Sullivan 2000)

Dubbed the 'Porsche of mobile phones' (Kaiser 1999) and 'our haute couture phone' (Nuovo, quoted in Steinbock 2001b: 274), as well as turning heads in the United States, the predecessor, the 8810, had caused waves and been wildly popular in the strategically important business and cultural hubs of Asia-Pacific such as Hong Kong (Ling and Arnold 1998). For its part, the sibling cell phone

8210 was launched in Paris Fashion Week (Steinbock 2001b: 274). The 8860 relied on the power of celebrity, being associated with various models, film stars, and directors. Like the Apple Mackintosh desirable laptop computer, the 8860 also benefited from informal or formal product placement: 'cameos of the 8860 appeared in everything from *Sex and the City*, a suggestive television show, to *Hanging Up*, a recent Diane Keaton movie' (Steinbock 2001b: 274).

Nokia was not only acclaimed for its distinctive reworking of the cell phone, it was felt to signify larger things. I have been relying on Steinbock's account to suggest the importance of design to Nokia. Steinbock, in fact, believes Nokia to stand for a larger paradigm shift and renewal in production and consumption itself, design-become-demotic. There is something significant going on in this hyperbolic reliance upon and blazoning of design, but I would like to leave this theme briefly and consider Nokia's innovation along the very seam where the lines between technology and society are typically drawn: the user interface.

Nokia's embrace of the user

As we have seen, the Nokia way places a high value upon research and develop-ment, and also upon a highly literate, flexible, and reflexive corporate culture. It is no surprise, then, to find that Nokia's employees have well documented their work. Nowhere is this more readily presented perhaps than in a book about its design practices and precepts edited by three serving and former staff, containing case studies from a range of Nokia researchers and designers. As its subtitle suggests, the book sets out to document how *Nokia Changed the Face of the Mobile Phone*, an achievement it encapsulates as *Mobile Usability* (Lindholm, Keinonen, and Kiljander 2003). It describes the design and development of a number of import-ant features in the Nokia cell phone during the 1990s, those innovations mentioned earlier that became generally accepted as part of cell phone communications in general. Their master-theme of the Nokian designers in this collection, held out to coincide with Nokia's corporate vision also, is that of how to understand that elusive, fickle, expert yet ignorant, belated yet avant-garde figure of the user.

In the second half of the 1990s especially, one of the difficulties Nokia faced was how to sell its phones to an expanding number of new markets, each with its own distinctive cultures and subcultures. Nokia's reinvention of itself as an inter-national company and global brand posed for it the challenges of other corporate behemoths. For a cell phone company, however, there are perhaps some more profound and subtle difficulties and implications, given the place of the material object of the phone in culture and communication. It is too costly to conceive and make anew a cell phone for each cultural grouping, or phase of life-cycle, or (shifting) market segment, so design needs to fashion sufficient bridges among different cultures and users (Fig. 3.1).

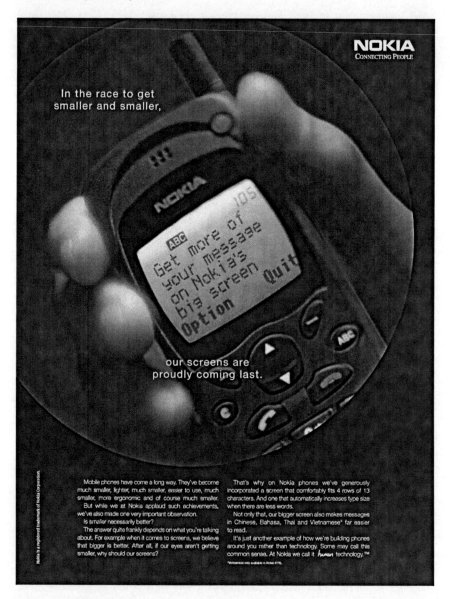

Figure 3.1 Nokia's cross-cultural phone design.

To come to grips with this task, Lindholm, Keinonen and Kiljander emphasise the importance of drawing upon the sorts of ideas about the use, consumption, domestication, and social shaping of technology that circulate in much cultural and social research on cell phones, including my own. Significantly they suggest a definition that collates a number of previously different, or even incompatible understandings of the user:

a mobile phone user is: an information processing unit accomplishing tasks; an actor in varying physical and social contexts; a consumer with a lifestyle; an interpreter of socially constructed meanings; a locus of different motivations; a member of a culture; an object and an initiator of continuous change.

(Lindholm, Keinonen and Kiljander 2003: 94)

This is a fascinating envisioning of the user as a hybrid, dynamic, and relational entity, and one commodified, yet powerful. Faced with the challenge of mapping and knowing this user – or at least stabilising her sufficiently to design an object to put into production – the Nokian designers invoke the idea of considering the 'whole culture':

Designing for people who seem exotic to us is hard because we cannot take any codes or interpretation frameworks for granted. We need to step back and look at the whole culture to be able to evaluate the relevance of even our task-level questions, must less the right solutions. *Cultural end-user studies* are the way to attain global user interface design.

(2003: 94)

There is a conundrum in this, of course, because of the dynamic, relational, and inextricably interwoven interdependence of technologies, their users and designers:

designers of new technologies have never seen the world for which they are designing. The very existence of novel technologies changes the situation in which they are used, and the use changes the products. So understanding users means understanding how they change as the society around them changes in general, and specifically how they change through interaction with the products that we introduce.

(2003: 93–4)

Interestingly, the case study that is introduced to illuminate this process is set in India, the country along with China that is now keenly studied and courted as a new economic power and huge emerging market. Understanding cultural specificity becomes an imperative for multinational profitability:

The vast potential of mobile market opportunities can be wasted if we are not prepared for each different culture entering the mobile information society . . . If we don't understand our markets well enough from the perspective of end-user needs, the new features we create will not be accepted and – even worse – we won't necessarily know why.

(Konkka 2003: 98)

To respond to such 'end-user needs', flexibility of design is required:

> Responding to culturally varying end-user needs doesn't always have to mean completely different products for each market area. Quite small user interface issues can sometimes make the difference. For example, the user's ability to add Hindi greetings or religious symbols to a message adds a great deal of emotional value to short message service (SMS) in India among its Hindu people. Hindu music in ringing tones and other alerts would do the same. The scalability and variability of the whole product to suit different cultures is a basic requirement for cultural adjustment.
>
> (2003: 98)

One researcher describes how her interdisciplinary research team approached an end-users' needs study in India in 2000. While general, aggregate figures on the Indian market were easily available, such information was not adequate to guide the particularities of design:

> The numbers can be used to construct a macro image of India as a mobile phone market, but they were far from sufficient to guide the design and localization of products for end users. Our project aimed at going from numerical abstractions to the concrete levels of users' lives. We were there to explore culture-specific factors, which could potentially affect user interface design.
>
> (2003: 99)

The team for the study included the Finnish researchers from Nokia – compromising a linguist, a usability specialist, a psychologist (Konkka) – and local Indian usability experts and translators. The research was avowedly limited in its objectives and informed by the 'contextual inquiry' method. Its main empirical explorations were an interview study in Delhi and user observation in Mumbai. In doing this, the ethos was the 'researcher has to become the user's apprentice' (Konkka 2003: 101). One set of findings related to the translatability of the user interface. The Nokia 3210 had contained the world's first Hindi user interface, and the researchers were keen to find out how it had been received by Indian users:

> We found that the technical terminology in our first Hindi release was rendered in literary and somewhat old-fashioned language. The results revealed that many technical terms would have been more understandable in English written with the Hindi (Devanagari) script. For instance, the terms *call divert*, *data*, *fax*, *call register*, *prepaid credit*, *incoming call alert*, and *infrared* don't have good Hindi analogs. In spoken language Hindi and English are mixed, and sometimes Roman script is used to write Hindi . . . We have done our best to

make the UI [user interface] as localized as possible, but we haven't paid enough attention to the fact that much of the language is in fact localized as English.

(2003: 108)

This is an important lesson, but even if this is acknowledged there remain real difficulties in translating the user interface, as Konkka openly admits:

We still don't know, however, if what we did is right or wrong. Localization is not that straightforward because understandability is not the only criterion. Native language can be important as such, and using local language shows respect for the local culture . . . The language will be modernized this time around [in the next version of the Hindi user interface], aiming at a better combination of understandability and respect for the appropriate Hindi expressions.

(2003: 108)

In concluding her report on the Nokia Indian fieldwork study, Konkka advocates such contextually oriented inquiry as a palpable way to conduct research useful for design, vividly remarking that the 'results have been felt, heard, smelled, and seen' (2003: 109). She goes even further to claim something even further for the researcher (and by extension the company for which she works): 'The researcher stays for a while as a living representative of the people and the culture where she or he has been. The researcher in effect becomes the messenger' (2003: 110).

It is worth pausing at this point to consider not only the limits of Konkka's contention here, but whether her position is indeed representative of Nokia's cultural turn more generally. To recapitulate: the dilemma for the late modern cell phone company is how to insert its product into the lives of consumers, so such purchasers will continue to buy this commodity and the various services that flow through it. Nokia has moved beyond imagining itself in the early years as a solely Finnish company (albeit one trading internationally), through enlarging its identity to project itself as European, to becoming truly international. It now employs workers from and in many countries and cultures, is listed on stock exchanges around the world, and borrows its rhetorics from global commercial culture and management discourse, but its Finnish workers and location are still a stabilising influence in the 'Nokia way'. How then does it ensure its phones 'connect' through the consumers of the new economic giants of the twenty-first century?

To do this effectively Nokia *must* engage with the question of culture – a dilemma other corporations face too. The problem in doing so, however, as not only Konkka's account reveals, but also other contributions to *Nokia Usability*, as well as a burgeoning literature on the user and usability from a number of different standpoints, is how to deal with the user's tendency to baffle or exceed the expectations of the designer. I suppose I am wondering here whether real engagement with the user would be an ongoing project involving far greater participation in design, corporate government, and ownership of the technology, that Nokia, or most of its competitors, are prepared to consider. It would also involve a far more profound questioning of the cultural politics of technology and design.

Certainly the position of embracing the user, and deploying innovative techniques such as contextual inquiry, is an important step forward in grasping the cultural dimensions of cell phone technology. For the researcher, using a few weeks' or months' acquaintance to see themselves as a 'living representative of the people and the culture where she or he has been', avoids the inconvenience of positioning the users as ongoing equals and participants in the conceptualisation, decision-making, and shaping of the technologies in their lives. Such a view is in keeping with Lindholm and Keinonen's overview of how Nokia manages the design of user interfaces (2003). They describe how the Nokia design team works on a new mobile phone user interface concept, and then when they are satisfied it goes on a 'design verification world tour . . . typically conducted in several countries, including a selection of the following: East and West coasts of the United States, Japan, Hong Kong, mainland China, and a few European countries' (2003: 149). However, such research on a design is more in the province of fine-tuning:

> Rarely does a tour reveal anything radical; radical problems will have been ironed out before the designers packed the suitcase and set out. Regardless of their culture, people tend to approach logical usability problems and goal-oriented tasks much the same way throughout the world. Cultural differences have more to do with preferences in graphics and vocabulary than with the core interaction. Therefore the logical mode of dialogue can be global, whereas displays designed for Europe and Japan have to be extremely different.
>
> (2003: 149)

Some of the pitfalls of this world tour approach are actually posed in another contribution to *Nokia Usability*, where Nieminen-Sundell and Väänänen-Vainio-Mattila (2003) point out not only the unfinished, dynamic, and open-ended character of products – 'products *keep changing after the launch phase*' (2003: 122) – but also the profound implications of culture:

> Culture as a source of meanings should thus be included in the analysis and acceptance of products. But, instead of just adding 'culture' to the traditional model of human–computer interaction, a more radical step is to reconceive

the whole product development chain as a locus for creating and reproducing culture. Socially shaped meanings are inscribed in or attached to products, which then are transferred to the everyday life of the users to become what they will.

(2003: 124)

Clearly my discussion here relies upon one collection of inside perspectives on the processes and meanings of Nokia design practices at a certain historical moment. It needs to be greatly expanded, not least with further studies and accounts of design and the conceptualisation of the user within Nokia as well as other cell phone companies (for a thoughtful consideration see Green et al. 2001). More-over there is a substantial, growing, and engaged interdisciplinary literature on cell phones and design, including studies that delve into cultural and intercultural questions (for instance, Yu and Tng 2003). Nonetheless, I do think this discussion does reveal the importance of culture, cultural work, and the production of culture, for the task of understanding how the cell phone comes to inhabit daily life, and what significances attach to it when it does.

Planet Vodafone

So far I have explored the development of cell phone culture through the perspective of a leading handset manufacturer, namely Nokia. The phone manufacturers and other equipment manufacturers (often referred to as 'vendors') have been very important but are only one part of the story. Another group of corporations that have played a leading role in the invention of cell phone culture have been the network providers. My case study here will be of perhaps the largest dedicated international mobiles company: Vodafone.[4]

Vodafone had its beginning in a company called Racal, specialising in the manufacture of radio communication units for the military. Racal was established by Ray Brown and Calder Cunningham (and its name was formed from the first two letters of their first names), but its driving force was the son of a docker, Ernest Harrison, whom they recruited as company secretary and chief accountant in 1951. Racal floated on the stock market in 1961, and by 1966 Harrison had assumed its chairmanship. It was in the early 1980s, however, that Racal's fortunes were really to rise, along with those of the newly emerging cellular phone market. Cellular phones had been introduced into Britain with the awarding of a licence to Cellnet, a consortium of British Telecom and the company Securicor. When bids were called for a licence for the second cellular telephone network in late 1982 Harrison worked closely with his colourful colleague Gerry Whent to develop and submit Racal's proposal. As the name of the network, they chose Vodafone (*vo*ice and *da*ta). Lacking telecommunications experience, Racal was a rank out-sider, but they won the bid, and Whent proceeded to set up a new company called

Racal Millicom to develop the network, basing its headquarters in the market town of Newbury, Berkshire. Once again we encounter the theatre of the 'first ever call' being made by a celebrity: this time the 'first ever' mobile call in the UK was made by comedian Ernie Wise (of Morecambe and Wise fame) on 1 January 1985 from St Katherine's Dock in London to Vodafone's base in Newbury. Vodafone was the first carrier to launch in the UK, and its pitch for the business market dovetailed nicely with the rise of Margaret Thatcher's enterprise culture, as the biographer of its most well-known Chief Executive Officer Chris Gent observes:

> Fuelled by the Thatcherite belief in the power of market forces, many young men and women were making good money in business. They saw even the cumbersome mobile handsets in production at that time as an essential new status symbol, one every bit as essential as the best champagne or a fast car.
>
> (Merriden 2003: 28)

A condition of the licence prohibited Vodafone from selling directly to the public, so a wholly owned subsidiary, Vodac, was formed in 1984 to be the service provider for the network.

According to its official corporate history, in 1987 Whent committed 'Vodafone to aggressively develop mobile telephony internationally in the long-term, by entering consortia formed to bid for licences, and by rigorously identifying opportunities for acquisition' (Vodafone 2005). At this stage Vodafone enjoyed the largest mobile network in the world. In the same year Vodafone made important moves in mobile data services, creating Vodata as its 'voice and data' business, especially to develop and implement its voicemail service Vodafone Recall. It also marketed other 'value-added' services, including information lines such as the *Financial Times* CityLine and the motoring organisation AA Roadwatch. Paging services were still popular, especially among business users, so Vodapage was launched with a paging network claiming coverage of 80 per cent of the British population. In 1988 20 per cent of ordinary shares of Racal's telecommunications division were floated on the London and New York stock exchanges. It was not until September 1991, however, that Racal and Vodafone de-merged fully in the then largest de-merger in British corporate history, and Vodafone Group, as an independent company, was listed on the London and New York stock exchanges.

Vodafone was an early participant in the second-generation GSM cell phone network, first in the UK in 1991. In the same year, Vodafone collaborated with Telecom Finland in the world's first international roaming call (allowing a customer to travel to another country and use their home network to make calls). In 1994, Vodafone's Vodata was the first UK network operator to launch data, fax, and SMS on the GSM network. One of the innovative products Vodafone launched early on was the pay-as-you-go product, something that very much shaped cell phone culture – especially for young users. It has been claimed that the concept of a pay-as-you-go cell phone was first developed by the Irish mobile carrier Eircell, which was started in 1986 as a division of Telecom Éireann, before eventually being acquired by Vodafone in 2001. Apparently Eircell introduced the pay-as-you-go system as a world first with the *Ready to go* brand, an innovation instrumental in making the cell phone a mass-market product in Ireland (*Wikipedia* 2005d). The *Ready to go* product was advertised with the song of the same name by the British band *Republica*. In 1996 Vodafone was the first UK network operator to launch a pre-paid package for its analogue. The package required no contract and no credit check, and was avidly taken up by young users.

In 1997 Chris Gent succeeded Whent as the Vodafone CEO, and radically reorganised the corporation. Whereas previously there had been six wholly owned providers of Vodafone service, these were now replaced by three: Vodafone Corporate, Vodafone Retail, and Vodafone Connect respectively (Merriden 2003: 37). Gent's most audacious efforts were to come in his daring mergers and acquisitions. As a study of mobile network operators and internationalisation has pointed out, it was in the 1980s that cross-border telephony relationships intensified, with fundamental shifts in how markets and ownership were viewed with privatisation and competition (Gerpott and Jakopin 2005: 635). From the early 1990s, the barriers to entry across national and regional markets were lessened with the widespread adoption of the GSM standards, and internationalisation deepened.

In Vodafone's case such changes saw it seek to become involved in the lucrative but still rather fragmented and underdeveloped US market. As we saw in chapter 2, the US had long been in the forefront of developing cell phone technology, pioneering its research, development, and deployment. Yet owing to the way its markets were created by regulators, service was delivered by many, many players, and end-to-end connectivity across the country (through roaming, for instance) was difficult to achieve. The fragmentation of the market was compounded by the decisions made by industry and policymakers regarding adoption of second-generation cell phone technology, and also the norms that had been accepted regarding pricing, including the custom that the receiver of calls be billed. One successful operator at the end of the 1990s was AirTouch, a mobile operator created from the telco Pacific Telesis in 1994. AirTouch had achieved much, not only in the US market, but also in Europe through joint ventures to bid for licences and operate networks (Merriden 2003: 42). Gent managed to snatch AirTouch from under the noses of the newly merged Bell Atlantic/GT. Pipped at the post, Bell Atlantic/GTE turned around and struck a deal with Vodafone AirTouch to create a new mobile company in the USA, called Verizon Wireless – affording coverage of some 90 per cent of the population. Vodafone was the minority shareholder initially, though with 45 per cent of the business, leaving Bell to hold the rest (2003: 47).

Flush from its US acquisition, Vodafone turned its attention to consolidating in the European market. After a series of tactical manoeuvres involving a number of mobile operators,[5] Vodafone pulled off a hostile takeover of Mannesmann, Germany's giant mobile company, with which it had previously co-ordinated on various joint ventures. Mannesmann had its origins in steel tubes, mining, and engineering, but in 1990 was the first private firm awarded a German cell phone licence (Merriden 2003: 51–3). Within two years it was the leader in the cell phone market, outpacing Deutsche Telekom, the former national telecommunications carrier. It also entered into joint ventures in Europe's other largest telecommunications market, Italy (creating the mobile phone network Omnitel, with Olivetti) and France (partnering with Vivendi). Vodafone acquired Mannesmann at a high price, with an impressive yield (Merriden 2003: 54). Mannesmann had also acquired Orange, in a bid to make itself too large to be easily digestible by Vodafone. Because of European competition regulation, Vodafone was obliged to divest itself of Orange, which it sold to France Télécom in October 2000.

Interestingly, Vodafone's takeover of Mannesmann was received with a good deal of hostility by the German public and press. The merger was seen as a clash of corporate cultures and perhaps also of visions for telecommunications: the frictionless international capital co-ordinates of Vodafone colliding with the corporate governance model of German corporations such as Mannesman characterised by a network of ownership and links of interconnected large companies and banks, with aspirations too for partnerships and consensus among shareholders, managers, and workers. (There is evidence to suggest that the German corporate governance system largely remains intact, despite changes represented by Mannesmann, and that there is no systemic shift to the Anglo-Saxon model (Heinze 2001, 2004)). In all this manoeuvring, Vodafone does have a strong claim to be a genuinely international cell phone firm. In their study of the degree of internationalisation and the financial performance of fourteen European mobile network operators in the years 1997–2003, Gerpott and Jakopin found that by the end of 2003 Vodafone was the only one 'with truly global business activities' (2005: 635).

We have seen that for Nokia brand development during the 1990s was an important priority, as it was also for other handset manufacturers. Brand development became important for mobile network operators around the world also, but it was an uneven process. There may be underlying reasons for this in consumption:

> Mobile service users in developed markets are a fairly fickle group, seemingly willing to switch brands without much concern as to whether the new service is likely to be much different to that currently consumed – which in general it is not. It is as yet unclear whether the mobile market can ever

develop strong brand loyalty, but operators understandably prefer to believe in that possibility.

(Curwen 2002: 177)

One factor that conditioned Vodafone's approach was that a condition of its licence was that it was not permitted to sell directly to its users and thus develop a direct relationship with them. Rather Vodafone and its competitor Cellnet were required to act as wholesalers to service provider intermediaries who offered the retail mobile services. Cellnote and Vodafone enjoyed a duopoly network arrangement from their launch in 1985 until One2One (owned by Mercury, competitor to British Telecom in fixed-line services) entered the market in 1993, followed by Orange in 1994 (their licences were awarded in 1991). While the new competitors made significant and growing inroads into the mobiles market, Vodafone and Cellnet continued to enjoy market power and high rates of return (as found by Oftel in its 1999 consultation (Oftel 1999)). Nonetheless Orange and One2One were allowed to retail air-time directly to end-users (though they were also obliged to sell wholesale services to other service providers upon request) (Oftel 1996).

As a counterpoint to the case of Vodafone, it is worth briefly considering the case of Orange, and how it constructed its brand and identity. Orange prided itself on the care it put into crafting, marketing, and so establishing its brand, and especially in distinguishing itself from among the then over seventy other service providers in the market (Oftel 1999). Its approach was to focus on the attributes and perceptions of a mobile (its utility and ability to conjure up desire) rather than foregrounding the technology:

> The brand had to be something that people would engage with on an emotional level as well as delivering tangible benefits to them. The team refined the core brand idea from four options – the manager, the innovator, it's my life, it's my friend. The result was 'it's my phone' which combined the best elements from the four . . . Market research found that people thought the name [Orange] was distinctive and friendly, extrovert, modern and powerful . . . An orange square with 'orange' simply written in lowercase white lettering was the concept that shone through . . . After extensive customer research into people's likes and dislikes of their current providers, Orange defined its values that helped shape the personality of the brand. These are honest, straightforward, friendly, refreshing and dynamic. WCRS [advertising agency] created the award winning launch advertising campaign and our brandline 'the future's bright, the future's Orange' was born. The campaign deliberately avoided images of mobile phones to show that Orange was about communication and customer benefits, a more personal approach.

(Orange 2005)

Clearly this account is the 'official' story available from Orange's website, but what it conveys is how Orange still wishes to be perceived: as a company with a fresh, new, simple approach to cell phones. This was indeed the reputation it earned for itself at the time as a very impressive, almost textbook branch launch, and it tried to reinforce this perception through keeping its service offerings easy-to-understand and grasp.[6]

Vodafone and Cellnet had established their businesses by offering relatively long contracts, and by what, in the mid-1990s, were relatively high rental or access fees and call charges – something that is probably representative of other providers around the world. This may have suited the business customers and relatively well-off upper- and middle-class customers the cell phone companies focused upon in the first decade of commercial operation. However such pricing strategies and packages were not so attractive to younger people with typically different financial and user profiles, nor to many other users who were not motivated by such a strong need for mobiles at this stage to be able to sign up to fixed contracts with hefty payment. The difficulty was that mobile providers had not shrugged off the traditional telecommunications public utility attitude to customers ('subscribers'), and adopted common marketing and transaction strategies for other retail goods and services. This is where Orange came into its own, later rivalled by that most brand savvy of companies, Virgin, one of the new entities called 'virtual mobile network operator' (or VMNO). Orange's own history adds a mythical gloss, but certainly it did mark a turn in the commercial construction of cell phone culture:

> Orange began building a strong, fresh, clear identity that set it apart from the clutter that characterised a market littered with high-tech jargon and complicated pricing. It was the start of revolution. Orange innovations like simple Talk Plans that offered real value for money, per second billing, Caller ID, itemised billing free of charge, and direct customer relationships changed people's attitudes about mobile communications.
>
> (Orange 2005)

In June 2001, the Orange image developed in the UK market was used to rebrand the Itinéris brand used in France. As Curwen notes, 'it is fairly unusual for a market leader to be rebranded, and even more so for it to adopt the tag-line, in this case, "The future's bright . . . the future's Orange", established in another country' (2002: 174).

The emergence of such a focus on brand and new ways to market to encourage the consumption of mobiles by a new entrant such as Orange required a response from already established competitors. Although Vodafone had introduced important new offerings such as pay-as-you-go airtime it was not until after their spectacular merger and acquisitions that the importance of brand was really grasped.

While it was comfortably established in Britain, it was not well known in its new European guise, as owner of Mannesmann, nor in the crucial emerging markets elsewhere especially in the Asia-Pacific. Vodafone had tended to associate branding with the sponsorship of sporting events such as the Derby or the English cricket team, a custom now taken to underline its Anglo-Saxon origins. Further, Vodafone simply was not spending as much on advertising as its competitors (Merriden 2003: 106). In the eyes of some commentators, Vodafone faced quite a challenge: 'the Vodafone brand can be said to lack any kind of "personality" . . . having collected a set of assets that are being marketed under a variety of brands in different markets, Vodafone is in need of a global brand image' (Curwen 2002: 177).

To build its brand, Vodafone signed a four-year £30 million deal with Manchester United in early 2000. The phone company's then CEO Peter Bamford declared:

> This ground-breaking agreement goes beyond a pure shirt sponsorship and will bring a new range of mobile information services to a loyal, massive supporter base. There is additional business potential in the bringing together of the world's largest telecommunications company and the world's best-known football club.
>
> (*Guardian* 2000)

Although Manchester United was an English football club, because of the developments in global sport and media culture it enjoyed an international following. According to Merriden, the agreement was a watershed for Vodafone's brand:

> Manchester United is no ordinary club. With over a £1 billion in turnover each year only the likes of Real Madrid (sponsored by Siemens IC mobile) and Bayern Munich (sponsored by Deutsche Telekom) rival it in sheer size. More importantly for Vodafone, the exposure that Manchester United commands is global. Manchester United players are treated like gods in the Far East, where the fan base is huge with, for example, more Chinese Manchester United fans than there are English ones.
>
> (Merriden 2003: 108)

Vodafone was trialling and selling not only mobile handset and voice telephony but also new mobile Internet and content services to the most ardent of football fans, who could see:

> highlights of the Manchester United matches and watch classic goals on their mobile phones whenever and wherever they chose. Vodafone also designed a United Pay as You Talk mobile phone that it planned to sell to fans selected

through direct mail from the club's supporter database . . . And it kicked off a series of direct marketing projects to promote its new manUmobile WAP portal and text messaging services . . . [offering] goal alerts, match reports and team news . . . audio interviews, video clips and merchandise offers.

(2003: 108–9)

A crucial but tricky part of the new arrangement was how Vodafone was to ensure it benefited from one of Manchester United's stars, who had become a brand name in his own right. This was footballer David Beckham, who was the face of Vodafone during the period of its greatest global expansion. In August 2002, he even assented to having his voice on the company's voicemail service:

David Beckham is lending his voice to Vodafone's official voice-mail service, the first celebrity ever to allow such an extraordinary endorsement . . . Screen savers, games and quizzes for mobile phones, as well as ads starrring Beckham, form part of the two-year deal which will make use of the footballer's status as a global icon. The mobile giant intends to use him in promotions around the world because he appeals to football fans and fashion followers alike.

(Day 2004a)

Following its Mannesmann acquisition, Vodafone faced a problem with its lack of visibility and brand awareness in the two big European markets of Germany and Italy. Its other major image, brand, and advertising campaign, therefore, featured German racing car driver Michael Schumacher and his preferred vehicle, the glamorous Italian steed Ferrari.[7] Despite this buoyant rebranding, one journalist remarked that while 'Vodafone's confidence has been reflected in a raft of extensive sponsorship deals aimed at making the mobile phone company as ubiquitous as Coca-Cola . . . something seems to be going wrong on Planet Vodafone', with a plunge in its share price and concern that it has 'yet to prove that is huge subscriber base – 83 million customers in 29 countries – can be turned into hard cash' (Doward 2001).

There is much else to say about the ways in which Vodafone, and indeed other network providers, have made a contribution to cell phone culture. Certainly Vodafone, like its competitors, is stretched to understand and keep pace with the new technologies and services now issuing into the marketplace. (Its response to an early form of mobile content, for instance, is represented in the Vodafone Live! portal.) Nonetheless we can see in this case study how Vodafone emerged from its English beginnings to navigate the then huge cell phone market of the USA, the changed circumstances of European governance and markets, the proverbial emerging markets of Asia and elsewhere, to work on its brand and the sorts of identities it wished to project. The deployment of celebrity, especially in the vast and increasingly transnational leisure and cultural economy of sport, has been vital to this.

Changing cell phone culture

Much has changed in our understanding of the conditions of culture in the short period since the Sony Walkman, or even since it was studied. A great deal has shifted too in how cell phone culture is produced. In my treatment here, I have sketched two influential instances of the production of cell phone culture in Nokia and Vodafone. In many ways, however, these are episodes from a 'classic' Europe and North America dominated period of the creation of cell phone culture, now being thoroughly refashioned. This was the period especially from the mid to late 1980s to the mid to late 1990s, a decade in which phone manufacturers and equipment suppliers and network operators, and a growing number of new intermediaries (such as phone, air-time, and content wholesalers and retailers, and various types of third-part suppliers and partners), sought to make and secure a mass consumer culture for cell phones, with global reach and local intelligibility and purchase.

What the subsequent development of the cell phone has made clear is that the need for detailed studies of cell phone culture has been produced in particular cultural and linguistic contexts. We do now have such studies emerging, such as two useful studies on Chinese cell phone culture. Jing Wang's important study of cell phone branding in China, for instance, looks at the 'shifting brandscape of China's mobile phone market' (Wang 2005: 189) and how music has played an important role in this, not only as something now available over mobiles that is associated with 'cool culture', but also as an important and coeval marketing tool. Wang shows the close relationships among fashion codes, music culture, and cell phone advertising and identities, and how Motorola's reinvention of itself as a global entertainment brand (with the funky and well-received 'Moto' tag) saw it affiliate itself with emerging, edgy artists, and what was seen as avant-garde. She also provides evidence for how difficult and tenuous it is for global multinationals to suture their products to local identities and subcultures. In their study of cell phones and advertising in China, Christina Spurgeon and Michael Keane offer a fascinating account of how a national firm, the Ningbo Bird brand of cell phones, negotiated the production of cell phone culture (Spurgeon and Keane 2005). As Spurgeon and Keane show, within three years of entering the market in the late 1990s, Bird became the top-seller, displacing global brands such as Motorola and Nokia but also becoming an exporter to South-East Asia, India, and Russia.[8] What is especially interesting about Spurgeon and Keane's account is not only how Bird appealed to functional and fashionable markets but also how in the confection of a national firm it incorporated discourses of the 'global', European high-technology and cosmopolitanism in its advertising.

Those attempting to grapple with the changed social and economic relations of consumer technology and culture that the cell phone in particular represents, recapitulates, and prognosticates, have sought to theorise the 'cultural economy' (du Gay and Pryke 2002), the 'new economy', or, in a discourse that has captured the imaginations of policy makers, industry, and scholars alike in different places, the 'creative industries' (or 'creative economy'). These new ways of seeing the production of culture have revealed new dimensions and configurations of how cultural and media industries relate to each other, how a particular media culture fits into the general ecology of communications and media, and how these relate to larger industrial, economic, and political arrangements in transformation. Further, there is now growing recognition of the importance of how the production of culture unfolds and is inflected in different settings. Most important of all, perhaps, is the keen sense we now have of the inextricably intimate and manifold hinges between production and consumption, something to which I will now turn.

Part II
Consuming the cell phone

4 Txt msg: the rise and rise of messaging cultures

The story [of SMS] has a slight resemblance to those of the Norwegian fairy tale character Askeladden, who picks up all kinds of items that he encounters given the presumption that it may come to use some day. In the adventure they always do, resulting in a massive success.

(Trosby 2004: 192)

When they had the campaign that allowed you to send SMS for two cents a piece, we pretty much sat there all day with the mobile and probably sent a few hundred messages in all . . . For three or four hours we just sat on the bed sending messages to one another.

(Sanna, Finnish fourteen-year-old, quoted in Kasesniemi 2003: 21)

Texting in the Philippines is transforming conventional fairytales. Not unlike a Cinderella-themed narrative: the ballroom can be conceived as cyberspace, where instead of dancing, Cinderella and the Prince text one another. The fit of the glass slipper can be compared to text skill. The fairy godmother can be envisioned as technology; the evil step-mother, the cost of pre-paid calling cards; and the three evil step-sisters: a stolen phone, a faulty SIM card, and no signal.

(Elwood-Clayton 2003: 235)

So far I have focused on the production of cell phone culture, considering narratives of its early history, especially as a portable voice telephony artefact, and then reviewing, in chapter 3, how influential corporations, in particular Nokia and Vodafone, made important contributions through their ideas of use, branding, and advertising. In this chapter, I wish to turn to another, interlinked aspect of the 'circuit of culture', cell phone culture – namely consumption.

To explore consumption and cell phone culture, I turn to a celebrated, almost proverbial episode: text messaging. There has been much fascination in studying, cataloguing, and debating the varieties and intricacies of text messaging, and how it has modified social, media, and cultural practices. Rather than repeating this work here, or drawing on new, empirical work, my intention is interpretative.

What I wish to do is to attempt a history, or perhaps a historiography, of text messaging, to gain insights into its place in cell phone culture. Text messaging is not only an intriguing case study in cultural consumption and user experimentation, as we shall find out later; what it signifies for cell phone culture is at the heart of much public and commercial disquiet and contention about the future of mobile media.

Doing the history of text messaging

Text messaging has been the subject of much animated debate and study, including two book-length collections (Glotz and Bertschi 2005; Harper, Palen, and Taylor 2005), but I have been able to find only one scholarly account of SMS history (Taylor and Vincent 2005). As I have already mentioned, there are many difficulties at this relatively early moment in doing the history of cell phones, let alone text messaging. Nonetheless, thinking about the development of text messaging provides an occasion to think about how such history might be done. What I would like to draw upon here is the influential approach to understanding the itineraries and adventures of technology offered by actor-network theory, which not only offers many challenges to traditional theories of technology, as I suggested in chapter 1, but also opens up new historical and cultural-theoretical approaches (Fig. 4.1).

Figure 4.1 Gordon Hill (left), who is morse coding the same message as nine-year-old Ben Wichester, who is sending an SMS, at the Powerhouse Museum, Sydney, 14 April 2005.

Textual beginnings

> Txt msg ws an acidnt. no 1 expcted it. Whn the 1st txt msg ws sent, in 1993 by Nokia eng stdnt Riku Pihkonen, the telcom cpnies thought it ws nt important. SMS – Short Message Service – ws nt considrd a majr pt of GSM. Like mny teks, the *pwr* of txt – indeed, the *pwr* of the fon – wz discvrd by users. In the case of txt mssng, the usrs were the yng or poor in the W and E.
>
> (Agar 2003: 105)

As Jon Agar notes, text messaging was considered to be something of a minor service (Agar 2003). However, this insight is more complicated than it appears. Certainly at the start, technology designers, manufacturers, and cell phone companies had been preoccupied with transferring telephone capabilities and culture to the cell phone platform. The development of the first-generation analogue cell phone transmission systems around the world is evidence of this. However, especially in the move to develop digital transmission systems for the cell phone, and standards that would embody these and promote common technologies, as well as in anticipating their implementation, consideration had been given to the data transmission capabilities of cell phones. With the growth of data communications from the 1960s onwards – and the use of modems over telecommunications networks, the dawning of the Internet, not to mention telex, videotext, teletext, and fax services – data services over cellular and wireless technologies were of some interest (there is a historical parallel here too, of course, given that wireless telegraphy was a precursor data service to its cellular radio antecedents).

In telecommunications, among the most robust and perhaps best-engineered forms of data services were those associated with the Integrated Services Digital Network (ISDN). The ISDN system involved a dedicated digital network that provided data as well as voice channels on the same subscriber line – something not possible again in a widespread manner until voice over Internet protocol started to become widely used over broadband connections. At a certain stage ISDN was seen as the natural progression path for telecommunications networks (for example Dorros 1987), but owing to the typical pricing policies in the 1980s and early to mid 1990s still shaped by older telco culture and slow to change (cf. ACCC 1998), as well as the fast emerging mix of alternative technologies (not least the Internet, faster modems for dial-up connections, then broadband) (ASTEC 1995), ISDN (often archly referred to as '*It Still Doesn't Nothing*', failed in most countries to move beyond its base of business clients to domestic customers. Given the prominence of ISDN in telecommunications circles, it was unsurprising that it was contemplated in early visions of GSM. In the list of basic requirements for GSM services in the first action plan in December 1982, it was stipulated that the 'services and facilities offered in the public switched telephone networks and the public data networks . . . should be available in the mobile system' (Hillebrand 2001c: 264). In 1985, however, a concept for data and other services was agreed that borrowed important structural elements from ISDN, yet recognised that 'GSM is not a mobile ISDN' (2001c: 266). Although there were some who supported GSM having data capabilities and channels akin to ISDN, the difficulty faced was that there was neither capacity in the system nor the means to gain the relevant efficiency needed from the scarce spectrum. ISDN was also a more stable service, as customers were just connected to one fixed line in their telecommunications carrier's network as opposed to the emerging issues in mobile telephony with the need for roaming in other countries and services provided by a range of competing providers.[1]

Instead of fully encompassing data, GSM was optimised for telephony, remembering that one of the abiding issues in the 1982–5 period was the transition for cellular phones from having their natural place in vehicles to becoming hand-held. Those participating in the standards-setting judged it was feasible to envisage a range of data services with data rates up to 9.6 kbs, a level that expectations quickly exceeded. Such data services, for the 'mobile office' (Hillebrand 2001c: 266) were what are termed circuit-switched (the fundamental, historical mode of telephone networks) rather than packet-switched (for a succinct primer on this distinction pivotal to Internet technologies, see Clarke 2004). With these constraints in mind, what was proposed was short message transmission:

> GSM was seen at that time as a car telephony system (the discussion on the viability of hand portables in the same network was still ongoing). So a typical application scenario was a plumber or other technician doing some repair work in the customer's home could receive short messages in his car waiting in front of the home. Another scenario was to enable a user to receive a short notice while he was engaged on a call.
>
> (Hillebrand 2001c: 266)

Ironically, because of its technical characteristics, SMS 'can be seen as the first packet switched service' in GSM (2001c: 266), and so a harbinger of what was to lie ahead in the transformations of the mobile Internet and media. SMS comprised three services: a message sent from a handset by someone ('mobile originated'), a message received on a handset by someone ('mobile terminated') and a message sent to many handsets ('point to multipoint'). This latter service, also newly created for GSM, was also called 'cell broadcast', a service 'somewhat similar to teletext on television, where a series of information messages can be sent to users, based on their location' (Cox 2001: 289).[2]

Within the European consortium developing the GSM specifications, Norwegian engineer Finn Trosby was entrusted with the responsibility of convening a 'Drafting Group on Message Handling'. This group produced a draft specification in November 1978, which set out key elements of the services, the network architecture, protocols, principles for routing of messages, and how the dedicated SMS handling service centre would work (Hillebrand 2001d: 413–14). One of the most important facets of SMS set in this phase was that SMS would be a store-and-forward service, analogous to email or the postal service. Also owing to the specifications of the transmission and priorities accorded to SMS, they could be 'transmitted to mobile stations in idle mode or involved in a call' (2001d: 414).

While the work in this period was crucial and, according to GSM historian Hillebrand, formed the 'basis of the tremendous success in the market' (Hillebrand 2001d: 414), it is important to note signal omissions and exclusions. Take, for instance, the possibility of sending and receiving SMS via not only cell phones but also fixed line phones too, something that is now being slowly introduced. Hillebrand laments that:

> I tried to interest the ISDN community to work with us on a compatible SMS service in the ISDN. This would have provided a standardised access to and from ISDN users. But the initiatives did not fall on fertile ground. Therefore the SMS did not provide a standard for the access from and to fixed subscribers.
>
> (Hillebrand 2001d: 414)

In contrast the composing and communication of SMS from an external keyboard and display (such as a computer screen) was developed in phase two of GSM, and implemented in 1994–5 (Holley 2001: 420). In 1992–3 a number of important 'advanced enhancements to SMS' were devised and incorporated, such as 'immediate display messages';[3] the use of SMS to allow voicemail messages to be sent to the user; and data storage improvements (Holley 2001: 420–1). The awkwardness and laboriousness of using keyboards was something that received much attention at about this time, especially through the introduction of keyboards with more characters as well as predictive text-entry systems (Taylor and Vincent 2005: 78).

The salient aspect of SMS is, of course, its famous terseness, both a constraint but a fabulous spur to communication. Early on, SMS was conceived as having a maximum message length of 128 octets (an octet is a byte of eight binary digits usually regarded as an entity) (Hillebrand 2001d: 408). By 1987–8 180 octets was possible but 160 was agreed upon (2001d: 414). In 1994 the possible length of a message was extended by allowing long messages to be split across a number of SMS (called SMS concatenation). This allowed SMS to be, theoretically at least, 'up to 255 segments of 150 or so characters', though using this full capability would be expensive so smaller groups of messages were thought more likely, as 'when Nokia introduced its picture messaging based on SMS concatenation in 1998' (Holley 2001: 421). To create further space, SMS compression was attempted from 1996 onwards. Finally, with the growing interest in ringtones and other sounds and images over cell phones, SMS was enhanced so as to deliver these multimedia in a message.

A defining element of digital textual communication is what languages are able to be represented. This matter has been widely discussed in relation to the Internet, especially when the basic code for email, American Standard Code for Information Interchange (ASCII), held sway (see, for instance, Nolan 2004), and has important implications for cell phones also. Holley notes that:

> the original SMS character was based on the set proposed for the European paging system . . . supposed to provide for the majority of European char-acters, including uppercase Greek characters, however it didn't include several characters needed in Eastern Europe, and even omitted some Northern Euro-pean characters. Coupling that with the expansion of GSM into the middle east and far east, it was clear that some major enhancement was needed.
>
> (Holley 2001: 421–2)

After much debate in the 1993–5 period, the solution adopted was a character set used for Unicode.[4] This way forward did have its own limitations: 'This character set allows transmission of the vast majority of characters in the world but of course uses more than twice the space of the original GSM set' (Holley 2001: 422).

A short but rich reflection upon the making of SMS is told by Finn Trosby, who was introduced earlier for his key role in devising the technology. Trosby begins by noting, bathetically, that:

> the reason for writing an article on 'the birth of SMS' is not to reveal a 15 year old story about huge achievements in terms of complex protocols and chal-lenging combinations of radio, data and network design . . . The SMS . . . is definitely one of the simplest compounds of the GSM system.
>
> (2004: 187).

Rather for Trosby:

> SMS is a story about innovation. SMS was indeed a true newcomer . . . SMS . . . was an extremely simple messaging service tailor-made for GSM . . . The major part of the GSM community expected the circuit switched data and fax services to be the most important non-voice services, and SMS to be more like an add-on that might increase the attraction of the GSM system without any commercial significance. The years to come proved it to be the other way round.
>
> (2004: 187)

Trosby summarises the merits and flaws of the design – the simplicity and use of available 'in-house' capabilities of SMS, for instance, versus lack of forethought of envisaging and designing for future possibilities such as group chat or message templates.

After acknowledging various individuals for their respective roles in SMS development, he tells a fairytale as a way to address the '[t]ricky part: what can we learn from the SMS adventure, if anything at all?':

> The story [of SMS] has a slight resemblance to those of the Norwegian fairy tale character Askeladden, who picks up all kinds of items that he encounters given the presumption that it may come to use some day. In the adventure they always do, resulting in a massive success.
>
> (2004: 192)

This bricoleur approach is quite different from what is possible later on:

> Trying to imagine the same situation today, it is not hard to imagine the average modern executive immediately tearing the SMS concept . . . into pieces. 'When there is no extensive and convincing text of market analysis, there should be no further transfer to a lengthy and costly design and production process.'
>
> (2004: 193).

To amplify this point, Trosby compares SMS with a number of other potential similar technologies:

> The strange thing is that if one imagines the modern product development filtering on all other services than SMS, they might have passed the checkpoint procedures without difficulties. The speech service was a banker, no one doubted that there was a substantial potential of migrating telephony from the fixed to the mobile networks. The fax service also had a high standing: fax had been a popular service in the fixed networks for years! The circuit switched data service also had its fixed network parallels that made perspectives of a high usage probable. Thus, for all three services it would have been fairly easy to produce convincing arguments in the context of today's product development forums why they should all be profitable. In this way, we can very well envisage a situation where the methods of today would have accepted fax and circuit switched data – the failures – and discarded SMS – the success!
>
> (2004: 193)

At the time in which he writes his history, Trosby is painfully aware of the new, determining context of telecommunications reforms – the 'huge paradigm shift in the business of telecommunications: leaving the age of monopolies and entering the age of the liberalised markets' (2004: 194). He contends that 'previous telcos could afford that luxury' of allowing the technique of a 'hunch':

> 'Hunch' is what you get when – in between the tightly scheduled tasks of today's demands – you are allowed to stray into areas of terra incognita without almost any other purpose but to explore . . . today's chatting crowd can be happy that the GSM system definition phase occurred well within the era of the previous regime.
>
> (2004: 194)

Trosby's narrative of SMS is only one, among many, and it recalls a particular vantage-point of a classic technical and scientific scene of innovation, in the relatively early phase of SMS development in the 1987–90 period. It is revealing of the creative and improvisatory thinking and action in which engineers and scientists engage, and other actors in technology also, but also reminds of the importance of attending closely to the accounts and actions of such agents.

Finding uses for SMS: Nordic writing

I have recounted in some detail the originary scene of SMS in a setting that is customary and familiar, namely that of standards-setting collaborations and institutions, peopled by engineering, working with each other, and seeking to understand and imagine the uses and users, and markets, of a new technological system, and implement optimum solutions. Much of this work though available in the technical literatures has not been widely acknowledged in, or articulated with, studies of the social and cultural bearings of the cell phone. To pursue such an object, I wish to delve at some length into the histories of how users were enlisted, or enrolled themselves, into text messaging.

At the stage when SMS only had 160 characters, in limited languages and character sets, there were additional constraints from mostly only having small keys as input devices, and rudimentary typeface displays on evolving screens. SMS was a store-and-forward technology, then and still offering poor quality of service or assurances of receipt of message. Reception permitting, an SMS is sent from a handset to a dedicated server in the network, and from there is despatched to the intended receiver. Assuming the receiver's handset is within range, the SMS can be received relatively quickly, within seconds. If either sender's or receiver's handset is not in range or turned on, the network is programmed to try again to send the SMS (for a pre-set duration, typically seven days). All the reassurance a sender can receive is that the SMS has actually been despatched from the handset to the network, not, however, that the message has in fact been successfully received by the addressee.

Two accounts would appear to be commonly circulated about the first SMS message ever sent. A young Nokia engineer is credited (according to Agar 2003), or it is thought that the first message was sent in Britain (according to sources on the Internet; also the source of Rheingold's claim that the 'first text message was sent in December 1992 in the United Kingdom' (Rheingold 2002: 15). Whether these claims are accurate or not, initial commercial visions of SMS were limited and aimed at business users:

> [I]ts broad-based appeal was initially as a unidirectional system for sending 'mobile terminated' messages to customers, such as voice mail notifications. Early SMS campaigns to promote the delivery as well as receipt of messages, rare as they were, almost exclusively targeted at business users and positioned the service as a second-rate add-on to voice transmissions . . . the industry was caught largely off guard by the upsurge in SMS usage (particularly among young non-professionals).
>
> (Taylor and Vincent 2005: 79)

To illustrate the attitude at this time, Taylor and Vincent quote a 1990 marketing brochure from the then network of GSM operator suggesting that generally a user would make a voice call to an operator who would then type in a text message for despatch (2005: 79–80) – clearly conceiving SMS on the model of existing paging services. Despite the limitations, or rather because of the constraints,[5] of these human and non-human factors shaping SMS, what emerged in many countries and subcultures was a rich ensemble of one-to-one, or one-to-many, text communications.

The first widespread takeup of text messaging is identified with the Nordic countries, especially Finland ('Nokia land') as Eija-Lisa Kasesniemi wonderfully documents in her 2003 *Mobile Messages*, still the most comprehensive study of text messaging cultures (and indeed of GSM cultures). In 1995, an interconnect agreement was signed between the two main mobile operators in Finland, allowing users to send SMS between networks. As occurred elsewhere, this connectivity was a precondition of widespread use, and the SMS boom then occurred in 1998:

> Instead of delivering certain predetermined types of information, the messages became communication for all and their contents came to deal with everyday life: 'Your basic, everyday messaging. Boring actually', said 15-year-old Maaret of her messages.
>
> (Kasesniemi 2003: 161)

In 2000, nearly 1 billion text messages were sent in Finland, a country with a population of only 5 million (Kasesniemi and Rautiainen 2002: 170). Kasesniemi and Rautiainen suggest that text messaging 'captured the interest of the youngest generation of Finns in 1998' and 'like TV and the Internet, has established itself as part of the adolescents' everyday life as a teenager' (2002: 171). They found that suddenly 'instead of talking about calling and changing color covers on their cell phones, all teenagers wanted to give their views on text messaging' (172). Very quickly then a culture of text messaging formed, with its own 'terminology, customs and social norms' (177). Kasesniemi and Rautiainen noted the development of vocabulary to describe unique features of text messaging culture, and they also noted this culture 'grows out of the unique circumstances of teenage life': 'The contents of the messages exchanged by teenagers range from contraception to death. Teens send messages on weekdays to ask for help with homework, and on Fridays they use SMS to locate friends, find dates or purchase alcohol' (2002: 177). Among the cultural practices they document are circulation of chain messages, and collective reading and composition (177). Also one issue in text messaging culture was the relative evanescence of messages. The early cell phones with text message capability had little memory in either the handset or the SIM card to store and retrieve messages. Until the widespread availability of protocols such as the wireless Bluetooth standard, that allowed phones to connect to other storage devices (such as computers, or memory cards) or printers, phone users could not easily print out or store messages. Many resorted, therefore, to copying cherished messages by long-hand writing:

> While some teens retain the most important messages on their cell phones, others have begun a movement to counter the perishable quality of text messages. Many teens copy their messages into calendars, diaries or special notebooks designed for collecting SMS messages. This practice of message collecting is an important part of text messaging culture.
>
> (2002: 178)

As the Finnish example shows, one of the reasons young people took to texting was a tactic of consolidating and shaping their own shared culture, in distinction from the general culture dominated by their parents and other adults. Texting became involved in a wider reworking of youth culture, involving other new media forms and technologies and cultural developments. Moreover, as Kasesniemi concludes, 'teenagers have been the pioneers of text messaging in Finland' (2003: 161) – something that became commonplace of messaging cultures elsewhere.

'Text capital of the world'

By 1999–2000, text messaging had been adopted in a number of countries, especially by young people as we have seen in the cases of pioneering uses in the Nordic countries. Texting quickly become implicated in the shaping and transformation of gender and sexual identities and practices. I want to turn now from the European, 'hyper-developed world' (Suchman 2002) to Asia, and the case of another country in which texting was widely and quickly taken up, and much remarked upon as a major part of cell phone use: the Philippines.

The diffusion of the cell phone in the Philippines has been very rapid:

> The cell phone has joined earlier commodities such as radio and television in most Filipino homes. But the mobile phone has achieved this level of penetration much faster than was the case for radio and television . . . Compared to other domestic goods, the mobile phone has enjoyed the quickest rate of diffusion in Philippine households. Cell phone ownership is becoming a major index of modernity and the basis for a new form of inequality.
>
> (Pertierra 2005a; see also Pertierra 2002 and 2003)

Although statistics on texting are difficult to verify, it is often claimed that usage in the Philippines far outstrips that of other countries, as, for instance, in this representative statement: 'Presently Filipinos send over 200 million texts daily, about 10 texts per user. This contrasts with Europeans who send about 3 texts daily' (Pertierra 2005a; cf. Ling 2004).

One of the reasons that texting became popular in the Philippines, as elsewhere, was its perceived affordability. Also it was experienced as relatively more reliable compared to expensive, poor-quality, fixed-line networks, not to mention problems with drop-outs and coverage of mobile voice telephony (Strom 2002). The irony of the perceived affordability is, in the Philippines as elsewhere, that relatively low-income users elect to pay significant proportions of their income on texting and cell phone, compared to other household goods (Elwood-Clayton 2005: 200). Indeed the whole issue of cost and affordability is a very complex one, and great care needs to be taken with citing cost as a factor in the take-up of text messaging. It is now recognised that the phenomenon of poor and low-income users choosing a cell phone over other commodities or communication technologies is something that requires study (Donner 2003, 2005; Elwood-Clayton 2005: 200), and probably has not received the attention it has merited owing to the focus and location of mobile scholars in first-world, richer countries as well as the construction of poor countries as suffering a 'deficit', or being located on the other side of the 'digital divide', so that their communication and media patterns and choices have not been explored.

With this provision in mind, we can discern important cultural reasons for the salience of text messaging in the Philippines:

> The Philippines is primarily an oral society and speech is often used to maintain and reproduce traditional hierarchies . . . Texting combines the informality of speech with the reflectiveness of writing. Informants claim that

it is easier to express certain aspects of themselves by texting than through direct speech. They feel more in control. But they are also less sure about the effects of their messaging. Many see texting as an opportunity for fun and even deception. Hence, this medium lends itself to exploring new relationships and topics.

(Pertierra et al. 2002: ch. 7)

An intriguing feature of texting in the Philippines is the availability and consumption of text manuals: 'Copious numbers of text how-to-books are sold in the bookstores . . . "Text to Text", "Ring Tones and Grafix", "The Lord is my Text-mate" ' (Elwood-Clayton 2005: 196). These guides on appropriate language, phrasing and diction, as well as how texting is best and properly used, and how it fits into contemporary manners and mores, are prevalent in a number of other societies as well, such as China (as Angel Lin's reading of SMS manuals sold to migrant workers in China has shown, see Lin 2005c) and also Indonesia (Barendregt 2005).

One of these new areas which texting is opening up is sexuality:

It is safe to say that texting is contributing significantly to the public emergence of a sexual subject, hitherto limited to a private discourse [with sexual jokes and messages]. Texting has also expanded the scope of social relationships, making it possible to include strangers [as in the case of using cell phones to flirt and conduct affairs].

(Pertierra et al. 2002: ch. 7)

Elwood-Clayton has expanded on the 'virtual strangers' theme to show that 'texting was uprooting traditional courtship, [had] re-integrated matchmaking into society, and had the potential to subvert traditional gender ideologies in the domain of young love' (2003: 226). Elwood-Clayton's most interesting findings relate to a topic now widely debated in cell phone culture: technology, gender, and agency. While noting the strong influence of traditional gendered rules of romance, especially for young women, she suggests that:

As texting is clandestine by nature, it enables secret dialogue away from parental eyes and provides a means of expression where young women do not have to adhere to traditional rules of gender conduct. Texting provides a site where young woman can *choose* alternative strategies and experiment with romantic agency without the stigmatization that is often associated with sexual proactivity.

(2003: 234)

In a latter study Elwood-Clayton delves into the 'dark side of SMS: hostilities in cyberspace among intimates', something brought about because of the new expectations SMS elicits among its users 'whereby friends' expectations of each others' accessibility increases, and in which lovers attempt to monitor one another' (2005: 196). In particular she argues that 'texting in the Filipino context is often a form of artillery in personal combats and can, in fact, propel and increase peril among social actors, at times manifesting in different forms of trouble and / or (symbolic) violence' (2005: 196–7). In light of these patterns of use, she proposes an addendum to her contemporary urban legend about texting Cinderella:

> we could see how easy it would be for one sister to sabotage Cinderella's chance with the Prince (by perhaps stealing his cell phone and telling the prince she no longer loved him and to not text him again). Or perhaps the Prince, after winning his sweet Cinderella, would get bored and begin initiating anonymous text relationships with other women.
>
> (2005: 217)

There is much more to be said about text messaging in the Philippines, and it will be interesting to see what its various 'careers' and trajectories become, settling down into patterns alongside other old and new media and communications. What I wish to turn to now, however, is the way that text messaging in the Philippines became synonymous with activism and the use of cell phones for new ways for people to form groups and organise: in short, the power of the cell phone to create new forms of collective activity, whether crowds, mobs, or publics.

Coup d'text

Howard Rheingold's 2002 book *Smart Mobs* has been widely discussed for its vision of social revolution and new technologies. Rheingold sees text messaging as the harbinger of such new, powerful forms of collectivity, studying emergent uses around the world. Significantly the chapter of his book devoted to 'Smart mobs: the power of the mobile many' opens with a recounting of the celebrated over-throw of President Joseph Estrada of the Philippines in January 2001:

> President Joseph Estrada of the Philippines became the first head of state in history to lose power to a smart mob. More than 1 million Manila residents, mobilized and coordinated by waves of text messages, assembled at the site of the 1986 'People Power' peaceful demonstrations that had topped the Marcos regime. Tens of thousands of Filipinos converged on Epifanio de los Santos Avenue, known as 'Edsa,' within an hour of the first text message volleys: 'Go 2EDSA, Wear blck.' Over four days, more than a million citizens showed up, mostly dressed in black. Estrada fell. The legend of 'Generation Txt' was born.
>
> (Rheingold 2002: 157–8)

Rheingold is careful to emphasise the social as much as technical nature of this revolution, yet still sees such developments, if rather ineffably, as leading to 'smart mobs':

> Smart mobs are an unpredictable but at least partially describable emergent property that I see surfacing as more people use mobile telephone, more chips communicate with each other, more computers know where they are located, more technology becomes wearable, more people start using these new media to invent new forms of sex, commerce, entertainment, communion, and, as always, conflict.
>
> (2002: 182)

As his earlier, prescient book *Virtual Community* (Rheingold 1993) did for the Internet, so *Smart Mobs* has compellingly fused and circulated a set of ideas about cell phones and their successor pervasive, wearable and mobile technologies, something I will touch upon in my discussion of moblogging in chapter 8. For the present, I wish to return to the matter of mobs and messaging in the Philippines.

The received view of the overthrow of the Estrada government is summed up in a remark attributed to Estrada himself: 'I was ousted by a coup d'text':

> It is commonly assumed that the mobile phone played a crucial role in EDSA2. Even its main victim, ex-President Joseph Estrada, seems to agree . . . What better imprimatur could one obtain for the importance of the cellphone – via text messaging and voice calls – in People Power 2?
>
> (Pertierra et al. 2002: ch. 6)

The text-toppling of Estrada is typically attributed to 'Generation Txt' – to the pivotal role played by text messaging and the new social category which marks it (apparently Generation Txt was 'first used as an advertising gimmick by cell phone providers to attract young users to their products'; see Rafael 2003: 407ff). The most detailed important study of text messaging and subjectivity in the Philippines questions the overriding role of the cell phone in the Estrada overthrow. Indeed as Pertierra et al. observe, in fact the 'coup d'text' phrase had probably come to Estrada's notice from the many text jokes circulating through this period (2002: ch. 6). Reviewing accounts of the events, as well as conducting interviews with participants, they offer a different account of the Estrada coup – something worth noting for our understanding of the development of text messaging. In early accounts of the link between the cellphone and the uprising, they discern a 'utopian vision of the mobile phone that is characteristic of "discourses of sublime technology" ':

> It focuses squarely on the mobile phone, and ignores the people who used it.

Moreover it strips the Filipinos who struggled against the Estrada government of their agency and gives it to the cellphone. Thus the technology is said to possess a mysterious force, called 'Text Power' . . . it is the technology that does things – makes things happen – not the people who use it.

(Pertierra et al. 2002: ch. 6)

The rhetoric of the technological sublime reappears a year late in an advertisement for the company Smart Communications, featuring an image of a cell phone screen with the assembled crowd during the crisis, under the caption 'Congratulations to the Filipino people for spreading and heeding the cry for truth!' (2002: ch. 6). Given the recrudescence of the technological sublime in digital media (on which see Bailey 2005; Mosco 2004; Nye 1994; Tabbi 1995), the detailed examination of precise details and forms of agency and co-ordination using cell phones is most instructive. Pertierra et al. find, for instance, that

> the cell phone did play an important role in EDSA2 [that is, the downfall of Estrada]. That role, however, was not the one for which it has usually been praised in the media since the event – namely, that of crowd-drawer par excellence . . . less than half of our survey respondents who took part in People Power 2 noted that text messaging influenced them to go. If people did attend, it was because they were persuaded to by an ensemble of other reasons.
>
> (2002: ch. 6)

The significance of the cell phone in the demonstrations lay elsewhere:

> firstly, in the way it helped join people who disapproved of Pres. Estrada in a network of complex connectivity . . . Secondly, the mobile phone was instrumental as an organizational device . . . In the hands of activists and powerbrokers from politics, the military, business groups and civil society, the mobile phone become a 'potent communications tool'.
>
> (Pertierra et al. 2002: ch. 6)

Precision is needed here, as Pertierra et al. convincingly demonstrate, to delineate the ways in which text messaging plays a role in activism. It is also useful to step back from the celebratory discourse on the cell phone and its powerful effects, and reframe this set of events as very much to do with the mutual construction of society and technology, in which culture is intimately involved. This involves placing both the technology of text messaging and the social and political forces manifested in this uprising in a much wider setting. For instance, in his account of the Estrada crisis Vicente L. Rafael terms the tropes of text messaging and activism evident in the discourses surrounding it as:

a set of telecommunicative fantasies among middle-class Filipinos . . . [that] reveal certain pervasive beliefs of the middle classes . . . in the power of communication technologies to transmit messages at a distance and in their own ability to possess that power. In the same vein, they believed they could master their relationship to the masses of people with whom they regularly shared Manila's crowded streets and utilize the power of crowds to speak to the state.

(Rafael 2003: 399)

For Rafael, rather than possessing intrinsic politics in its own right, text messaging here is about a 'media politics (understood in both senses of the phrase: the politics of media systems, but also the inescapable mediation of the political) [that] reveal the unstable workings of Filipino middle-class sentiments. Unsettling in their relationship to social hierarchy, these sentiments at times redrew class divisions, anticipated their abolition, or called for their reinstatement and consolidation' (2003: 400). Thus Rafael compares the strong claims for the cell phone with earlier proto-nationalist fantasies associated with the telegraph and telephone by the colonial bourgeoise in the late nineteenth century: 'They imagined that these new technologies would afford them access to colonial leaders, enabling them to hear and be heard directly by the state' (2003: 400). Here we see once again the importance of how technology, its attributes, contexts, and uses are imagined, something also prevalent in my next case study of the development of text messaging.

Pagers, text messages and mobile e-mail in Japan

Japan is another country where text messaging became popular relatively early. In Japan, the forerunner to text messaging was the pager. Initially pagers were a technology shared among workers, being typically leased to a company or organisation rather than an individual (Okada 2005: 43). Initially pagers rang when receiving a call, and did not provide a callback number or other information. In 1987, however, NTT introduced a pager with a liquid crystal display capable of displaying numerals and letters:

This function changed the pager from a medium limited to receiving calls from one specific individual or location to one that could respond to calls from various sources such as the office, home, and friends. With this change, the pager was extended into private and personal uses outside of the office setting.

(2005: 44)

This 'personalisation' of pagers grew especially in the early 1990s as cell phones were becoming more popular and subscription charges became cheaper (also in 1993, subscription deposits were lowered). Younger people than before began using pagers, particularly female school and college-age students. By the mid-1990s users in their teens and twenties were predominantly the new subscribers to pager services. In 1995 Tokyo Telemessage released the Mola, a new pager that could receive text messages, which 'dramatically expanded youth pager uptake . . . young users began using the pager to exchange short messages in which words were assigned to sequences of numbers and codes' (Okada 2005: 44, 51). In the same year, users were able to buy rather than just rent the pager terminal. By mid-1996 there was a peak of almost 11 million subscribers, a quarter of these being 20 to 29-year-olds, and 35.2 per cent households with children between the ages of 15 and 19 (2005: 44).

The juvenation of pagers is a fascinating study in the sociotechnical interaction among companies, manufacturers, and users. The pager 'allowed girls to receive messages from various partners, and a new form of dialogue was constructed through the repeated exchange of pager messages' (2005: 44). As Okada explains:

> The method of communication popular among high school girls during that period is called *poke-kotoba* (pager lingo), which translates a specific sequence of numbers into specific words, generally using the first syllable of the name of a number as the 'reading' of the number. For example, 0840 is *ohayo* (good morning), and 724106 is *nanishiteru* (what are you doing?). The pager, which was designed as a medium to simply request a return call, evolved into a medium of interactive text communication via these girls' using the telephone keyboard for sending out messages.
>
> (2005: 51)

Pager manufacturers noted and responded to these communication practices, by adding a new function:

> that converted numbers into phonetic symbols. For instance, 11 became the symbol for *a*, and 21 became the symbol for *ka*. Until then, in order to translate *poke-kotoba*, the users needed a common reference or understanding to decode the digital sequences. With this new function, they were able to send messages that were readable by anybody.
>
> (2005: 51)

Keitai short message services were a response by the mobile carriers to the success of pagers. In April 1996 DDI Cellular Group launched the Cellular Text Service. This was followed by similar services by IDO and NTT DoCoMo (Short Mail), also by a text-messaging service for the personal handy phone, Cellular Moji Service, introduced by DDI Pocket (Okada 2005: 53; Matsuda 2005a: 35).

Matsuda notes, 'this type of service . . . has come to be called, collectively, short message. At the time, it was not possible to send messages between *keitai* subscribed to different service providers, and each provider had a unique service name' (Matsuda 2005a: 35).

These short messaging services were displaced, if not eclipsed, by J-Phone's introduction of SMS in October 1997 (Funk 2001: 22; Matsuda 2005a: 35). J-Phone was then the third-largest service provider in Japan, and was later to become Vodafone, and its launch of this messaging service 'caused J-Phone's share of young subscribers to skyrocket even as late as mid-2000, more than a year after the introduction of i-mode . . . [and its] share of overall *new* subscribers to jump into the number spot' (Funk 2001: 22). Not only did J-Phone's SMS help it to best its competitor KDDI and its much faster data services (in technical terms, cdmaOne services then operating at 64 kilobits per second or about six times faster than its competitor's offerings), it also helped key players developing i-Mode's service to reinforce the importance of the mass consumer market and affordable payments (indeed micropayment models) versus a focus on business users and more expensive renting of portals (Funk 2001: 22–3).

The Japanese love of text messaging has been widely noted, and typically claimed as 'one of the distinctive features of Japanese youths' *keitai* use' (Okada 2005: 49). Some researchers, such as Okada, have gone so far as to suggest the Japanese case may be unique:

> As researchers in other countries have noted, the heavy use of mobile messaging among youth is common in countries with widespread mobile phone adoption . . . However, the Japanese case is somewhat unique in that text messages far outpace voice calls for young people.
>
> (2005: 49)

What emerged eventually, however, was the popularity of *keitai* Internet email over SMS:

> Japanese users gradually chose this type of e-mail over short messages because it is cross-platform and allows for longer messages. From a user perspective, however, there is little difference between text messages sent as short messages and those sent as Internet e-mail. Users refer to both as *meiru* (mail).
>
> (Matsuda 2005a: 35)

Such *keitai* email supports relatively long messages of between 250 and 3000 characters and can also carry graphics, video, audio, and web links (2005a: 35). The attraction of *keitai* email was early on secured by its close link with simple but attractive forms of mobile content, distinguishing it not only from SMS but also from fixed line email:

e-mail is a very important part of the services offered by mobile content providers. For example, screen savers, which typically include various cartoon characters, are sent in e-mail. With more than 2.5 million subscribers [in 2001] for this kind of official service, there are more than 2.5 million of these e-mails sent every morning from the content providers to their subscribers. Further, there are many entertainment services that enable users to add these cartoon characters along with photos, ringing tones, and, in the future, video clips to their e-mail.

(Funk 2001: 35)

I will talk more about *keitai* mobile email, and the mobile Internet more generally, in chapter 9, but it is worth noting here that Matsuda emphasises that just 'as in Norway . . . and Finland . . . the user demographic that most commonly uses mobile e-mail is young and female' (2005b: 125).

Slow moving message: Hong Kong and SMS

There is much else to say about the domestication of SMS, and what I have described so far leaves out many important perspectives and alternative stories. Part of this work to be undertaken, I suspect, entails consideration of cases where SMS has not been so popular, has not been used or enlisted users. Haddon has pointed to the need to understand non-users, former users, and intermittent users, to appreciate how such indifference, forgetting, reluctance, or foreswearing shapes notions of uses and meanings of information and communications technologies themselves. Though it is not often talked about, and does not seize the public imagination, text messaging is not always a story of frenzied adoption.

In some places and among many groups, SMS has been relatively slow to gain users. One very large and important market often cited is the USA, where mobile messaging has remained rather dormant:

In the USA, text messaging was not popular, since phones were incompatible and the cost advantages mattered less to the affluent. (Additionally, beepers and pagers had a prevalence unmatched elsewhere in the world.) As a result, mobile culture is far less rich in the USA than in texting hotspots such as Finland, Italy, the UK or, particularly, the 'text capital of the world', the Philippines.

(Agar 2003: 108)

This is a reasonable starting point, though, as we have seen, pagers were an important precursor to SMS in Japan (and China too, it might be added), yet texting was significant in that country. As well as cross-cultural factors such as the relative amount of private versus public space in different societies, Rheingold explains the success of SMS as enabled by a circumvention of corporate telecom-munications carrier culture:

> NNT bypassed its corporate culture by creating DoCoMo and hiring outside Mari Matsunaga. Scandinavian and Philippine populations surprised unsuspecting telecommunications operators by embracing SMS. The Euro-pean and Asian adoption of SMS was made possible in large part by pricing policies that made texting less expensive than voice calls. U.S. operators did not bypass their corporate cultures.
>
> (2002: 22)

Rheingold also considers the question of why the USA has not yet grown a 'mainstream texting culture', noting two important American texting subcultures, and musing about whether such practices could spread virally:

> Hip-hop culture, streetwise and fashion-conscious fans of rap music, favor Motorola's two-way pagers, while young stockbrokers, suits, and geeks in the information technology industry favour the BlackBerry wireless pagers from Research in Motion. If the adoption barriers of incompatible technical standards and high prices for texting services disappear, might the cultural practices now incubating in these subcultures reach a tipping point and set off a mainstream fashion epidemic?
>
> (2002: 23)

There is much more to be said about messaging in the USA; however, the case I will turn to now brings into view one of the most mobile connected societies in the world, Hong Kong – often seen as a gateway to the booming Asian mobile markets.

Hong Kong has had quite a different experience of text messaging compared to many other countries. Its take-up and use of SMS is often lamented as much lower than other, much discussed, text and multimedia loving Asian counterparts such as Japan, Korea, or the Philippines, as represented in this 2004 overview:

> Hong Kong has a comparatively low mobile data penetration. Hong Kongers only send an average of 11 SMS per month compared to over 200 SMS per month sent by Japanese and Korean subscribers. Less than 1.5 per cent of Hong Kong mobile subscribers access the Internet from their mobiles compared to nearly half per cent of Korean subscribers and approximately 80 per cent of Japanese subscribers, over a fifth of whom only do so from their mobiles.
>
> (Waters 2004; cf. IT Matters 2002, also Telecoms Infotech Forum 2004)

There are a number of reasons adduced for Hong Kong's comparatively low use of text messaging. First, Hong Kong operators were slow to adopt interoperable SMS, allowing text messages be sent and received across networks (Hansen 2001). Secondly, in the early years especially, as we have seen, text messaging to date has been much easier for speakers of languages with Latin scripts rather than traditional Chinese scripts. The act of typing messages in English, for instance, is difficult enough, let alone typing messages in Chinese characters.

Hong Kong mobiles scholar John Ure notes that '[consumption] patterns as well as consumer adoption rates of [SMS] would seem to be influenced by both local cultural factors and local market conditions, such as the level and structure of prices' (Ure 2003b: 10). For instance, voice calls on cell phones in Hong Kong, and access to mobile telephony generally, have been perceived as very cheap compared to other countries, so there is not the price-based motivation for users to text to save money. Hong Kong is a very competitive, fragmented, and relatively small cell phone market (Cheung 2003). At the stage when SMS usage was beginning in Hong Kong, there were doubts about its profitability in the face of what were presumed to be technologies with far greater capabilities (Hansen 2001).

Worried about this, cell phone companies have tried various ways to create demand for text messaging services. An early service devised to attract young users by leading cell phone company CSL was 'I-DATE-U', an interactive scenario game based on four female characters. Claimed to be 'the first-ever virtual dating game on mobile phones', the game could run on basic SMS or via the 2.5G WAP (wireless access protocol)/GPRS (general packet radio service) technology. Users (presumably male) could ask questions and engage in conversation via text with characters (McKenzie 2001). Another service introduced to stimulate take-up was 'canned messages' (e.g. 'happy birthday'), prepared in Chinese, to save keying time. Another popular group of text services are text subscription and transaction services. For instance, Peoples Mobiles offered a mobile betting service, allowing customers to place bets on football and horse racing. M-commerce, such as payment by mobile (m-payment), has also been seen as a way of increasing revenue (Ramos 2003). Hong Kong has also moved to position itself for multimedia message services (MMS), with early implementation of interoperability across networks.

These commercial responses to use of SMS in Hong Kong seem to be in keeping with Angel Lin and Jim Lo's pioneering study of Hong Kong college students and SMS use. Lin and Lo discerned 'emergent trends and patterns of SMS use' in which 'gendered differences are most apparent, and bilingual linguistic identities also seem to be emerging among the high users' (Lin and Lo 2004; see also Lin 2005a). They cautiously concluded that 'new mobile communication technologies might interact with existing sociocultural and discursive practices to produce gradual change in these practices as well as in communicative practices both among and between males and females' (Lin and Lo 2004: 15).

There is another example of such interactions leading to text messaging cultures in Hong Kong. Harking back to my earlier discussion of the importance of texting in contemporary Filipino culture and society, this has been very much a diasporic media form. A high proportion of Filipino citizens work overseas, and make a substantial contribution to the gross national product through their remittances. The number of overseas Filipino workers reached 1.06 million on official September 2004 figures (National Statistics Office 2005); 49.3 per cent of these workers were male and 50.7 per cent were female (the latter having increased by 13.5 per cent over the preceding year). Hong Kong accounts for 12.4 per cent of the 820,000 overseas Filipino workers based in Asia. Especially prominent are the Filipina domestic workers ('maids'), who often live away from their families in the Philippines for many years. Typically they work six days per week, with Sundays off when they can be seen congregating in available public spaces downtown, as their own private space is very small (mostly a tiny room in their employers' apartment) (see for instance Constable 1997).

Hong Kong mobile companies have responded to the unique characteristics of overseas Filipino workers resident in their country, with specific offerings including SMS. In August 2004 CSL partnered with Smart, a unit of Philippine Long Distance Telephone Company, to offer cheaper text messaging than its competitors as well as voice call and other services, including money transfer via text message. In response another Hong Kong mobile company SmarTone joined with a Philippine mobile counterpart Globe (jointly owned by Singtel and Ayala) also to allow subscribers to transfer money via text to relatives and friends in the Philippines (building on their earlier service to allow airtime to be bought in Hong Kong and transferred to a relative or friend in the Philippines). The interplay between corporation and consumer conceptions of text messaging by Filipino workers in Hong Kong offers both new possibilities for place-making and communicative and cultural fashioning of migrant lives, identities, and transnational communities (McKay and Brady 2005). In this way cell phones are deeply implicated in both the resolution yet also the intensification of social and gender contradictions that stem from the violence of the conditions of contemporary capitalism, its modes of forced as well as chosen mobility, that displace people and tear asunder their relationships as they try to survive (Parreñas 2001).

I have only briefly touched here on the social and cultural aspects of SMS, MMS, and other 2.5G and 3G mobile data services in Hong Kong. Nor have I canvassed the complexities of the economic and industrial debates regarding cell phone developments, and the policy responses such as the Hong Kong Wireless Development Centre (www.hkwdc.org) (on such questions see work of the University of Hong Kong Telecommunications Research Project, especially Ure 2003a and 2003b; also Telecoms InfoTech Forum 2004). Nonetheless for the broader rethinking of cell phone culture, the Hong Kong experience is a very interesting one because it questions the assumption that text messaging can be universally regarded as a 'success', or that it has a particular trajectory. A history of text messaging needs to include and account for this case, not just for comprehensiveness, but also because it stands to tell us something about the shaping of this technology. Clearly the story of SMS is a more complex one internationally than commonly understood, and tracing the nuances of this is instructive for reminding us of the cultural specificity of theory too.

The 'success' of SMS

There is an assumption in the celebration or reviling, by turns, of text messaging, that it has been now proven a 'success'. Making such judgements about technology, or anything in history, is extremely problematic of course – not least given this is a quite new phenomenon. Further, as I have suggested above, the rise of SMS (or resistance to it, or simply lack of interest) is variable across cultures.

The difficulties of declaring one technology a 'success' and another a 'failure', or indeed, at a deeper level, of drawing neat boundaries around technologies, is nicely adumbrated in a classic opus of actor-network theory, Latour's 1996 *Aramis*. In *Aramis*, Latour offers a comprehensive account of a technology that was a 'failure' rather than a 'success': a French automated train system known as Aramis commenced in 1969 and was finally abandoned in 1987. By contrast, SMS may appear to be a case – at least so far, and in some places – of a technology that has drawn many elements into an alliance, and has succeeded (Latour 1996: 106). There is much to be added about the human and non-human elements enlisted in SMS, especially during the 1990s (not least the 160 character set of SMS as an actor in its own right). And the future is open, as to whether SMS will decompose.

In the light of Latour's work it is instructive to compare SMS with another technology that has, for some years at least, been judged a failure, namely Wireless Access Protocol. Discussed at length in chapter 8, WAP was an early attempt to capitalise on the take-up of the Internet, especially with the advent of the World Wide Web and graphic user-interfaces for the IBM-PC platform. It was widely regarded as a flop. However, with improved resolution of cell phones, a greater range of screen sizes, faster speeds, and a substantial base of users with WAP-enabled phones, the technology is now slowly becoming popular – and so offers an opportunity to see the reamination of this technology. Indeed WAP resembles Latour's Aramis, and what he calls the linear model of innovation, where the 'initial idea emerges fully armed from the head of Zeus. Then, either because its brilliant inventor gives it a boost, or because it was endowed from the start with automatic and autonomous power, it sets out to spread across the world. But the world doesn't always take it in' (Latour 1996: 118).

SMS, on the other hand, or thumb, seems to fit the translation or whirlwind model of innovation:

the initial idea barely counts. It's a gadget, a whatchamacallit, a weakling at best, unreal in principle, ill-conceived from birth, constitutionally ineffective . . . the initial gadget is not endowed with autonomous power, nor is it boosted into the world by a brilliant inventor . . . the initial gadget moves only if it interests one group or another, and it is impossible to tell whether these groups have petty interests or broad ones, whether they are open or resolutely closed to technological progress. They are what they are, and they want what they want . . . every time a new group becomes interested in the project, it transforms the project.

(1996: 119)

Of course, this distinction between the two models of technology innovation, and WAP and SMS, is too neat in itself. The symmetry will be well muddied if we add the case of the Japanese technologies of text messaging and mobile email, famously the i-mode system, discussed in chapter 9.

In emphasising the contingent and even potentially open-ended nature of technology, and also its simultaneously and co-operatively produced boundaries with the social, I reach similar conclusions to Alex Taylor and Jane Vincent in their SMS history, also inspired by actor-network theory. They set out to 'reveal that no simple path can be drawn to explain the developments in and uptake of technologies' (2005: 75), indicating the many and heterogeneous entities that have combined to bring what we understand as SMS about. This shows that the history of SMS, like any other technology, cannot be simply repeated – for instance, as a moral underwriting of the guaranteed, widespread, and lucrative take-up of MMS. In chapter 5 I will consider another case study in how the uncertain and serendipitous logics but also power relations of consumption have shaped cell phone culture – the less-known but equally significant case of disability and accessibility.

5 Cellular disability: consumption, design, and access

Text messaging is a widely known and discussed facet of mobile technologies, a phenomenon which demonstrates the need to appreciate the dynamics of consumption as well as production in order to understand cell phone culture. In this chapter, I further explore consumption, and how the needs, expectations, and desires of possible users are factored into the design of cell phone technology. This time I look at consumption of the cell phone from an angle still little known and understood: accessibility and disability.[1]

Often overlooked as media users and cultural agents, people with disabilities number approximately half a billion people worldwide. Estimates of people with disabilities in any population vary but figures of between 15 and 20 per cent are often cited in many countries (ABS 2004; Metts 2000; on the difficulties and politics of defining and measuring the incidence of disability see Abberley 1992 and Altman 2001). While people with disabilities have had accessibility problems with many technologies, they have also as a group been avid and often pioneering users. Yet in the history of cell phone culture, disability has played a significant yet overlooked role.

In this light, this chapter looks at the consumption of cell phones by people with disabilities and the responses to this by technologists, as a neglected yet richly illustrative component of cell phone culture. To give some background, in the first section I explain contemporary social, political, and cultural approaches to understanding disability. Secondly, I discuss the incompatibility of second-generation digital cell phones for hearing-aid users and Deaf people using tele-typewriters. Then I turn, thirdly, to users' cultural and social innovation, exploring Deaf people's use of short text messages (SMS). Fourthly, I contrast Deafness and cell phones with Blind people's non-use and use of SMS. Finally I conclude with reflections on disability, consumption, and cell phones.

Approaching disability and the cell phone

As yet the new ways of studying disability as an integral part of humanities and social sciences are still not well understood – especially when it comes to the undertheorised area of disability and technology. In this chapter I draw upon critical disability studies (Albrecht, Seelman, and Bury 2001; Snyder, Brueg-gemann, and Garland-Thomson 2002). Diverse and interdisciplinary in its constitution, critical disability studies critiques the dominant understanding of disability via the medical model, where disability is believed to be located in the individual's deficient, sick, or abnormal body. It also opposes the allied, and historically anterior, charity discourse of disability, according to which the person with disability is to be pitied and controlled by benevolent institutions (Stiker 1999). As it has emerged in the United States, Canada, the United Kingdom, Europe, and Australia, critical disability studies theorists typically propose a sociopolitical approach to disability. For instance, British theorists of the social model propose a distinction between an individual's impairments (the bodily dimension) and disability which is socially produced (exemplified in the barriers society unfairly creates for the person with impairments) (Barnes and Mercer 2003). Developed with my friend and collaborator Christopher Newell, my approach seeks to go beyond classic social model accounts by acknowledging the wide range and varieties of impairment and disability; by acknowledging the interaction among gender, sex, race, class, and age in the social relations of disability; by seeking to understand the important cultural dimension of disability; and in proposing the importance of technology in the contemporary social relations of disability.

To date there has been little scholarly work at the intersection of the literatures of social study of science and technology, those of cultural and media studies, and those of critical disability studies (Goggin and Newell 2005c). This is also the case with regard to networked digital technologies now so pervasive and ubiquitous in many countries. Accessibility for people with disabilities is often now a focus of discussion yet still more often honoured in the breach (Goggin and Newell 2003). Important initiatives have been taken in the area of the World Wide Web to make the Internet accessible, yet the overlapping cluster of software, hardware, and networks associated with online communications is proving far more intractable. As the Internet merges with mobile and wireless devices, inclusive and accessible technologies for text, video, and voice communications have been overlooked or only slowly eventuated. As the National Council on Disability has noted:

> There are limitations that make cell phones either inaccessible or difficult to use (and, therefore, possibly undesirable). People who have visual impairments may have the most difficulty reading the display and accessing visual information. People who are deaf or hard of hearing may have difficulty carrying on a verbal conversation and detecting auditory alerts. People with a

mobility disability may have difficulty making accurate inputs and simultaneously handling the phone and manipulating the controls. People who have cognitive disabilities may have difficulty understanding metaphors that are used and remembering how to access information.

(NCD 2004: 102–3)

The topic of access generally, and accessibility for people with disabilities specifically, has been much ventilated over the past decade, not least under the not especially helpful rhetoric of the 'digital divide' (Warschauer 2003). Access is certainly important as a concept but it needs to be placed within a general account of technology, culture, and the social. In this chapter, however, my focus is squarely on disability, and indeed the politics of bodies and ability, as an integral part of cell phone culture.

Designing disability: the case of digital cell phones

As we have seen in chapter 2, cellular phones were commercially introduced around the world from the late 1970s, commencing with in-car phones. When hand-held cell phones became available from the mid-1980s onwards these were very bulky. Obviously, at this stage, the cell phone was difficult for many people with disabilities to hold and use. With advances in miniaturisation, computerisation, and manufacturing, cell phones became smaller and lighter. This made them easier to use for some consumers, but more difficult for others because of the dexterity and nimbleness demanded by tiny buttons and interfaces. Many people with disabilities did use cell phones for a range of purposes, including safety, security, and mobility assistance. There is much further to say on first-generation cell phones and people with disabilities (with important perspectives in Von Tetzchner 1991 and Roe 1993), but I will now turn to second-generation digital technologies.

When second-generation cellular systems were introduced around the world from the early 1990s onwards, their new features opened up new possibilities but created new forms of exclusion also:

The present trend of marketing mobile phones that are smaller but with an ever-increasing number of features, ranging from memory store to calculator functions, is good for many people – but not for everybody. Blind people cannot use text-based information on the screen at all [including phonebook maintenance and use], while those who are partially-sighted have great difficulty with very small displays. Voice outputs are of no use to deaf people and may be difficult for those who are simply hard of hearing. The extensive range of network based facilities like automatic answering and voicemail: functions, text messages and call progress announcements require either useful vision or useful hearing, if not both. The Internet-based applications, such as sending and receiving Emails, surfing the net and engaging in e-commerce, are all visually oriented and so exclude blind consumers. Manufacturers and service providers seem to give low priority to solving these problems, for example by offering alternative output modes.

(Shipley and Gill 2000)

Here cell phones illustrate the general proposition that when technology is reshaped it is because of certain sorts of imagined users and use, with particular sorts of 'normal' (or rather normalised) bodies and abilities. Typically people with disabilities do not fit into these categories of the normal (sometimes referred to as 'normate'), and are often not seen either as fitting the ideas of public markets that such normal bodies support. New designs which might allow other uses, by people with disabilities for instance, come often by another route:

Yet some problems are being overcome: hands-free operation is now offered on some models, not in response to demand by disabled people who have difficulty in using a very small keypad, but because it is wanted by drivers who wish to use their mobile phones in a moving vehicle.

(2000)

For people with disabilities there were also significant difficulties with second-generation cell phones, overlapping other sites of conflict over the technology (such as fears that electromagnetic emission from phones or towers might cause cancer). Not long after the new digital mobile system had been developed and was starting to be introduced commercially in a number of countries in the early 1990s, it was revealed that this technology emitted a high level of electromagnetic interference. Once the existence of these cell phone emissions became widely known, there was much public agitation, indeed panic, as I examine in chapter 6. While the potential for cell phones to cause damage to health and safety was much noticed, there was much less public discussion, let alone awareness, of an associated matter: such interference had the potential to cause a buzzing sound in people's hearing aids, as well as actually making the phones difficult to use for people with hearing aids (Berger 1997; Burwood and Le Strange 1993; ETSI 1993; Joyner et al. 1993; NTAD 1994; Roe 1993). Internationally, phone companies, governments, and regulators put much effort into managing the public outcry. In doing so, they appeared to be motivated by a concern that this new, expensive technology might not be adopted by consumers, despite widespread support from governments.

In effect, cell phone companies regarded hearing aids *rather* than cell phones as the principal problem needing to be addressed. Attention was directed to the need for hearing aids to cope with higher levels of electromagnetic emission, something that was seen as important given the wide range of technologies emitting such signals – not just cell phones. A European standard was introduced in 1990 requiring hearing aids to be immune to emissions from cell phones. Research was also conducted on removing the source of emission further away from the hearing aid, and eventually 'handsfree kits' were designed for hearing aid users as a solution. Even this solution did not provide assistance for many, and other tactics were required on the part of the disability movement. In Australia, for instance, the disability movement needed to invoke the human rights and anti-discrimination law framework in order for the matter to be successfully addressed: the Human Rights and Equal Opportunity Commission (HREOC) conducted a public inquiry into the matter, which resulted in a conciliation some eighteen months later (Goggin and Newell 2005b; HREOC 2000). Despite such interventions and measures such as 'hands-free kits', the problem remains – and is only partially solved in some countries with the availability of the alternative digital mobile technology, CDMA.

In early 1996 the US FCC convened a summit of the wireless industry, hearing industry, and consumers in an effort to resolve the hearing aid and cell phone compatibility matter (Berger 1997; Victorian 1998). This meeting precipitated the formation of a dedicated taskforce under the aegis of the American National Standards Institute (ANSI) to develop a standard on immunity and emissions requirements and test protocols, which devices are required to meet (Victorian 2004). This work culminated in an American standard (namely ANSI C63.19, see ANSI 2001; also Victorian and Preves 2004). In July 2003, the FCC reopened hearings into the issue. It gave federal imprimatur to the ANSI C63.19 standard, and also ordered a rolling timetable and further accessibility improvements. Other requirements included that within two years every major handset manufacturer and service provider must offer at least two cellular telephones that reduce interference to a level defined in the standard; and that by early 2008, half of all cell phone handsets have interference down to these levels or less (FCC 2003; Victorian 2004).

A related aspect of the construction of disability in digital cellular telephony lay at the intersection of a newer technological system and an older one, with their overlapping yet distinctive cultural practices. Deaf people in a number of Western countries, especially the USA, had developed a rich repertoire of communications and cultural practices using an early form of text communications. Devised in the early to mid 1960s, this technology was variously called the Telecommunications Device for the Deaf (TDD), teletypewriter (TTY), Deaf telephones, or just text telephone (Lang 2000). TTY communication involves two keyboard devices being connected to the telecommunications network to send and receive text messages. Many Deaf people own their own text phones, and, to meet the requirements of legislation such as the 1990 *Americans with Disabilities Act*, TTY payphones may be found in public places such as airports. From its inception this form of text phone communication by Deaf people relied on the Baudot standard developed for telexes. With the advent and growing popularity of computers and online communication in the 1990s, devices and standards were developed such as V.18 that used the ASCII standard but incorporated the Baudot standard also (Hellström 2002).

The technical breakthrough that had made the TTY possible was a coupling device that allowed sounds transmitted over the telephone to be translated into data, and eventually, alphabetic letters (Lang 2000). Like modems, this meant that TTYs functioned compatibly (within limits) over the telecommunications network. TTYs also worked satisfactorily with first-generation analogue cell phones: 'Analog systems work fairly well with teletype devices (TTYs). Some phones have built in modular jacks into which a TTY can be plugged; other phones can be used with an adapter' (NCD 2004: 103). However, the much vaunted second-generation digital system threatened this interworking or knitting together of technologies:

> Initially, digital systems did not work well with TTYs. Digital wireless transmissions inherently contain errors, but error correction techniques can reduce the problem for speech. Digital networks are less forgiving in the case of the tones generated by TTY devices, however, and the transmission errors can cause characters to be lost or changed, resulting in unintelligible messages.
>
> (NCD 2004: 103)

In his account of deaf people and telecommunications in Australia, Harper observes that:

> When the government decided to move from an analogue to digital telecommunications system in 2000, on the premise that it would improve the wireless network access to a wider range of the Australian people, it did nothing to find a solution for those who were losing a service – Deaf people using TTYs on an analogue mobile service.
>
> (P. Harper 2003)

The consequences of second-generation cell phones for the Deaf community were quite significant. In Australia, for instance, as the national relay provider, Australian Communication Exchange (ACE) argued:

> In the late 1990s, telecommunications access for people with a disability made a tremendous leap forward and the future looked positive . . . However, in three short years since 2000, more than half of the telecommunications network is now not accessible to people who are Deaf or have a hearing or

speech impairment despite the existence of the disability discrimination and telecommunications legislation [due to shut-down of the analogue network in 2000, and complete switch to digital mobile networks].

(ACE quoted in Goggin and Newell 2004: 416)

This experience was one shared by Deaf people around the world, underscoring the 'glocal' nature of mobile telecommunications: the shaping of this eminently global technology through local arenas. Internationally, it took concerted pressure from the Deaf community and their supporters, with alliances of users, scientists and technologists, academics, and interested industry across national, regional, and international settings, and also the invocation of general disability discrimination legislation in various countries, before the cell phone manufacturers and telecommunications carriers took this problem seriously.

In the USA, for instance, the Federal Communications Commission, which played a central role in the reshaping of telecommunications and disability through the 1990s (Goggin and Newell 2003), issued a requirement in 1996 that carriers were responsible for ensuring connection of 911 (emergency) calls over digital wireless networks for callers using a TTY. Certainly this was only the beginning of the process: 'The deadline for compliance was extended repeatedly as various wireless carriers worked to provide a solution' (NCD 2004: 104). An industry group, the TTY Forum, comprising carriers, wireless handset and infrastructure manufacturers, TTY manufacturers, telecommunications relay service providers, and disability consumer organisations, worked from 1997 onwards to ensure the networks would be able to carry 911 calls via TTY by the mid-2002 deadline set by the regulator (Harkins and Barbin 2002; NCD 2004). A number of larger providers met this deadline and implemented wireless TTY compatibility, including AT&T Wireless Systems, Cingular Wireless, NexTel, Sprint PCS, T-Mobile (formerly Voicestream), and Verizon Wireless (TAP 2002). Despite this, a number of carriers still petitioned the FCC for an extension.

There were certainly some genuine difficulties faced in the endeavour of achieving compatibility of cell phone networks and handsets with TTY devices. These included redesign to accommodate the speed and tone of TTY Baudot signals and 'setting standards for the interface between TTY devices and digital wireless cell phones operating with several different digital standards' (TTY Forum 2002; NCD 2004: 105). At the end of the process, however, there is evidence to suggest that in the USA reasonable compatibility has been reached between cell phones and TTYs in non-emergency situations, though difficulties still remain with wireless 911 TTY calls (especially related to some of the equipment used by operators or emergency services answering calls) (NCD 2004: 105). However, not all cell phones are compatible with TTYs, and consumers have been urged to test their TTY with their wireless provider (TAP 2002). Elsewhere the problems of TTY and mobile compatibility also remain.

Seeing telephony: deaf people and text messaging

We have seen how the needs and desires of hard-of-hearing and Deaf cell phone users were not initially understood or envisaged as part of the design of second-generation digital mobile networks. Also that this set of design and consumption issues has not been widely noticed and discussed. To explore these issues further I now turn to a case which has received significant publicity, Deaf people's invention of text messaging.

Deaf people have long used text communications. As we have seen, from the 1960s onwards Deaf people had established a set of communicative and cultural practices around the TTY. Coupling TTYs with cellular devices, something attempted by some users with analogue cell phones, offered new telecommunicative possibilities for Deaf people. While the introduction of digital cell phones made mobile TTY communications difficult, another unexpected possibility was gradually opened up – text messaging. While a definitive history of the Deaf adoption of SMS has yet to be written, the outlines of this episode have now become widely known:

> The deaf have taken to this technology as an answer to their prayers. As texters in countries like Australia, Britain, and Israel, where the mobile phone service providers have agreed to interconnect their networks, they can take their means of communication with them as far as they can go and reach anyone who has a mobile phone.
>
> (Power and Power 2004: 334)

But although there have been few detailed studies of Deaf people's adoption and use of text messaging (an exception being Bakken 2005), one central theme in available accounts is that users can now communicate with other Deaf and hearing people without the intermediary of a human TTY relay operator. Power and Power point out that abbreviating text has 'long been familiar to [Deaf people] because it is used in TTY conversations', and that the characteristics of the SMS genre 'suit the sometimes-limited English of Deaf people' (2004: 335). Indeed there is some evidence to suggest that the rate of use of SMS among Deaf people is higher than their hearing counterparts (P. Harper 2003; Power and Power 2004).

Certainly Deaf people's creative use of cell phones caught the attention of mainstream media:

> Over the last few years, the mobile phone has emerged as a popular device for what at first may seem an unlikely user group: the deaf and other people who are hard of hearing . . . This usage shows how a group of people can take

up a technology that was not initially designed or marketed to them, and adapt it to suit their own needs and purposes.

(Wurtzel 2002)

Service providers in a range of areas including emergency services, police, and education institutions began to realise the potential to reach Deaf people via SMS.

Just like the rise of text messaging in general, once mainstream cell phone companies noticed the Deaf community's avid use of text messaging, they were keen to market to Deaf consumers, and also publicise this use for wider, public consumption. In September 2001, for example, Vodafone New Zealand sponsored 2001 Deaf Awareness Week:

> Text messaging is more than just a youth craze turned mainstream – it also gives deaf people the chance to communicate via mobile phone . . . Vodafone New Zealand's GM Company Communications, Avon Adams said it was good to see text messaging providing options for the deaf community. 'Text messages are free to receive and only 20c to send to anywhere in the world. They open up a realm of possibilities to deaf and hearing impaired people who can't make use of voice-based communications,' said Ms Adams.
>
> (Vodafone NZ 2001)

Redesign of the technology in light of such use was slower in coming: 'As the technology was not developed with this community in mind, operators and manufacturers have been slow to tailor offerings for the deaf and hard of hearing' (Wurtzel 2002). One problem for Deaf people is that SMS only supports asynchronous rather than real-time interaction (P. Harper 2003) – as it is a store-and-forward technology resembling email in this respect – despite the often very fast communication it can often afford. Also text messages need be written in hearing languages such as English rather than native sign language, and the frequent text messaging required by Deaf users can be quite costly.

Despite such challenges, Deaf users have also avidly taken up devices such as text-messaging pagers and portable digital assistants – with the T-Mobile Sidekick becoming a cult object among some communities of users (Kilner 2005). Mobile devices are also being used with Internet protocol relay services, for instance with America Online and MCI's 'My IP-relay' service launched in 2004 (AOL and MCI 2004). This enables Deaf people to have their phone calls transcribed by relay operators, and sent to them over the Internet, and then to have their instant message replies read back to the hearing person by the relay operator (LaVallee 2005).

As new textual media, the cell phone and associated technologies, are deeply involved in significant and hotly debated transformations in Deaf identity and community: 'These technologies have begun to alter how Deaf people contact and communicate remotely with each other' (P. Harper 2003). Like wider debates regarding cell phones that have had an important function in shaping this media culture, there are those who praise the utility, function, freedoms, intimacies, and sociability such technology brings to Deaf people and others who lament the threat to older social forms. For example, face-to-face contact and gatherings have been much prized by Deaf communities, not least as a way to communicate via the visual and tactile medium of native sign language. In this respect Deaf clubs have been an important social and cultural institution, and fears have been expressed that the mediated communications offered by SMS, instant messaging, and the Internet will lead to an attentuation of social ties and cultural norms, and the disappearance of important customs (see Kunerth 2005, and response from Laird 2005). These fears have been more generally raised regarding cell phones, and have a long history in the reception of new media (Marvin 1988; Winston 1998). I would also suggest that notions of the cell phone are being socially and culturally shaped by the innovations of these users, and their imaginings of the technology. Thus SMS takes its place in a historical ensemble of technologies and communicative and cultural practices, including TTYs, fax machines, and, more recently, electronic mail and instant messaging (Bowe 2002; Lang 2000; Power and Power 2004).

Blinded by SMS

From the celebrated Deaf use of SMS, we now move to a contrasting case where a disability culture and its desires and needs regarding a technology have not been reflected in values, design, or narratives of use. In doing so, I am mindful of the problematic, dynamic, yet intensely invested categories of 'Deaf' and 'Blind', and the entire vexed taxonomic enterprise of knowing the truth of a person via an impairment label (for a critique of this see the opening chapter of Goggin and Newell 2005a).

As with people with disabilities in general, and Deaf users in particular, a useful starting point is the thesis that for Blind users the cell phone has gone hand-in-hand with new personal and collective possibilities. As Jolley notes:

> People who are blind have enjoyed the flexibility that results from mobile communications. Using their mobile phones they can find each other more easily in public places, and they have the added security of being able to make a phone call if they are lost or feeling endangered.
>
> (Jolley 2003: 27)

Yet, to propose an antithesis, the technology has not been imagined or designed with Blind users in mind.

Jolley usefully summarises a number of taken-for-granted features of cell phones that Blind people most often cannot use:

People who are blind have very limited access to the standard features of mobile phones. In general terms they can only make calls by manually entering the number to be called, and they can receive calls if the phone rings or vibrates. But they do not know the battery strength, the signal strength, if the PIN has been wrongly entered, if calls are missed, if the phone is accidentally on divert, or anything else that is shown on the screen. They cannot use the menu system, the telephone directory system, or anything but the most elementary speed dialing features. And, of course, they cannot use SMS. These features have been introduced gradually, as network services have been enhanced, and as new models of mobile phones have been released.

(2003: 27)

People with low vision also face problems:

Many people with low vision find it difficult to find a mobile phone with a large enough, brightly lit screen that they can comfortably read. So if they cannot read the screen, people with low vision face the same denial of access to the features of their mobile phones as do people who are blind.

(2003: 27)

The author of a comprehensive series of articles on cell phone accessibility for Blind users for an American Federation of Blind publication (Burton 2004, 2005a; Burton and Uslan 2003, 2004a, 2004b; Burton et al. 2003) offers this account:

In the early days of cell phones, when they were used only to make and receive calls, accessibility was not a major issue. As long as visually impaired people could tactilely identify the control buttons on the cell phone, it was no problem to make and receive calls. However, they were left out of the loop when the evolution of cell phones brought display screens and other new advances, such as phone books, text messaging, and e-mail, into the mix. Although people who are visually impaired were still able to perform the basic functions of making and receiving calls, the manufacturers did not design these new phones in a way that would allow them to independently access the new, more advanced features. There was no text-to-speech functionality to accommodate cell phone users who are blind, and there were no display screens with the visual characteristics, such as large fonts or highly contrasting colors, that would accommodate users who have low vision.

(Burton 2005b)

As cell phone manufacturers and service providers did not collectively envisage and design mobile technological systems with affordances and capabilities for Blind users, it has been largely left to specialist disability technology providers to design purpose-built workarounds. This could only be done with high-end phones such as Nokia's Symbian Series 60 that allowed third parties to add software programs and applications to cell phones (Molloy 2004). The company Cingular Wireless, for example, has licensed for the US market a software application called TALKS. TALKS is able to read screen-based menus, instructions, and content, and convert these into synthetic speech, using either the phone's speaker option or plug-in earphones or headset. Another application is Mobile Speak. It is designed to work with the Symbian series 60 operating system, to be carrier independent, to access 'most of the functionality of the device', and is offered in a number of languages (to date mostly English and European languages but also Turkish, Arabic, and Chinese). As well as a number of Nokia phones, it also works with the Siemens SX1 (Mobile Speak 2005). Another product is offered by Code Factory, a Spanish developer of 'software solutions for the blind and visually impaired' (www.codefactory.es). Code Factory also offers a related product called Mobile Accessibility, 'a complete mobile phone solution for the blind and vision-impaired' (Code Factory 2005). There is much to be said about the politics of artefacts here, and the inscription of the boundaries between mainstream and specialist technology. However, one index of these matters is the prohibitive price of adaptive software.

As well as applications for or adaptions of existing phones, in 2003 Spanish technology company Owasys announced the world's first cell phone specifically designed for Blind people. (After all, producing a *national* cell phone has been an important project for some countries, so why not a *disabled* cell phone?) When the phone was exhibited in Britain a company representative explained their thinking:

> We thought there were parts of the consumer market whose demands were not very well covered by the big players . . . From our conversations with ONCE (the blind people's organisation in Spain) and RNIB here in the UK, it was clear that there was a need among blind people for a product like this.
>
> (Adams-Spink 2003)

It is not clear to what extent Owasys's dedicated product has been taken up by Blind users, or whether most are more comfortable with a screenreader or application option (at least those who can afford it, and have the skills and training to use it). One difficulty may be slow and costly progress on approvals in different countries. In addition, the Owasys phone has fewer features than a phone running a screenreader, and carries a comparable price to a high-end phone plus screen-reading software.

As the capabilities of mobile devices expand, so too do creative options emerge, extending the capabilities of the cell phone for Blind people. In mid-2005 Motorola announced a software upgrade for one of its phones, to enable text to speech reading of menus, messages, and other screen-based phone features. A technology company called vOICe, – 'See with your ears!: Wearable Bionics used by the Blind Aim: Vision through Brain Plasticity' – has developed an aural camera phone designed for Blind users (The vOICe 2005), which translates images into soundscapes which are transmitted to the user via headphones (Sandhana 2003). The company has a utopian vision for its innovation:

> Within a decade, second-hand camera phones could become an affordable platform for use of The vOICe by blind people living in developing countries! These phones can at the same time serve many general communication, Internet access and computing needs for the sighted poor, while doubling as a digital camera.
>
> (The vOICe 2005)

There is other software now available that allows a person to use a phone camera to identify the colour of objects (via a 'talking color identifier'). These offer ingenious, if relatively untested, reinterpretations of the visual cultural and multimedia features that now ship with the majority of cell phones.

If such options are in cell phones and mobile technologies are available for disabled users, these also reconfigure technological and cultural possibilities for all users. Significant numbers of Blind people are indeed now using text messaging and other data features on cell phones, as well as portable digital assistants, wireless laptop computers, and other devices. These innovative uses of mobile and wireless technologies build on and complement other media innovations of Blind users, such as braille, radio, Internet, audio recording, podcasting, blogging, talking books, and new digital publication standards such as Daisy (www.daisy.org). Outside Blind community and cultural lists, websites, journals, and circles, there is little recognition in other audiences of innovative uses of cell phones (cf. Goggin and Noonan 2006). Not surprising, perhaps, that progress in reshaping cell phone technology for Blind users is still slow at the time of writing (HREOC 2005).

Noonan's 2001 appraisal of the situation sadly remains a valid diagnosis:

> there are only two significantly developed zones of [blindness] accessibility momentum – PC access, predominantly via Microsoft's Windows32 operating systems; and Web accessibility, predominantly driven by the WAI [Web Accessibility Initiative] . . . This is important to consider when we note recent projections in the IT industry that more than half of the internet connections by 2002 (or 2005 in other estimates) are expected to be from non-PC devices. This means that they will be from technologies which, currently, have no means of accessibility to their visual output. This raises the important question as to how people will be able to access set-top-boxes, WAP-capable mobile phones, personal organisers, smart domestic appliances and the like, which are solely visual (and non-textual) in output.
>
> (Noonan 2000)

The implications of such an impasse in technology are far reaching. SMS is now intensively used around the world, especially by young people, and is often an important aspect of cultural participation and social membership. Such emergent norms mean that Blind people's lack of access to SMS, and neglect in the design and shaping of mobile technologies more broadly, can lead to significant social exclusion.

Cell phones and next-generation disability

As the sources cited here make clear, study and discussion of disability and the cell phone is largely to be found in the specialised technical, service provider, or advocacy literatures and fora. There is still little discussion of disability to be found in telecommunications, new media, or Internet studies literature, and these are even fewer scholarly discussions of social and cultural aspects of mobile communications technologies. In seeking to stimulate such inquiry, I have been able to sketch only briefly three different case studies in disability and the cell phone. There is a great deal of empirical work that remains to be undertaken, first to establish the histories of disability and technology touched upon here, and second to debate and theorise these. This is an important research agenda, not only as a matter of human rights and justice but also because these narratives unsettle our taken-for-granted theories of technology. From a different perspective, I would note that Internet, games, and new media studies have made much of the role of the user in appropriating, domesticating, developing and actually producing networked digital technology and its associated cultural forms and content. There is much interest among cell phone and mobile technology scholars in questions of use and consumption. People with disabilities are mostly overlooked as users, consumers, and audiences, when they could be profitably credited as everyday, do-it-yourself consumer-producers of cell phones and media.

To understand cell phones and disability adequately, indeed cell phone culture in general, one needs to confront some deeply ideological notions (or myths) of technology. The term ideology is appropriate because it marks the operation of power: the social construction, or shaping, of disability in technology has decisively to do with relations of power (Goggin and Newell 2003). It is often very puzzling to those dedicated to the pursuit of accessible technology for people with disabilities that time and time again new technology brings not the much vaunted benefits (indeed salvation), but instead insidious new forms of exclusion, regulation, and control. Why, the proponent of accessible technology asks, if accessibility and 'universal design' are such simple, fruitful, and potentially profitable principles (NCD 2004), do we nearly always find that technologies are designed without imagining that people with disabilities will be among their users? My suspicion is that stubbornly resistant aspects of achieving inclusive technologies form part of a larger project of dismantling the oppressive power relations of disability in our societies, in which, *mutatis mutandis*, people with disabilities have long been seen as *other*, indeed, all too often still, as inhuman (Goggin and Newell 2005a).

While power is very palpably to the fore here in the construction of disability and accessibility in cell phone culture, it also is very much a part of other aspects of the technology. I will discuss a different aspect of power as we now move from consumption to representation and regulation – and the subject of mobile panics.

Part III

Representing and regulating the cell phone

6 Mobile panic: health, manners, and our youth

The adverse health effects most often linked with mobile phones in media reports were brain tumours, other cancers, headaches, and brain damage.

(Stewart Report 2000: 21)

There are a few teachers who claim that getting pupils to carry out written work using phone text language is better than nothing. How sad is that?

(Tino Ferri, National Association of School Masters and Union of Women Teachers, quoted in Hurley 2003)

In scenes that hit a new low even for such a sick craze, Caroline Monk – who has lost her hair from chemotherapy – was hit in the face and punched to the ground by a boy aged 12 to 15 just for the hell of it. Then four other thugs piled in, branding her a 'slaphead' and filming her on a mobile phone so others could gloat over her ordeal. The gang only broke off when she screamed 'I've got f***ing cancer!' and left the scene weeping tears of pain and rage . . . [she] is now recovering on spiritual retreat in Ibiza.

(Cummins 2005)

To understand the cultural object of the cell phone we look at how it has been imagined and represented. So far in this book I have discussed some of the meanings associated with cell phones, and also the social practices with which cell phones are customarily identified. There are a wide range of representations of cell phones that have been important to how different societies and cultures have made sense of this technology. In this chapter, I wish to focus upon this one noticeable and persistent feature of the representation of mobiles: panics.

Stanley Cohen's classic study of the mods and rockers and how they were viewed in mainstream British society revealed a wide gulf between the insider experience of the practices and customs in these subcultures as opposed to the menace or danger it was thought to hold to others (Cohen 1972). Informed by criminology, sociology, and deviance theory, Cohen's account highlighted the role media play in creating such moral panics. The concept of moral panic was an emphasis that was taken up and developed by Stuart Hall and his co-authors in *Policing the Crisis*, a study of news, media, and young people that became greatly influential in cultural and media studies (Hall et al. 1978). Hall and his collaborators were also interested in how discourses about the threats posed to social order by particular subcultures were created and sustained. They firmly related this to a broader account of capitalist society and its sophisticated yet pervasive exercise of power through hegemony, and ultimately through the norms, values, and routines of the media. Since *Policing the Crisis*, accounts of moral panic have formed an influential part of media theory (see, for example, Eldridge, Kitzinger, and Williams 1997). Indeed, there have been a number of full-length treatments of moral panics: one such study is much influenced by North American sociology (Goode and Ben-Yehuda 1994), while two other accounts reprise formative British sociological explorations of moral panic (Critcher 2003; Thompson 1998).

For my purposes here, I have found Thompson's work helpful, particularly his suggestions for an extension of moral panic classic accounts such as Cohen and Hall et al. The first of these is risk, inspired on the body of work on 'risk society' by Ulrich Beck (1992) and others. Thompson suggests that moral panics are phenomena 'characteristic of the modern "risk society" '. The pertinence of risk to moral panics has been queried (Ungar 2001), but in pointing to the importance of risk in understanding moral panic, Thompson tackles two of the most difficult questions in approaching the notion: namely, what it is about modernity that gives rise to moral panics, and how moral panics differ across cultures and nations. Moral panic theory, as Thompson notes, has been a distinctive contribution of British sociology, and, it might be added, British cultural studies (Thompson 1998: 141–2). What Thompson suggests is that the nature of the media in a particular setting is important for the occurrence of moral panics, especially its centralisation – and so relatively rapid and homogeneous relaying of news and images.

The theorisation of media and its relationship to power leads to the second framework Thompson wishes to incorporate, namely the rich and ambiguous concept of discourse. Thompson characterises his own project as seeking to:

> locate the study of moral panics within a sociology of morals, focusing on changes in forms of moral regulation and reactions to them . . . moral panics are often symptoms of tensions and struggles over changes in cultural and moral regulation.
>
> (1998: 142)

If we accept this argument, then moral panic theory stands to be especially useful for the insight it yields into reframing the object of a societal discussion. A furious even explosive public discussion or scandal around a particular phenomenon may not be actually about its purported object. Rather at stake may be something quite different, such as the management and control of certain groups in society. Representation then is closely allied with another of the elements of the 'circuit of culture', namely regulation.

Even in this brief discussion it is evident that cell phones pose considerable challenges for moral panic theory, as equally do other new media today, such as the Internet, which are harbingers of great cultural and media transformations. How one explains moral panics depends upon the account of media one gives. So, for instance, Thompson suggests that one reason for Britain's unique status as a veritable test-bed for moral panics is the dominance of its national news media in setting and shaping a news agenda. An important issue in explaining moral panic is considering the relative weight of the dynamics of group behaviour as opposed to the media. At issue is the question of where social problems are collectively defined (Best 1990; Jenkins 1992; Thompson 1998). Moral panic theorists have convincingly pointed to the media as the key place where such definition occurs, and thus as a generative site of moral panics. There have been quite a number of earlier technologies that have also been at the epicentre of moral panics. One of the most striking recent examples is video games, dubbed 'video nasties', the subject of furious debates and a number of studies in the 1980s and 1990s replaying concerns about media and violence (Barker 1984; Buckingham 1996; Critcher 2003: 79–80). Such phobic objects are associated with particular deviant affordances, and with social groups that require invigilation and regulation.

One challenge to such accounts is the pace and reach of media transformation, and to what extent this changes the dynamics of media representation, institutions, and audiences, and so the shaping of panics. Cell phones, of course, are intimately involved in this redefinition of media, offering new pathways for the circulation of anxieties, as well as themselves being triggers of moral panic.

It is with these thoughts on moral panic in mind that I wish to analyse and reframe some important ways that cell phones have been culturally represented, and become implicated in debates over social regulation. Clearly my starting point is indeed to see cell phone anxieties as a species of moral panic – what I am calling 'mobile panics'. Among other things, I would like to analyse representations of cell phones to see if there is not a better way to shed light upon what is at stake in this recurring demonisation of the cell phone (cf. R. Harper 2003). First, then, I discuss the discourse on the health effects of emission from cell phones or transmission towers. Secondly, I examine the key role young people play in mobile panics, focusing on the panic over mobiles' threat to literacy and cultural values. Young people also function as the fulcrum of the third mobile panic I discuss, namely mobile bullying as represented in the case of 'happy slapping'.

Cellular risks

Since the recognition of radiation, especially in the development of nuclear technologies, there has developed a sense of both its curative and beneficial powers but also the harm it might cause. In the early 1990s concerns emerged about the adverse effects to people's health and well-being due to cell phones. It was feared that the intensity of electromagnetic radiation from cell phones being clasped to people's heads while making calls, or carried around close to their bodies in pockets, around necks, or on belts, could raise the temperature of tissue and organs, and through prolonged contact lead to tumours, cancers, or other illness. Also, there were widespread fears of the radiation emitted from transmission towers, especially when located in sensitive locations, for example near areas where children congregated, such as schools.

Electromagnetic radiation was not only something emitted by cell phones, it was becoming more widespread with the use of radio waves and spectrum for carriage of signals by a number of other information and communication technologies. As we saw in chapter 5, a little-publicised consequence of electromagnetic radiation of second-generation digital phones was interference with hearing aids, something to which cell phone manufacturers and carriers responded by seeking to encourage the development of devices with better immunity or resistance to radiation. The interference issue paled into relative insignificance in comparison to the potentially far graver consequences of electromagnetic radiation to human lives.

It is important to place the panic over mobiles and health in the history of discourses of danger from new technology (cf. Lasen 2005: 41–5). This is something emphasised by Chapman and Wutzke in their study of the media's role in the construction of cell phone as health threat in the 1995 case of protests against a mobile transmitter base station in Sydney. The first thing they note is the almost entirely sympathetic coverage of the event:

> With momentary exceptions, all media coverage inhabited the same definition of the issue assumed by the protesters: that the residents were quite understandably concerned about their children's health, were engaged in a classic David-versus-Goliath struggle, and were pursuing justice.
>
> (Chapman and Wutzke 1997: 614)

Following classic media theory, they muse that as a 'big news story, the dynamics of this story are *prima facie* sociologically interesting as a case study in newsworthiness', but that it was a second issue that was most interesting: 'what were the characteristics of this issue that allowed a situation posing health risks that were almost certainly infinitesimal to be regarded by residents as worthy of impassioned action and the attention of the media?' (1997: 615–16). To explain this, they draw upon a model proposed by P.M. Sandman that contends that the 'idea of risk needs to be reconceptualised to take account of the relationship between the risky situation or agent (which [Sandman] names the "hazard") and the strength of people's responses to these situations' (Chapman and Wutzke 1997: 615; Sandman 1989, 1995). In this case Chapman and Wutzke found few applicable predictors for reducing community outrage, with the exception of chronic consequences and plenty of benefits. Accordingly, Chapman and Wutzke draw the conclusion that the figure of the mobile phone tower appearing in this suburb activated quite a number of long-held predicates of hazard, as listed by theorists such as Sandman, but also redolent of long-lived myths of technology.

While cell phones would certainly seem to fit into such mythical traditions and media frames of reference, what is it about mobile phone technology that might trigger such a panic? Something shared with other moral panics is that it is perceived to affect a vulnerable population:

> all news coverage concentrated solely on the children in the kindergarten said to be at risk. Later, when the transmitters were moved adjacent to a club frequented by elderly patrons, the outrage re-emerged in further media stories. Towers throughout Australia sited in factory grounds; in the back of fire-brigade stations or beside highways have attracted little community outrage.
>
> (1997: 618)

The hinging of this mobile panic on the pathos of vulnerable children led directly to regulatory initiatives to address this, such as specifying that mobile towers be located further away from child-care centres or schools where there are larger concentrations of children.

Whereas this may be seen as evidence of policy being shaped by social and cultural perceptions, it is important to note that there are intertwined scientific reasons for such policy. Indeed one critic advancing such an argument also issues a corrective to Chapman and Wutze's account, suggesting that it was not that the mobile towers issue demonstrated palpable public irrationality (Mercer 1998; cf. Jong and Armstrong 1997). To the contrary, there was, and remains, a rational basis for positions put by many of the protesters. At the core of this is the complexity of scientific reason regarding technologies, including mobiles in this case, and the multiple ways such scientific knowledge interacts with culture and society. Hence the broad public ramifications of recurrent scientific and technical controversies:

> A predominant feature of many risk debates is the existence of an underlying scientific/technical controversy. Such controversies often involve differing expert perceptions of the existence or magnitude of a hazard and differenti- ated 'attentive publics' and activist groups. Even disputes that may not

originally involve scientific disagreement, because of the social significance of scientific legitimation, may well attract scientific and technical disagreement.

(Mercer 1998: 291; see also Jasanoff 1986; Martin and Richards 1995; Nelkin 1979)

As public concern mounted in many countries regarding the health effects of cell phones, the very legitimacy of the technology, not to mention its business prospects, was being seriously questioned. A key moment in the public understanding of the science involved here, but also in governmental, industrial, and cultural legitimation of the cell phone, lay in the decision of the British government to establish an independent expert group to examine possible effects of mobile phones, base stations, and transmitters on health. The Expert Group's work represented perhaps the first comprehensive, independent, and open investigation into an extremely confusing and contested topic. The group reported in 2000, concluding that:

> the balance of evidence does not suggest mobile phone technologies put the health of the general population of the UK at risk. There is some preliminary evidence that outputs from mobile phone technologies may cause, in some cases, subtle biological effects, although, importantly, these do not necessarily mean that health is affected. There is also evidence that in some cases people's well-being may be adversely affected by the insensitive siting of base stations . . . Overall, the report proposes that a precautionary approach be adopted until more robust scientific information becomes available.
>
> (Stewart Report 2000: iii)

To arrive at this conclusion, the Expert Group in particular dissected the two key and interlinked areas of understanding how radiofrequency fields from mobile phone technology function, and reviewing the scientific evidence of adverse health effects. Since this time, many other scientific studies have been conducted, refining the areas of agreement and disagreement on mobiles and health effects. What remains interesting about the Stewart Report is that it also directly tackled the mobiles and health panic.

The Expert Group took seriously the concerns expressed by the public regarding the health effects of mobiles. It reviewed UK media coverage in the period between January 1999 and February 2000, as well as seventy-six television and radio programs broadcast during this period:

> Seventy-nine per cent of the media reports alleged adverse health effects from mobile phones and base stations, whereas nine per cent concluded that there was too little rigorous scientific evidence to arrive at a conclusion, or reported no adverse effect. Overall, the safety of mobile phone handsets

achieved more coverage than the safety of base stations, although local newspapers tended to report more on issues relating to base stations. Other aspects of safety that were covered included concerns that driving while using a hand-held mobile phone was dangerous.

(Stewart Report 2000: 21)

The Stewart Report also reviewed the information available to the public from various sources other than the media, including the telecommunications industry. It found that the mobile phone manufacturers had tended to provide clear information to and better communication channels with the public than network operators, urging improvements given the 'public continues to distrust the operators in the area of public health' (2000: 22). The Expert Group was also critical of the role played by the National Radiological Protection Board, the government agency that supported its deliberations, in not better informing the debate and so leavening the media 'scare' stories (2000: 24–5).

As these criticisms reveal, the Expert Group was concerned to dispel the public worry, concern, and distrust concerning mobiles. It believed good communication to be one part of the solution to this problem, and the other associated, central strategy to revolve around information. It recommended that this should be addressed by the industry, but that responsibility should also lie with the state:

> We are concerned that too much of the information that is currently presented to the public regarding the health aspects of mobile phone technology is misleading . . . We therefore believe that it would help if Government provided clear advice on this topic in the form of a leaflet circulated to all households . . . This leaflet should be developed in concert with industry, which has already produced some good leaflets.
>
> (2000: 25)

This emphasis on the role of the state to provide guidance to its citizens in understanding technology is an interesting one. It relies on the much debated 'deficit model' of science communication; namely that the public would understand the beneficial purposes of science and technology if only its lack of knowledge ('deficit') was remedied (Dickson 2005; Irwin and Wynne 1996; Sturgis and Allum 2004).

Over and above the problems with the deficit model of communication implicit in the Stewart Report, it is worth reflecting that governments have had to manage a number of conflicting roles and perspectives on technology, reflecting different views and interests of sections of the populace as well as different ministries. I think there are grounds to suggest that the industry and its partners in government communications, in telecommunications, and in economic ministries, regulators and agencies across the world were very worried when concerns about health effects of cell phones arose in the early 1990s, and wished to downplay and manage the ensuing panic – because they did not wish to see the goose killed off as it was about to lay its golden eggs. Here I would depart from Adam Burgess's otherwise convincing analysis and critique of how public fears regarding cell phones were constructed (Burgess 2004). Burgess is rightly scathing of the extremely problematic way in which the cell phone came to be lumbered with unjustified expectations of danger and health risk, and he is scathing about simple-minded, reactive blaming of the cell phone industry for such ills on society. However he neglects to acknowledge the active, shaping role of the industry as public and media relations manager, not to mention participant in the conduct and funding of some of the research dissected in the inquiry.

My view would be that as scientists, industry, bureaucrats, and citizens dis-cussed and debated the health effects over the next decade, the health effects issue was normalised through a combination of micro-regulatory and policy responses, reassuring scientific evidence, and behavioural and technological adaptations, in the service of the precautionary principle. Dormant but remaining a concern, the gross social and cultural facts of usage were taken to have largely trumped health scares, as the Stewart Report observed: 'The continuing rapid growth in the use of conventional mobile phones . . . indicates that most people do not consider the possibility of adverse health effects to be a major issue' (2000: 26). This is certainly the case regarding the use of cell phone handsets, but something of a panic is very much active in relation to base stations: 'Given the much lower exposures to radiation from base stations than from handsets, the greater public concern . . . about the former is paradoxical' (2000: 26). The Stewart Report explained this in terms of perceived control and benefit:

> individuals can choose whether or not to use a mobile phone, whereas they have little control over their exposures from base stations. Furthermore, people derive a personal benefit from the use of a phone, but gain nothing directly from the presence of a base station close to their home or place of work. If anything they may suffer a loss of amenity and perhaps a reduction in the value of their property.
>
> (2000: 26)

It is no coincidence then that the cell phone, one of the most oft-cited contempor-ary indices of modernity, should be accompanied by a number of panics. That one of the most widespread and potentially damaging of these regards its threat to the body, and the body's well-being, also represents one of the greatest fears of modernity – the frailty and mortality of the body. The discourse of risk was key to how the potential crisis over health hazards was managed, and continues to be.

Cell phone as threat to culture

The folk devil in a moral panic is most often the figure of a young person. As we have seen, cell phones are closely identified with young people. Like a range of other technologies, young people, including children, have indeed been avid adopters of mobiles. While they are often given credit for their technical facility and dexterity with mobiles, their association with the technology is often regarded as a social problem. There is the use of mobiles for illicit purposes. There is the high level of debt incurred by young people in owning and using a mobile, often the first time a young person has used credit. There are the possibilities that mobiles offer for co-ordination of activities and greater independent communication with peers. There are the panics about the introduction of camera phones because of their potential use by paedophiles and others to take photos of young children.

Because of their prevalence and availability, their portability, their intricate incorporation into the patterns of everyday life, and, increasingly, their function as *media*, mobiles have posed considerable challenges for the conduct and regulation of private and public spheres, and the boundaries and relationships that pertain to and traverse these. In this section I will discuss the panic activated by cell phones that traverses the time-honoured terrain of culture itself. To do so, I will focus on two facets of this: first, the fear that, widely used, cell phones will lead to a decline in literacy, and so pose a fundamental threat to cultural values and canons; second, the anxieties regarding the threats that cell phones pose to sociability and accepted norms of communication.

At the opening of this book I have remarked that cell phones have often been seen as the antithesis of what a 'culture' is and stands for. Especially prior to the use of cell phones for artistic and media purposes, they have been typically discussed as something that threatens the processes of cultivation and learning around which pedagogy and citizenship revolve. Examples abound, but take this representative article:

> Scotland's schoolkids are turning into a generation of illiterates – because of mobile phone text messaging, experts warned last night. Many youngsters now write in the abbreviated gobbledegook, rather than standard English . . . Judith Gillespie, development manager at the Scottish Parent Teacher Council, said: 'There must be rigorous efforts from all quarters of the education system to stamp out the use of texting as a form of written language as far as English study is concerned . . . You would be shocked at the numbers of senior secondary pupils who cannot distinguish between "their" and "there". The problem is that there is now a feeling in some schools that pupils' freedom of expression should not be inhibited, so anything goes.
>
> (Hurley 2003)

The article provided proof of the depth to which 'text message kids' have stooped:

> The following is an excerpt from an essay written in text language by a 13-year-old girl at a leading state secondary school in the west of Scotland [with translation] . . .
>
> My smmr hols wr CWOT. B4, we usd 2go2 NY my bro, his GF & thr 3:@ kds FTF . . . Bt my Ps wr so:/ BC o 9/11 tht they dcdd 2 stay in SCO & spnd 2 wks up N . . . I ws vvv brd in MON . . . 2 day, I cam bk 2 skool. I feel v 0:-) BC I hv dn all my hm wrk. Now its BAU . . .
>
> In English
>
> My summer holidays were a complete waste of time. Before, we used to go to New York to see my brother, his girlfriend and their three screaming kids face to face . . . But my parents were worried because of the terrorism attack on September 11 that they decided we should stay in Scotland and spend two weeks up north . . . I was extremely bored, in the middle of nowhere . . . Today, I returned to school. I feel very saintly, because I've done all my homework. Now it's business as usual . . .
>
> (Hurley 2003)

Anecdotes with a similar theme have been widely circulated and reported, often featuring specimens of the linguistic usage also (indeed the anecdote regarding the essay with an excerpt was reproduced, without acknowledgement, in a later more critical piece on the implications of text message language (Boyd 2003)).

It is difficult to establish, however, how widely text message language has crossed over into other linguistic contexts and genres, and indeed become absorbed into languages more generally (although at least one study is under way, namely by Baron). There are now a number of studies that suggest that text messaging does not have the direct and baleful effects on language competency and literacy suggested by detractors. For instance a Swedish study concluded that 'language use in text messaging is to be regarded as a variant of language use, creatively and effectively suited to the conditions of SMS and the aims for which it is used' (Segerstad 2005: 331). Similarly Ling's sociolinguistic account of texting emphasises its situated and appropriate nature, as exemplified by the practice of the teenage women he studied: 'This is not to say that the writing of teen women is the polished prose of Margaret Mead, Toni Morrison, or Virginia Woolf. These are short and slapdash messages intended for immediate response' (Ling 2004: 165).

We certainly need a better understanding of how text message language works, and how it relates to other linguistic trends and also the intertwined processes of technological, social, and cultural changes. There are distinct parallels here with fears over literacy and civilisation occasioned by other new technologies.

The linguistic changes occasioned by the Internet, specifically email, brought great anxieties. We are now able to understand such processes, comprehending these as part of the complex dynamics of language change in which new usages associated with new media technologies and communicative practice play an important but not necessarily deleterious part (Baron 2000; Crystal 2003, 2004). Baron's work on email and instant messaging tellingly points out that technological change is only one variable that influences the direction of language, along with social, cultural, economic, and political change (Baron 1998, 2000; Baron et al. 2005). Also that different languages stand to develop in different ways, with new media being one factor. At stake here is a clash over different models of language, schematically rendered as the yawning chasm between the 'prescriptive' (urging adherence to a norm or standard) and the 'descriptive' (taking a neutral view on changes in language, but rather seeking to ensure that accounts of language accurately describe what users say and write and communicate) (Crystal 2000, 2002, 2003).

Closely associated with fears of the deterioration of language in the face of text messaging are worries over the preservation and transmission of culturally ordained or at least highly prized texts and reading practices. Here text messaging and new features of mobile media have provided a new twist on concerns that cultural literacy in the broader sense will be diminished, as students by inclination and the infusion of new critical literacy pedagogies hone their skills in languages of mobiles, Internet, and television rather than the putatively more refined and sophisticated artefacts of literary canon of novels and poetry. For their part, advocates of critical literacy have contended that skills in using, reading, viewing, and listening to mobiles and other newer media can and should become a part of a relevant but also rigorous curriculum and pedagogy (Luke 2000, 2003a, 2003b). Another response to these criticisms advanced by such detractors has been initiatives to incorporate mobiles into literary activity – for instance, with the transmission of literary texts over mobiles (a Chinese novel; short texts; poetry), or the inclusion of text message haiku into poetry contests. A rather more dialectical grasping of the mobile is the unfolding development of genres and idioms that are elicited by and explore the cell phone and mobile technologies as cultural technology. Suffice to say that the cell-phone-as-threat-to-culture-itself panic is not going away anytime soon, and that these cultural battles over the import of cell phones will continue to be fought. At this point, however, I will draw to a close this discussion, and move to my third study of mobile panic, one in which our youth and their manners once again figure prominently.

Mobile bullying and the curious case of 'happy slapping'

As I start to write about the moral panic on bullying I listen to a radio program dedicated to 'social change and day-to-day life' discussing the topic with an academic expert and a school principal. This serves to remind me once again not only that bullying is a topic that of recent times has been something of an *idée fixee*, but that bullying using new technologies such as cell phones and the Internet is something that really has seized the public imagination. Whereas public discussion of bullying has now moved from the association of bullying in schools and the schoolyard, and features bullying of and by adults in settings such as workplaces and universities, bullying via the instrument of the cell phone remains almost exclusively something that is associated with children and young people.

A most virulent strain of this discourse about young people, mobiles, and bullying was the English 'happy slapping' panic of late 2004 to mid-2005. 'Happy slapping' was coined to describe the phenomenon of people slapping someone in the face while filming their reaction with a mobile phone. Happy slapping seems to have emerged in the autumn of 2004, but as far I can tell it first appeared in the British media in January 2005:

> Schools are cracking down on the video phone 'happy slapping' craze sweeping London. Teenagers have been plaguing commuters on trains and buses in the capital [London]. They slap strangers in the face while filming their reaction on mobile phones. Head teachers at several schools have confiscated mobile phones after pupils were found recording the attacks.
>
> (*Mirror* 2005a)

Several things about happy slapping are defined at the outset: it is an epidemic; it is something that young people, especially teenagers, engage in; and schools and teachers are trying to stop it. In its early guise, happy slapping is more voyeuristic prank than menacing violence. For instance, the Alcatel 'One Touch 756' mobile offered by Virgin, is described in the *Mirror* by one of its technology writers as the 'budget video-equipped handset' that 'should prove popular with the "happy slapping" generation' (*Mirror* 2005d). Within three months happy slapping had apparently become widespread:

> In one video clip, labelled Bitch Slap, a youth approaches a woman at a bus stop and punches her in the face. In another, Knockout Punch, a group of boys wearing uniforms are shown leading another boy across an unidentified school playground before flooring him with a single blow to the head. In a third, Bank Job, a teenager is seen assaulting a hole-in-the-wall customer while another youth grabs the money he has just withdrawn from the cash machine. Welcome to the disturbing world of the 'happy slappers' – a youth craze in which groups of teenagers armed with camera phones slap or mug unsuspecting children or passersby while capturing the attacks on 3g technology.
>
> (Honigsbaum 2005)

Just how the 'youth craze' developed is unclear, but one version has it that:

> According to police and anti-bullying organisations, the fad, which began as a craze on the UK garage music scene before catching on in school playgrounds across the capital last autumn, is now a nationwide phenomenon. And as the craze has spread from London to the home counties to the north of England, so the attacks have become more menacing, with increasing numbers of violent assault and adult victims.
>
> (Honigsbaum 2005)

The exact numbers of happy slapping incidents was unclear, with only a handful of confirmed arrests and convictions – though there would appear to be much higher figures reported of cases investigated, such as the British Transport police reporting some 200 investigations in a six-month period from late 2004 to April 2005 (Honigsbaum 2005).

Media attention focused on a relatively small number of cases. Some of these were relatively trivial if shocking:

> Earlier this month James Silver, 34, a freelance journalist, was attacked while jogging on the South Bank in London. While one youth blocked his path, another hit him with a rolled-up magazine. When he spun around another teenager – who had been hiding behind nearby scaffolding – leapt out and hit him hard in the head. When he staggered to his feet he noticed the rest of the gang were jeering and pointing their mobile phones at him.
>
> (Honigsbaum 2005)

Other cases were very violent indeed, most grievously in the case of sixteen-year-old Becky Smith, who was attacked by teenagers in her Manchester home, lost consciousness, and suffered temporary paralysis. The assault was filmed on mobile phone, and circulated around her school – only to be viewed by her thirteen-year-old brother Craig. The case was reported upon ten days later on May 20: 'Thugs beat a girl of 16 unconscious and filmed the attack on a mobile phone in a sick craze called Happy Slapping' (Disley 2005a; see also *Guardian* 2005; S. Jones 2005). A sixteen-year-old girl was later charged and arrested for the assault. Amid the outrage, her mother called for a ban on the offending technology: 'The school should get rid of video phones, or are they going to wait until someone has been murdered before they take the phones off the kids?' (S. Jones 2005). Ironically reports of the case were accompanied in at least one newspaper by the publication of photos of her bruised face.

The following day, 21 May, there was another reporting of a happy slapping incident, accompanied by a photo of the victim, Caroline Monk, girlfriend of television star Matthew Wright: 'This woman has cancer. She was punched to the ground and then photographed on a mobile phone by teenage yobs. She is the latest victim of happy slapping' (Cummins 2005). The depravity of the happy slappers appeared to have plumbed new depths. The reporting of happy slapping cases conjured up lurid pictures of senseless ultra-violence harking back to Stanley Kubrick's 1971 film, *A Clockwork Orange*:

> A terrified teenager is tied to a railing in a dark stairway. His face is marked with a black pen. The voice of a vicious thug taunts his victim, hitting him repeatedly while another yob films the disturbing act on his mo phone . . . Torture and extortion of this nature appear to be an escalation of the 'happy slapping' craze . . . Jan Harlan, the late director's brother-in-law, who helped to make the Oscar-nominated film, said that such violence was 'beginning to make *A Clockwork Orange* seem like *Bambi*'.
>
> (Zimonjic and Hastings 2005)

As the happy slapping panic metastasised, the police took the lead in publicising the threat and their responses. They were soon joined by various organisations with a concern for young people and bullying, such as *Bullying Online* (www.bullying.co.uk), a charity providing information and strategies for children and parents concerned with bullying in schools:

> Liz Carnell, the director of victim support and lobbying organisation Bullying Online says the use of internet or mobile-related bullying is on the increase and that schools are failing to address the problem . . . The problem with cyber bullying is that technology allows a far greater dissemination of the abuse . . .
>
> (Hoare 2005; see also Honigsbaum 2005)

In this way, happy slapping was associated with bullying using mobiles and the Internet, already a well-established moral panic as we have seen (Hoare 2005). To deal with the epidemic, one school subscribed to a service called 'Text Someone', which allows pupils to use text messaging to report bullying using this medium (Hoare 2005).

One of the most interesting developments in the happy slapping episode, and something that confirms its candidacy for the category of moral panic, occurred when it became defined as a national social problem at the heart of youth deviance and urban crime in Britain. In early May 2005, the Blair Labour government was returned for a third term on a platform in which crime and anti-social behaviour had been a key electoral issue. Later that month the Deputy Prime Minister John Prescott welcomed a ban by a Kent shopping mall, the largest in Britain, on youths wearing baseball caps and hooded tops, 'the "urban crime" uniforms' (*Mirror* 2005b). In doing so, Prescott told BBC Radio that he had himself been the victim of intimidation by a group of eleven youths with hoods while at a service station the previous year:

> He [the assailant] came at me in a very intimidating manner but, of course, I now have security control. They appeared and [the gang] vanished. But what struck me about it is not only did they come with this kind of uniform, as it is, but they came with a kind of movie camera to take a film of any such incident. I found that very alarming.
>
> (Taylor 2005)

The possession of the video camera was something interpreted by the media as signifying a possible happy slapping attack (*Mirror* 2005b; Taylor 2005): 'Mr Prescott may have been targeted by a "happy-slapping" gang. Such gangs use mobile phones or digital cameras to film each other attacking their victims' (Taylor 2005). In the wake of the Becky Smith attack, Education Secretary Ruth Kelly announced a crackdown on unruliness in classrooms, saying such behaviour was 'particularly unacceptable and a symptom of what goes on in some groups in society' (Disley 2005b). One parliamentarian even called for mobile phone signals to be blocked in schools to stop happy slapping, and the government agreed to 'review' the situation (Temko 2005).

A decisive phase in the happy slapping panic was the release of a 'picture phone survey', a piece of research on bullying of young people. The research was commissioned by children's charity NCH in conjunction with Tesco Mobile, and was widely reported. Among its findings were that: 20 per cent of respondents had experienced some sort of 'digital bullying', 14 per cent by mobile text, 5 per cent in Internet chatrooms, and 4 per cent by email; 10 per cent said they had felt uncomfortable, embarrassed, or threatened by someone using a mobile phone camera to take a picture of them – and of these some 17 per cent believed the photo taken of them had been sent to someone else (NCH and Tesco 2005). The survey was based on interviews with 770 young people aged between eleven and nineteen in March–April 2005. Upon release it became a very influential tool around which to shape responses to happy slapping, with NCH adept at crafting a strong message:

> 'A mobile phone is one of a child's most treasured personal possessions,' NCH said. 'So if the mobile starts being used to harass a child, be it through text or camera phone bullying, it can seem like there is no escape . . .'
>
> (*Mirror* 2005c; also Carvel 2005)

NCH and Tesco also set up a website to encourage children experiencing text bullying to talk to a friend or adult (www.stoptextbully.com) as well as a dedicated 24-hour mobile service (NCH and Tesco 2005). As the efforts of this non-governmental actor in concert with a cell phone company stakeholder reveal, there is a fine, if not indistinguishable, line between researching and seeking to redress real concerns about cell phone mediated bullying and participating in the construction of a moral panic.

Happy slapping is a fascinating case because while it was taken seriously by some sections of the media, moral entrepreneurs (such as *Bullying Online*), and the state, it was at least received in a comic, if not ironic and questioning fashion. For instance, happy slapping became jocularly mentioned by columnists and in particular those writing about sport ('Short of putting on hooded tops and filming the whole thing on a mobile phone, Arsenal could not have delivered a more contemptuous slap to the Manchester United face' (Kelner 2005)). There were a number of journalists and commentators who explicitly queried the panic.

> May was not a good month to be aged under 16. Following New Labour's re-election pledge to foster a 'culture of respect', childcare was off the agenda and child-panic replaced it. Subsequent events seemed to justify this mood . . . The term 'moral panic' is employed far too lazily these days. Orchestration by the government and the media of public concern is hardly a new phenomenon. Nor does calling something a moral panic imply that such anxieties are entirely spurious. Yes, there is a debate to be had about children, but it is not this one.
>
> (Brooks 2005)

> [W]hile this hi-tech development [happy slapping] may be new, the social phenomenon of unruly kids terrorising respectable adults is as old as the hills . . . This is not an attempt to mount a defence for the worst of these louts on their strange tiny bicycles. But to pick on a lot of kids just because they wear hooded tracksuit tops is not only unfair, it is a viewpoint which ignores history.
>
> (O'Sullivan 2005)

> [I]s happy slapping a genuine trend or media hype?
>
> (Akwagyiram 2005)

Manufactured or not, happy slapping turned back upon one of the moral panic theorists critiquing it. Graham Barnfield, journalism lecturer at the University of East London, and, like myself professional-moral-panic-sceptic, was unwittingly signed up to authenticate the happy slapping media epidemics. Barnfield had been invited to participate in Trevor McDonald's ITV *Tonight* programme on happy slapping, in which he was asked to watch happy slapping footage on a laptop in a club, while being interviewed for his response. Previously sought out by the media for comment on reality TV, and the way that humiliation had become entertainment, he is adamant he did not suggest a causal link between television and happy slapping, but exactly this was suggested in the ITV press release that the BBC and other media outlets based their stories upon (Hoare 2005). The *Mirror* reported, for instance, that:

> Dr Graham Barnfield, of the University of East London, said he blamed TV shows like Jackass and Dirty Sanchez which screened people doing pranks for fuelling the fad. He said: 'Kids watching are thinking "Maybe I could stage my own scenes of pain along these lines." '
>
> (Disley 2005c)

Fortunately for Barnfield, the story of his unwitting participation in the happy slapping moral panic became a sympathetic and instructive narrative for consumption by readers of the *Guardian* higher education section (comforting for other academics licking the wounds of their mauling at the hands of the media):

> Reading the BBC news headlines on the internet one night last month, Graham Barnfield came across references to an academic blaming TV shows for the 'happy slapping' craze. 'My first thought was, here we go again,' he says. 'Yet another berk falling for the theory of copycat behaviour' . . . further reading revealed that Barnfield himself was the berk in question.
>
> (Crace 2005)

Though Barnfield contacted the BBC, which corrected the story on its website, it was too late:

> Within a week, Barnfield had drifted into a surreal world. Not only were his views being misquoted in the British, New Zealand, South African, German and Indian media without a single journalist bothering to check for accuracy, he was also being misrepresented as an expert on happy slapping, a title he had never claimed for himself.
>
> (Crace 2005)

In any case he did become an expert on happy slapping, but was not called upon again by the media as a commentator on this (Crace 2005).

Getting the panic message

There is a broad range of different considerations at play in the three quite distinct cases of mobile panics I have reviewed here. The salience and importance of risk as a new element of moral panic is certainly clear in the case of cellular phone and health effects. Literacy and language anxieties and the contemporaneously described moral panic of happy slapping both display classic features of moral panic and are very much about the regulation of a deviant population (namely ill-mannered, feckless, and subversive young people). They are also accompanied by new developments such as a kind of knowing, reflexive use of the term 'moral panic' itself to name yet the phenomenon almost in the process of constructing it – not to mention the shrinking, critical distance, and indeed porous relations among the spheres of journalism, charity, government, and scholarly theorists of moral, mobile panics themselves. All things considered, there *is* something striking and important that continues to go on which does justify the concept of moral panic, and which has been not only germane but indeed highly significant in the development of cell phone culture.

Settling into the haze of a summer as I reflected upon mobile panics and where they fit into cell phone culture, the city in which I live was unexpectedly and violently gripped by one in which these things mattered very intensely indeed. In early December 2005, there was a race riot on the popular Cronulla beach, south of Sydney, in which hundreds of young people, young men especially, gathered on a weekend to protest the incursions into their playground of surf and sand of visitors from the more culturally diverse suburbs to the west, especially young men of Australian-Lebanese and 'Muslim' cultures. In the ensuing days, there were violent raids and assaults back and forth across Sydney's beaches and suburbs, involving almost farcical yet deadly earnest efforts to identify people of 'anglo' or 'Middle Eastern' appearance (often specifically 'Lebanese') respectively, and threaten or bash them. Having been caught largely unawares and been initially slow to respond, the New South Wales state government responded with a massive show of force and repression, passing new laws to curtail accused and offenders' rights, ostentatiously policing all beaches north and south, and 'locking' down whole suburbs. The race riots were widely reported in the international press, and jolted, of course not for the first time, the city's self-image of a cosmopolitan, multicultural nation. At the very heart of this state of siege and the panic that gripped those living there was a mobile panic: the spark that was widely believed to have set off this conflagration was a racist text message.

In the days leading up to the riot racist text messages had apparently been circulating calling upon concerned 'white' Australians to rally at Cronulla to defend their beach and women.[1] The volume of such text messages and emails also increased in the wake of the riot (certainly I received one personally from a phone number I did not recognise). New messages were being sent to exhort Lebanese-Australians and others to fight back. Media commentators, police, government officials, and many others held such text messages directly and centrally implicated in organising the riot and in the violent scuffles that followed. There were calls upon the mobile companies to intercept and ban such messages, though it was pointed out that text messages were usually only held for twenty-four hours and were more difficult to regulate than it was to tap phone calls. Nonetheless this mobile panic drew a direct and immediate response from the state government, which included provisions allowing the confiscation of cell phones and outlawing sending, receipt, or keeping of racist or inflammatory text messages. For some days police proceeded to stop cars and board buses and demand to inspect mobiles, checking and reading text messages, arresting at least one person for being responsible for banned text messages. Predictably perhaps, media outlets sought out experts on text messaging and cell phone culture for commentary, including myself, and most mainstream media appeared interested in portraying a fascination for texting and reinforcing its pivotal role in the riots. In participating in media interviews, I found myself torn between wishing to attest to the significance and importance of cell phone culture and texting, and being extremely sceptical about its alleged power in shaping these events. One of my colleagues did provide the ritual mention of 'swarming' and 'flashmobs' that fitted nicely, while I mostly sat this dance, or rather panic, out.

While the panic was focused on the deadly power of the cell phone to conjure up a howling mob, what was lost was the formidable, if not implacable role of old media, and cultural representations more generally, in all this. The text messages in question, to which the initial riot was attributed, had actually been read out on one of the country's highest-rating and most influential talk-radio programs, by its well-known conservative host. The contents of such messages had also been detailed in print media, especially tabloids, and been widely discussed. As in the 'coup d'text' of Philippines President Estrada discussed in chapter 4, the actual use of text messages and cell phones in the conceiving, co-ordinating, and improvisational dynamics of the riots remains quite unclear. While little retrospective interpretation at all has emerged regarding the riots, it certainly felt that the police and state overreaction and the arrival of the traditionally hot and lethargic Christmas, combined with the underlying structures of power and feeling to achieve the reinstitution of calm, or rather perhaps the habitual, much less invisible expression of whiteness as usual. The policing of the crisis had certainly been fuelled by the mobile panic, but setting law enforcement the task of bringing those text messages to book was probably like asking them to catch the wind.

For analysts, as well as police, the novel and salient appearance of texting also has a certain lure. Yet in concentrating on the deadly power of the cell phone to conjure up a howling or smart mob, or in the fascination with the new modes of transmission of mobile devices, it is important to give credit to the formidable, implacable role of media, and cultural representations more generally, in all this, as they are transmitted, received, interpreted and circulated through old as well as new modes, channels and technologies.

7 Intimate connections: sex, celebrity, and the cell phone

Why can't the English teach their royalty not to speak? If the Princess of Wales was indiscreet over her cellular telephone, it was probably because she, like most people, misunderstood how easily such conversations can be intercepted . . . Assuming it was real, it was about as private as a harangue in Hyde Park . . . it may seem surprising that it took so long for an enterprising audio paparazzo to claim to have recorded royal intimacies.

(Ramirez 1992)

Dear Victoria . . .

You are rumoured to be looking through David's pockets and shoes for evidence. I did the same thing. My husband hid his mobile phone in his shoes at night, and I crept on all fours to steal it and read the messages. It makes you feel like the lowest of the low to demean yourself by checking up on the man you are supposed to love and trust . . . I think however hard it is for you to do, you must find out if David has been unfaithful. Speak to those involved yourself. Maybe even have the courage to ring Rebecca Loos to hear her version of events . . .

Best wishes

Rachel Royce

(Royce 2005)

Names and numbers from Paris Hilton's cell phone have been stolen – possibly by a hacker – resulting in the private phone numbers of numerous celebrities being posted on the Internet . . . This may turn out to be Ms. Hilton's greatest contribution to mankind . . . My only regret about the Hilton incident is that my name wasn't in her phone book. I'm hurt.

(Magid 2005)

The meanings that we associate with technologies are vitally important to how such technologies are shaped. How we imagine and represent technologies – what we take them to stand in for – has a great deal of influence (not always but in many circumstances) on the 'small' techno and media cultures they inaugurate and sustain, but also on how such technologies, their uses and significance fit into the larger cultures we inhabit. There are links also, as I have indicated in chapter 6, between such representation and systems of social regulation – mobile panics being an excellent case-in-point of powerful representations of cell phones with pervasive and strong social and even political consequences. In this chapter, I turn to another salient facet of representation and regulation, the way that the cell phone is represented in terms of systems of sexuality and celebrity.

In popular culture, the arrival of telephones resulted in considerable anxiety about the boundaries and relations between public and private spheres. With the new possibilities they represented for communicating with lovers and intimates, as well as friends and families, telephones were the subject of public discussion expressing and working out these troubling new mores, the reformulation of social rules and appropriate etiquette. At the boundaries of acceptable behaviour, and posing dangers to respectable families and citizens, were the uses of the telephone for licentiousness and adultery, and other threats to the ordained gender and sexual hierarchies. The arrival of hand-held cell phones as a new form of portable telephony ushered in new protocols, genres, and practices for mediated communication for romance. Much has been written on cell phones, intimacy, and sexuality, but it certainly is apparent, like other new technologies before it, that the cell phone's irruption into the scene of communication unfroze certain aspects of social relations, opening up new opportunities for behaving and relating differently, and especially promising (or threatening) to be signally implicated in the dynamic contemporary redrawing of boundaries between public and private spheres. There are already considerable literatures on such topics, and important studies underway; what I wish to focus upon here is the way that the particular unintended effects of cell phones for romance have captured the popular imagination.

There are many stories, much gossip, and urban (and rural) myths that circulate on the age-old topic of amorous infidelity, telling tales about relationships that lovers wished to keep secret from their other partners, marital or otherwise. The cell phone has added a new twist to these stories because it features as a new way for lovers to communicate without other intimates knowing. Where drama occurs, however, is when one lover inadvertently overhears a phone call, finds a voicemail message, or reads a text message that reveals that their loved one is having an affair, as this news item underlines:

> Italy's love affair with text messaging is having an unexpected consequence: cell phones have become a leading give-away of secret affairs. Snooping spouses are finding amorous messages, as well as inexplicable phone numbers, stored in the memory of mobile phones.
>
> (Rachman 2003)

There are many everyday stories of how cell phones figure in the mediation of such illicit romances, but what I will focus on here is how we learn about such topics from media representations and narratives, and their luminary protagonists – celebrities.

It is now a commonplace to observe that we live in a world obsessed with celebrity. While many commentators decry this development, this is not necessarily helpful for understanding what is going on here in contemporary culture and media. We now have a number of important studies that attempt to do precisely this: to inquire into the function and significance of celebrity (such as Marshall 1997; Rojek 2001; Turner 2004). Celebrity is an important way that consumers of media understand and position themselves in the culture of contemporary capitalism. The lives of celebrities offer representations of exemplary figures that consumers can invest with their desires, and upon which they project and work through the social contradictions which their lives straddle. The multifaceted importance of this is brought out in Graeme Turner's definition of celebrity as:

> a genre of representation and a discursive effect; it is a commodity traded by the promotions, publicity, and media industries that produce these representations and their effects; and it is a cultural formation that has a social function we can better understand.
>
> (Turner 2004: 9)

Before moving on from this discussion of cultural and media theory of celebrity it is worth noting an important, recent development in celebrity, namely the presentation of celebrity as something that can be experienced by everyone. The production of ordinariness as a defining feature of the contemporary mediascape, evidenced in the 'reality television' phenomenon (Bonner 2003), promises that 'ordinary' people can become celebrities – and crucially that the unexceptional textures of their lives can become part of the staging of this celebrity (Turner 2004).

In terms of the cultural representation of the cell phone, the first thing to remark is that celebrity is put to work most obviously in advertising and marketing. Actors, television stars, sporting celebrities (Andrews and Jackson 2001; Jackson and Andrews 2005), and other celebrities have become the 'face' of cell phone brands, advertising, and promotional campaigns. Cell phone manufacturers, carriers, and retailers work with advertisers to craft a desired association between their service or handset and the celebrity. However, the relationships between celebrity and cell phones that I wish to explore here are those unauthorised deployments of celebrity that arise in the appropriations and inventiveness of popular culture, that are not welcomed, or at least officially anticipated, by cell phone corporations and their advertising partners. As the cell phone has developed, key to its representation in popular culture has been a series of spectacular scandals over unauthorised interception of phone calls, messages, and images of celebrities.

So, in my first case study, I examine the alleged interception and taping of cellular phone calls that were key to the early 1990s release of the tapes of conversations between Prince Charles and lover Camilla Parker Bowles ('Camillagate'), then Princess Diana and her intimate James Gilbey ('Squidgygate'), as well as a number of cell phone tappings of minor royal notables. From adulterous voice telephony, I turn to my second example, that of the new possibilities for assignations and affairs that text messaging offers, as the case of British footballer David Beckham and alleged paramour Rebecca Loos illustrates, and, furthermore, the SMS philandering of Australian cricketer Shane Warne with various putative lovers. Finally, I close by briefly canvassing even richer possibilities for eavesdropping or the opening and reading of epistolary fictions highlighted in the case of the hacking of reality TV starlet Paris Hilton's smartphone, involving not only the watching of amateur video but theft of addresses, data, and potentially even identities.

Phonetapping the royal romance

Voice calls on the first-generation analogue cell phones could be easily recorded using scanning equipment (Ramirez 1992). This led to the unauthorised taping and release of conversations between many people, including quite a number of political leaders around the world. One of the most controversial incidents, however, centred on that great institution of contemporary celebrity, British royalty, and in particular, one of the most loved celebrities of postmodern times, Princess Diana (Ang et al. 1997; Davies 2001; Kear and Steinberg 1999; Richards, Wilson, and Woodhead 1999).

On New Year's Eve 1989, Princess Diana conducted a wide-ranging conversation with her longtime close friend, James Gilbey, Lotus car-dealer and heir to the gin fortune that bore his family name. Diana spoke of her decision to leave her husband Prince Charles, and Gilbey repeatedly called Diana 'darling' but more insistently 'Squidgy' (some fifty-three times in fact). A transcript of the tapes was finally published in the *Sun* on 23 August 1992, under the headline ' "Dianagate" tape of love call reveals marriage misery'. The *Sun* was pipped at the post by the US *National Enquirer*, which went to press with the story four days earlier, but did manage to pre-empt a book on the royals detailing the transcripts (Blundell and Blackhall 1992). Competitor the *Daily Mail* billed its version of the story as 'Diana in love tape mystery'. Excerpts from the tape were also broadcast on an Irish radio network (Millership 1992). The next day the *Sun* modified its line to 'Hunt for the Diana tape spy'.

In an entrepreneurial move, the *Sun* then made the tapes available to curious listeners on a premium rate telephone service. Such listeners could also call a special phone and hear the twenty-three-minute tape for themselves at a mere 48 pence per minute. The recording attracted over 100,000 callers over eleven days: 'In the latest embarrassment for the scandal-hit royal family, thousands of Britons on Tuesday rang a telephone hotline to hear a tape recording allegedly of Princess Diana chatting intimately to a mystery male admirer' (Elgood 1992). Though once outrage grew, the *Sun* made it known that it would be donating its share of the proceeds to a charity (Mullin and Henry 1992). Finally the Independent Committee for the Supervision of Telephone Information Services (ICSTIS), as the regulator of such premium rate telephony, ordered that the service be withdrawn, deeming it an unreasonable invasion of privacy and as such a breach of the ICSTIS Code of Practice (Hamilton 1992). In explaining his decision, the ICSTIS Chair drew an intriguing distinction between reading the transcript and hearing the voices themselves:

> We thought there was all the difference in the world between reading it in print and actually listening to the voices. Anyone who has heard it as we have heard it must be profoundly affected by listening to these voices with all the silence, the stresses, the emotional content that comes across.
>
> (Sir Louis Blom-Cooper, quoted in Hamilton 1992)

Such pathos, reminiscent of what Roland Barthes would have called the 'grain of the voice' (Barthes 1985), was lost on the *Sun*, which criticised the ruling and straight away put a new tape on a new line at a standard rate.

The 'Squidgygate' tapes had been offered for sale to *Sun* reporters in January 1990 by Cyril Reenan, a seventy-year-old retiree who was in the habit of listening in to non-commercial radio frequencies. There emerged, however, considerable doubt about the provenance of the tapes. Diana and Gilbey had been approximately 100 miles apart at the time, making such a recording technically impossible, using the equipment Reenan had available. Reenan himself revised the date of interception and was publicly repentant about selling the tapes once the transcript was published (*Guardian* 1992). Though another amateur radio buff also claimed to have recorded the call, this 'lucky ham' theory has been criticised as implausible (Alder 2003; *Guardian* 1993). Instead, many commentators have suggested that the tapes were made and then rebroadcast by intelligence agencies at the behest of the royal palace, in an attempt to tarnish Diana's reputation (Alder 2003), a position put forward persuasively by politician and journalist William Rees-Mogg:

> These tapes, at least the two Wales tapes, were relatively sensational. When sensational conversations can be leaked, it is natural to suppose that they are selected from a wider group. The tapers cannot have struck 'Squidgy' or 'Trousers' first time. In early 1989 someone, and almost certainly not Cyril

Reenan, the 70-year-old retired bank manager of Abingdon, was systematic-ally spying on the royal family. That someone subsequently used these taped conversations to damage the reputations of both the Prince and the Princess of Wales by leaking them to various competing newspapers.

(Rees-Mogg 1993)

The transcript of the call finally published by the *Sun*, it is suggested, is an amalgam of the two amateur recordings. Certainly there was a pattern of both Charles and Diana enlisting the media in their battles, as the palace officials did also. The government of the day was not interested in pursuing the matter further, with the Home Secretary declining to hold an official inquiry into the bugging of the royal family (Wintour and Norton-Taylor 1993).

Further impetus was given to this explanation when the story broke about the leak of another intercepted telephone call. In November 1992 the *Daily Mirror* carried the transcript of an eight-minute tape of Prince Charles talking with his long-time lover Camilla Parker Bowles. This episode was dubbed 'Camillagate'. (There was also a third tape passed to media, a recording of a conversation between the Duchess of York and a male friend.) The full transcript was published by the *Daily Mirror*, but not until it had been issued in the Australian women's magazine *New Idea* (*Guardian* 1993), 45 per cent owned by Rupert Murdoch's News Corporation (whose News International also owned the *Daily Mirror*'s competitor, the *Sun*). As veteran royal watcher James Whitaker recalled with some pride:

A few months later, in December 1992, the *Daily Mirror* got hold of its own sensational tape which subsequently became known as 'Camillagate'. We recorded in detail a bedtime conversation between the Prince of Wales and Camilla Parker Bowles which had taken place on the night of December 18, 1989 while Charles was staying at the home of Anne, Duchess of Westminster. In it the Prince joked about 'coming back' as a Tampax.

(Whitaker 1996)

Mobiles scholars may care to note that Charles and Camilla also made jokes likening pressing a button on the phone to a breast: Charles 'hangs up saying he will "press the tit" – the button on the mobile phone he is using. Camilla replies: "I wish you were pressing mine" ' (London Observer Service 1993).

Three years after the Camillagate revelations, an alleged videotape of Diana frolicking in her underwear with lover James Hewitt was released and the *Sun* called to mind other illicit recordings (*Sun* 1996). The following year, the *Sun* once again reminded its readers of the cell phone tapes, holding them out as a barometer of the health of the monarchy:

> Over the past decade, the reputation of the Royal Family has sunk to a level few of us ever believed we would see. People haven't forgotten the disturbing revelations of the Squidgygate and Camillagate tapes. However, time is a great healer. We believe the Monarchy will survive. And one day Charles WILL be King. Camilla will probably be at his side at public engagements with the public's blessing . . . But she can never be HIS wife and OUR Queen.
>
> (*Sun* 1997)

The 'Squidgygate' and 'Camillagate' incidents were certainly decisive moments in how the British royal family, and the monarchy itself, surviving in vestigial form, was being parlayed into new conceptions of celebrity. Yet these were significant events also for the development of cell phone culture. Just as the lines demarcating public and private for celebrity were being renegotiated, not least with the active, willing construction of media personae by the royals themselves and their new media-practitioner myrmidons, so too were such spectacles a way of publicly discussing the new phenomenon of cell phone communications and how and in what manner such technologies could be used. As they became more widely used from the early 1990s, the politics of listening became more widely debated when cell phones were being used in crowded public places such as trains, buses, restaurants, and elsewhere. In the 'Squidgygate' and 'Camillagate' episodes, we also see displayed the ambivalence elicited by such overhearing: a prurient and unapologetic fascination with eavesdropping, alternating with an outraged sense that privacy is paramount and must not be violated.

Seeing the signs: dangerous text liaisons

The 'Squidgygate' and 'Camillagate' are but two of a number of examples of the role sex has played in the cultural representation of cell phones, and how this has been closely intertwined with the workings of celebrity. Because of the lack of security in their technical systems, first-generation cell phones were easily, or at least plausibly, able to be intercepted. Though, as the case of the royals reveals, the fiction of the amateur radio ham eavesdropper can be a screen for the involvement of security professionals with doubtless hi-tech gear and strategic and powerful ambitions. Nonetheless at least one phone company, Hong Kong-based Hutchison Whampoa, whom we will later encounter as a force-to-be-reckoned-with in third-generation mobiles (see chapter 10), took advantage of the opportunity to try to relaunch the failed Telepoint ('Rabbit') mobile telephone system by touting the secure nature of its communications:

> A new super-secure mobile telephone system that offers protection from the kind of 'listening tom' who bugged the Princess of Wales is launched today, marking probably the last chance for Telepoint, the 'poor man's mobile

telephone service' that was originally launched in 1988 and has, so far, proved something of a flop . . . [Telepoint is] a low-cost mobile communications service that allows subscribers to use their pocket telephones only if they are within 100 yards or so of a 'base station', usually a high street shop, railway station or airport. Telepoint phones cannot receive incoming calls and, in the early days, were tagged as 'the call-box in your pocket'.

(Atkinson 1992)

Despite this last hurrah for Telepoint, the technology did not get a second chance, especially with second-generation digital cellular systems coming on the market.

One of the much promoted features of these second-generation cell phones, especially the European GSM system, was their high level of security. Digital cell phones are much more difficult to intercept, especially because of the encryption of the signal.[1] The GSM encryption was significant, and those involved in devising it have claimed that it was 'first time ever that encryption functionality had been provided in a consumer device, and [that it] played its part in the liberalization of policy on encryption that today's security designers enjoy' (Walker and Wright 2001).[2] The encryption of messages has long been a way that spies have kept the meaning of their communications safe from unintended parties. The encryption features of second-generation digital cellular systems were only able to be cracked by security agencies, given requisite permissions and technical information (though early on in the development and launch of second-generation cell phones there were some anxieties about this on the part of law enforcement and intelligence agencies). The new digital cell phones were vastly more secure, however, than regular phone lines and analogue cell phones (and much more so than unencrypted Internet communications) so amateur radio operators were no longer able to intercept radio conversations (on the effectiveness of GSM security see Walker and Wright 2001: 397–401). Attention shifted, however, to other new features of cell phones, and the fertile possibilities they offered to unintended addressees of communications and messages.

One of the most publicised and widely followed cases involved a global celebrity already associated with cell phones through advertising: English footballer and model David Beckham. In early April 2004 the British *News of the World* carried allegations that the year before Beckham had had a relationship with one Rebecca Loos, at that time an employee of his management company SFX:

The lonely England soccer ace turned to the 26-year-old privately-educated daughter of a Dutch diplomat for comfort after feeling abandoned by wife Posh in their troubled long-distance marriage . . . in a story that will rock millions of Posh and Becks fans worldwide – we detail how the former Manchester United star secretly made love to Rebecca at two top hotels in the Spanish capital. How he sent her a stream of graphic text messages telling her what he wanted to do to her in bed. And how Victoria failed to see the signs that she could be losing her man.

(Thurlbeck 2004)

After breathless relation of their love-making, based on the testimony of a 'friend' of Loos, the story continued with their text messages edited and reproduced ('He became a txt maniac'). Other media also took up the story:

> David Beckham and his assistant Rebecca Loos exchanged scores of intimate text messages as they tried to keep their forbidden passion alive . . . Texting became a substitute for real sex . . . By their very nature many of these messages are extremely graphic and have been edited. They were passed to a newspaper by a friend of Ms Loos.
>
> (Jagasia 2004)

The *Daily Mirror* cut to the chase:

> David Beckham and his alleged lover sent each other a series of raunchy text messages . . . Details of their passionate texts are bound to shock Victoria Beckham who once said she would 'die of a broken heart' if her husband was ever unfaithful.
>
> (Cummins, Showbiz and Moyes 2004)

Beckham dismissed the claims, saying he was happily married. While football had been party to a number of scandals in the preceding months, Beckham had managed to keep his image unscathed until this (Kelso 2004). Of concern was that Beckham's potential in emerging markets specifically could be damaged:

> John Taylor, the chairman of Sports Impact, a sports sponsorship and public relations firm, said that the scandal could damage Beckham's commercial value. 'He is seen by a lot of ordinary people as a role-model father, modern husband and family man,' he said. 'It would hurt him in the Far East with the sort of companies specifically looking for those ideal family role models.'
>
> (Bird 2004)

Ironically, as I noted in chapter 3, Becks had been closely associated with Vodafone's push into text messaging, downloads, and other mobile data services. At the high-water mark of Becks's Vodafone advertising career, signing a multibillion pound deal in August 2002, he was hailed as the perfect global celebrity, pre-eminent in Asia:

> The mobile giant intends to use him in promotions around the world because

he appeals to football fans and fashion followers alike. 'David has the rare ability to appeal to such a wide range of people that he is the ideal person to promote our services globally,' says Peter Harris, Vodafone's director of sponsorship and media. 'He is the most recognised sportsperson in Asia.'

(Day 2004a)

After assessing the fall-out, Vodafone decided to sign Becks up for another year (Brooks 2004).

The hypocrisies and twists and turns of the crafting of celebrity aside, public discussion quickly turned from the putative infidelities of Becks to the treachery of the cellular technology itself.

> It may be good to talk but it can be dangerous to text. In its short history the mobile phone has claimed some high-profile victims. It has helped in the overthrow of governments, the tarnishing of the monarchy and now it threatens one of the most famous names in sport . . . What's gone mostly unnoticed – although perhaps not to the Beckhams now – is the way that we leave electronic footprints wherever we go in this increasingly connected world. They are, in most cases, impossible to eradicate. In the old days, it was a lot simpler: billets doux could be retrieved and thrown in the fireplace, making proof elusive for the accuser. Nowadays the reality is that text messages, like most forms of electronic communication, are stored not only on the devices that create and receive them . . . Even if you delete the incriminating messages from your phone, they are still there.
>
> (Arthur 2004)

One explanation offered, tongue-in-cheek, was that Becks was just trying to come to grips with the Spanish language:

> Anyone looking at the allegedly steamy cellphone correspondence without a mind hopelessly mired in tabloid filth will find a ready explanation for the conversations . . . I don't doubt that, should he ever wish to engage in the tricky art of text sex, his natural physical dexterity, powers of concentration and willingness to fillet his prose so ruthlessly will stand him in exceptionally good stead.
>
> (Mangan 2004)

Becks's troubles were compounded with the publication several days later of allegations of a second affair, with Sarah Marbeck (not a 'diplomat's daughter' this time, but a 'barrister's daughter'), allegations that also featured 'sex and text'. The revelations triggered new fears about the security of cellular phones, especially for celebrities: ' "I tell celebrities their mobiles are hackable". One leading [public relations consultant] . . . said he already advises clients not to leave messages and to avoid talking on the phone' (Timms 2004c).

As with the outcry over the publication of the Squidgygate and Camillagate transcripts, there were calls for the media to face greater regulation, to respect privacy. The Press Complaints Commission responded, revising its code of conduct to ban journalists from intercepting cellular phone calls, text messages, and emails. Becks's pragmatic response to the furore was to employ a new public relations specialist, downgrading the other two PR firms the Beckhams retained (Day 2004b; Timms 2004a). For her part, Loos agreed to an interview with Sky One, watched by over two million people (Timms 2004b), and proceeded to develop a short-lived career as a minor celebrity (echoes of Monica Lewinsky), appearing on *Celebrity Love Island*, and masturbating a pig on channel 5 reality television show *The Farm*.

Just not cricket

If the romantic career of text messaging had not been well established with the Beckham escapades, it certainly was confirmed in the case of another sporting celebrity caught in the cell phone limelight. Shane Warne is a famous Australian cricketer, well known in cricket-loving nations as much now for his amorous adventures as for his sporting prowess.

Warne was something of an early adopter of the cell phone for romance. In 2000, when he was playing for English club Hampshire, he was reported to have repeatedly sent text messages to Donna Wright, a nurse he met in a nightclub who spurned his advances. In a television interview at the time Warne denied that he was harassing Wright: ' "There was a bit of dirty talk and, er, she did talk dirty to me and I was reciprocating with her" ' (English 2005b). The press was having none of this:

> Mixed message
> Warne once had ambitions to be Australia captain, and the evidence is that tactically he would have been good at it . . . But the captaincy carries more with it than simply doing the business on the cricket field. It is necessary to conduct oneself properly off it.
>
> (Wilde 2005)

There were further text scandals. In August 2003 a South African woman ('mother-of-three'), Helen Cohen Alon, alleged Warne had 'pestered her with repeated sex texts' (English 2005a), as did a Melbourne woman two weeks later: 'Melbourne stripper Angela Gallagher claimed Warne swamped her with raunchy texts that led to a three-month affair after they met at a Melbourne nightclub'. In March 2005, another text message furore erupted: 'Spin king Shane Warne has become embroiled in another text message scandal . . . [he] is accused of sending the messages to a Wellington woman during the New Zealand v World X1 series last January' (Edmund and Crutcher 2005).

Yet another case surfaced in June 2005: a close friendship with a British woman, Kerri Colliemore, who acted as his confidant, emerged, described as his 'SMS mate' (English 2005c). This case was the final straw for Warne's wife Simone. The format established in media reporting of text affair allegations was adhered to in this crescendo, with the most salacious messages reproduced (*Courier-Mail* 2005). The Warne story offered rich material for the public discussion and representation of cell phones and romance:

> Armed with a mobile phone and basic literacy skills Warne becomes his own worst enemy. The spin king's penchant for bombarding women with lurid text messages has been well-documented over recent years. Now it has contributed to the end of his marriage. But Warne and long-suffering wife Simone, are not alone. Psychologists, private investigators and even mobile phone companies agree that text messaging is being used extensively for expressions of love (and lust), often with disastrous consequences.
>
> (Burke 2005)

In this instance, the Warne story also provided a hook for a follow-up piece on the addictiveness of text messaging:

> There are some people who just shouldn't have a mobile phone. Funnily enough they are usually the ones who swear they can't do without it . . . They are textaholics – obsessive compulsives who can't help but write text messages whenever they have a free hand . . . Australia's most famous textaholic, Shane Warne, who again has hit the headlines for his textual exploits, recently tried to kick the habit.
>
> (Finnila 2005)

Virgin Mobile even came to the party, and devised a technical solution:

> To combat the problem of making incoherent calls to bosses, former or current partners, Virgin Mobile has come up with a way users can blacklist numbers they don't want to ring while drunk. All users have to do is dial 333 and a phone number that they don't want to call and Virgin Mobile will stop all calls to that number until 6 the following morning.
>
> (Finnila 2005)

Warne earned himself a reputation as a serial philanderer, with a mobile twist: 'Shane Warne has played many a role in his record-breaking and controversial career. Champion cricketer and text-message villain spring to mind' (Timms 2005e). In the face of widespread ridicule and condemnation, however, there was only one thing to do – to go cold-turkey: 'Shane Warne has banished the one vice that has repeatedly threatened to derail his star-studded Test cricket career: his mobile phone' (English 2005a). This was less than a month after readers of the *Coventry Telegraph* were urged to text their answer to a quiz to win a prize of a signed Shane Warne cricket bat to mark the Stratford Cricket Festival. Despite the repeated reports of Warne's proclivities for text-intensive romance, and announcement of their separation, Shane and his wife Simone fled to Spain after the final text message scandal broke, affording this lovely coda:

> On Friday, *The Sunday Times* found Warne relaxing near the resort's pool sending dozens of text-messages – as Simone looked on. But if Simone was perturbed by her husband's frantic texting, she showed no sign of it. On the contrary, she seemed perfectly content to be beside him once more.
>
> (*Sunday Times* 2005)

Smart celebrity phone

From the inadvertent reading of text messages by others, I wish to finish with an intimation of the unfolding cultural representation of cell phones in their new incarnations as mobile media. This is the widely reported incident of celebrity heiress Paris Hilton, whose mobile phone directory, text messages, and images were stolen, and distributed over the Internet:

> The super-rich heiress is distraught that her pals' phone numbers and tawdry text messages were swiped and spilled all over the Internet by computer hackers. 'I don't know why this stuff always happens to me, but I wish it wouldn't anymore', the vampy 24-year-old told *US* weekly in her first inter-view since her cell phone was breached . . . Not only was her entire address book from her T-mobile Sidekick II posted on several Web sites, the hackers also accessed naughty photos of Hilton, including a topless shot of her making out with MTV Latin America veejay Eglantina Zingg.
>
> (Becker 2005)

The Hilton hacking episode was made-to-order, as a reporter remarked: 'The caper had all the necessary ingredients to spark a media firestorm – a beautiful socialite-turned-reality TV star, embarrassing photographs and messages, and the personal contact information of several young music and Hollywood celebrities' (Krebs 2005).

An additional ingredient was that the Hilton heiress had already been the subject of that peculiar kind of contemporary notoriety. Her reality television show *The Simple Life* (where Hilton and her sybarite friend Nicole Richie move in with an Arkansas farming family for a month) had just premiered when a video of her having sex with boyfriend Rick Saloman was, in the manner of these things, set loose on the Internet (*Wikipedia* 2006d). Avidly downloaded, the sex video made her name as a wild young thing (as the scenes of her interrupting sex to answer her cell phone were widely parodied) (*Wikipedia* 2006c).[3] In June 2004, the video was released on DVD under the title of *1 Night in Paris*, with Saloman, not missing a trick, as host. (Hilton later sued, and settled for a share of the profits – though claiming she would donate her proceeds to charity.)

The cell in question was the T-Mobile Sidekick II, a successor to the Sidekick, a phone with advanced data and wireless Internet capabilities akin to a portable digital assistant. It is otherwise known as the hiptop by its producer Danger (www.danger.com), and Triton PCS and Edge Wireless, who also offer it in the USA, as well as providers in Canada, Singapore, and Austria. The hiptop is marketed in the USA by T-Mobile under the name Sidekick, which targeted it to the 18 to 34-year-old young adult market. The hiptop site ('get away with it') is replete with mentions of funky, celebrity users (www.hiptop.com). As well as offering integrated Internet and messaging functionality, the hiptop backs up data on the provider's service, not just the device itself. These technical details are relevant to understanding how the hacking occurred. It was initially assumed that a hacker with great technical skills had pulled off the feat, but it transpired that a Massachusetts teenager had initially managed to access the T-Mobile server by persuading an employee to divulge information that allowed security to be breached (Krebs 2005). The hacker then was able to exploit a security flaw in the tool that reset user passwords, and so gain access to any subscriber's account if he or she knew the phone number (Krebs 2005). The teenager was sentenced to eleven months detention for the crime (Evers 2005).

Paris Hilton illustrates what Turner reminds us about contemporary celebrity, namely that the 'attribution of celebrity can occur without any significant achievement as its precondition and this is increasingly frequent within the media today' (2004: 22). The irony of the representations of the cell phone that Hilton as celebrity ended up mediating, is that, like Beckham, she was actually a promoter of the technology that undid her (*Gizmag* 2004). Indeed the interrelations between cell phones and celebrity are manifold, and we have seen the way in which *infamous*, typically heteronormative, instances of cell phones being turned against their star users have circulated widely, to become in their turn important representations that feed back into the shaping of cell phone culture itself. There is at least a double movement here. Celebrity has become more central to cultural and media industries, and to the experience of everyday life over the last two decades. In roughly the same period, we have seen the rise of cell phones, the Internet, and other new media. Here I have taken the annus horribilis of the English royal family to be emblematic of a certain set of representations about the unintended uses of first-generation analogue cell phones; then looked at the way that male, massively branded (at least in Beckham's case), sporting heroes figure the way the wayward nature of second-generation digital cell phones; and, finally, suggested that cell phones are now being represented via contemporary systems of celebrity as they move into the realm of multimedia convergence. It is this topic that I will investigate for the remainder of the book, starting with the phenomenon of camera phones.

Part IV
Mobile convergences

8 On mobile photography: camera phones, moblogging, and new visual cultures

There is a practice for people to exchange photos, and if there is a camera in your *keitai*, you can make custom wallpaper as well as exchange photos.

Takeo Uematsu, Sharp Corporation on the first camera cell phone.[1]

An erotic life is, for more and more people, that which can be captured in digital photographs and on video.

(Sontag 2004: 24)

A weblog is a record of travels on the Web, so a mobile phone log ('moblog'?) should be a record of travels in the world. Weblogs reflect our lives at our desks, on our computers, referencing mostly other flat pages, links between blocks of text. But mobile blogs should be far richer, fueled by multimedia, more intimate data and far-flung friends. As we chatter and text away, our phones could record and share the parts we choose: a walking, talking, texting, seeing record of our time around town, corrected and augmented by other mobloggers.

(Hall 2002)

In tracing the development and lineaments of cell phone culture, I have so far broadly drawn upon the 'circuit of culture' framework to discuss the production of such culture, its consumption, then, briefly, its representation and regulation. Through this also, I have from time to time noted how cell phone culture has developed through mechanisms of and changes in identity. My principal concern has been the evolution of cell phone culture, characterised first by voice telephony and then by new sorts of sociotechnical innovations, especially with the second-generation digital systems when mass take-up occurred. In the remaining three chapters of the book, my focus is on the cell phone moving centre stage into the theatre of media transformations that is still often referred to as 'convergence'.

Convergence indicates the merging of media and cultural industries associated with forms of the twentieth century such as radio, television, newspapers, magazines that came to be relatively well established in their cultural bearings. I certainly have reservations about this term: while it may have been revelatory in the early to mid 1990s, it is certainly not in the present day. The important task is the work of actually tracing the ways in which cultural practice as well as industrial structure and political economy is transforming across these sectors, and this is the subject of much contemporary study and debate, not least in industry, policy settings, specialist publications, and the increasingly influential public spheres of geek culture magazines, email lists, websites, and blogs. What I attempt here is to map the convergence of cell phones with other media, starting in this chapter with camera phones. In the first part, I recount the invention of the camera phone, and identify some of its uses and the ways in which it is involved in changing cultural practices and the significance of this. In the second part, I extend this analysis by looking at the phenomenon of mobile blogging (moblogging, or blogging using cell phones), in which camera phones have been integral.

The invention of the camera phone

Camera phones have not been in existence for long, yet have been very popular. A leading country for camera phone design and use has been Japan. The Japanese manufacturer Kyocera marketed the first *keitai* equipped with a built-in camera in July 1999. Called the 'Visual Phone', Okada recounts that the PHS VP-210

> [was] designed as a video phone, capitalizing on the relatively fast transmission speed of the PHS. The press release at the time of the product's introduction featured a scenario of distant grandparents talking to their grandson while viewing his face. However, the terminal weighed 165 grams and was slightly larger than the average handset, attributes not well received by users.
>
> (Okada 2005: 56)

The widespread adoption of the *keitai* camera commenced with the introduction of Sharp's SH-04 phone, manfactured for J-Phone. This was the first *cellular* camera phone and included a service called *sha-mail* (photo mail): '[the] handset weighed 74 grams and was the smallest of its kind among the prevailing products. The camera was 110 thousand-pixels, not very high in graphic quality, and it could only capture still images' (Okada 2005: 56). The availability of camera phones in Japan since has been phenomenal, as borne out by Steinbock's observation that by 'January 2004, some 60 per cent of mobile phones in Japan were camera phones, and in 2005 almost all mobile phones were' (Steinbock 2005: 185). Despite some trepidation, companies in other countries moved into mobile imaging quite soon after, with Nokia launching its integrated camera phone, the 7650, in November 2001 – and on its way to becoming market leader (2005: 184).

The uses of the camera phone developed in overlapping sets of cultural practices associated with ephemeral, one-time-use cameras. Fuji Film had developed a one-time-use camera (*Utsurun-desu*, or Quick Snap), 'which popularized the practice among teenage girls of taking snapshots of friends to keep as mementos. These young women made original photo albums of the snapshots and carried them around as precious lifestyle and friendship records' (Okada 2005: 58). The throw-away camera went hand-in-hand with the introduction in July 1995 of *Puri-kura*, or Print Club, a photo booth for making stickers:

> [*Puri-kura*] were set up in arcades and other entertainment and shopping sites and became a craze among youth . . . [Teenage girls] turned a section of their personal planners into a *puri-kura* album or created an exclusive mini-album for *puri-kura* stickers, which they always carried with them. It also became a very common practice to put a *puri-kura* sticker of a special friend or boyfriend on their pager or *keitai*.
>
> (Okada 2005: 58)

As I have discussed earlier, the decoration and modification of cell phones have become an important way that people express their identity. With the advent of the camera becoming part of the cell phone, various aspects of this do-it-yourself personalisation could be incorporated into the device: 'the *keitai* camera has come to encompass the production of customized wallpaper and some of the functions of *puri-kura* stickers' (Okada 2005: 59).

While there are still relatively few studies of the cultures of use of camera phones or mobile imaging in general (Koskinen, Kurvinen, and Lehtonen 2002), there are some recurring themes in discussions of the new technology. Central to these is a strong emphasis on the embeddedness in and orientation of the camera phone towards a technology of everyday life. A much-cited early piece quotes a survey in which the highest proportion of camera phone users report that they 'took photos of "things that they happened upon that were interesting" ', whereas the capturing of travel photos was down the bottom of the list (Daisuke and Ito 2003). For Daisuke and Ito, this is a

> striking testament to the everyday and ubiquitous uses of the camera phone. Within the broader ecology of personal record-keeping, archiving and communication technologies, camera phones occupy a unique niche. In comparison to the traditional camera, which gets trotted out for special excursions and events – noteworthy moments bracketed off from the mundane – camera phones capture the more fleeting and unexpected moments of surprise, beauty and adoration in the everyday.
>
> (2003)

There is some evidence to suggest social and cultural functions of camera phones are quite distinct from their digital stand-alone or analogue camera counterparts.

We certainly need to be cautious about forming judgements regarding this; however, the novelty and new function of camera phones, yet again like other new technologies, are a prime trope of the discourse accompanying them.

Authors of a Japanese study discern 'practices of picture taking and sharing that differ both from the uses of the stand-alone cameras and the kinds of social sharing that happened via *keitai* voice and text communications' (Kato et al. 2005: 305). They cite research showing that many of the kinds of photographs taken with camera phones are similar to traditional cameras, such as photos of friends, family and pets, and travel photos. However in their survey Kato et al. also note evidence of a 'new mode of pervasive photo taking when a camera is always at hand':

> *keitai* camera users are taking photos of serendipitous sightings and moments in everyday life (rather than of special planned events that have traditionally been documented by amateur photography) . . . [W]ith the *keitai* camera, the mundane is elevated to a photographic object.
>
> (2005: 305)

The sheer ubiquity of the phone is one reason for this. A cell phone is for many people the only other thing they always have with them other than their wallet or purse, keys, and watch. Previously few people would have carried a camera with them. Now they find themselves with a camera at their disposal more often and in a wide variety of circumstances. Also drawing on a Japanese study (conducted in 2002) France Télécom researcher Carole Rivière proposes that:

> When it becomes part of the daily experience of using a mobile phone, photography departs from the realm of the occasional, or even the exceptional, that gave it its traditional function. Moreover, the photographic act is disassociated from the possession of a unique, specific object, the camera, whose existence and representation consolidated the perception of photography as a specific practice reserved for certain occasions, for specific events.
>
> (Rivière 2005: 171)

She contrasts Pierre Bourdieu's account of the camera as emblematic of the family, regarded as its joint property and used at ritual events (Bourdieu 1965), with the status of the cell phone as 'primarily that of a "prosthetic" object' and so 'part of its owner' (Rivière 2005: 172).

The trope of the camera phone as an exemplary everyday form of image capture carries important cultural implications, especially when it is joined up with a narrative and rhetoric of technologies fit for use for all, a certain demotic turn in photography. Rivière writes of how such talk of the camera phone brings photography into the 21st century as an agreeable form of communication or language, one that can be used by anyone, anytime, anyhow. In this sense, it makes photography 'commonplace', stripping it of every intention other than for one's own pleasure and the pleasure of expressing something in the immediate present.

(2005: 172)

The implications of the demotic register of the camera phone typically are carried forward with a discussion of the way that each person now is able to represent his or her own 'news'. We can discern at least two sides to this radical personalisation of news-gathering.

For one thing, there is the claim that the means of making such imagistic representations of events are now placed in the hands of the multitudes, so everyone can aspire to that figure of modernist news and visual culture (Hartley 1992 and 1996) – the photojournalist. One exemplary instance of this is the leaking to international media of the digital photos of the US military torture of Iraqi detainees in the infamous Abu Ghraib scandal. There are troubling ethical questions about our investment as viewers in such widely circulated if not grossly iconic images, as raised by the late Susan Sontag (specifically Sontag 2004 but also her 2003 study; also Gross, Katz, and Ruby 2003). I am not sure, however, that such considerations were uppermost in the mind of US Defense Secretary Donald Rumsfeld, whose immediate response to the suspicion that the Abu Ghraib photos were taken by camera phones was to ban them (ABC 2004). Another haunting example of the cell phone-equipped citizen-journalist (or 'cetizen', to invoke a newly coined term) at work in the defiles of everyday life occurred in the terrible London tube and train bombings of July 2005. Digital stills and video images from blast survivors or onlookers with cell phones provided images, records, and narrative fragments, uploaded onto Moblog UK as among the first images to be seen (Lee 2005), then widely reproduced in national and international media. (Cell phones provided other, basic, functions also, such as providing light to assess injuries; Shaw 2006). Apparently after the July 7 bombings, the BBC's email address 'yourpics@bbc.co.uk' 'received over 1,000 images and mobile clips from the public' (Day 2005). To my mind, the most memorable, and certainly the most frequently reproduced, of these crepuscular, flickering images, perhaps, was that taken by a person struggling to ascend from the infernal scene of an underground tube, moving in a distraught crowd. Given the flood of potential images now available from de facto freelance photojournalists, new opportunities have emerged for cultural intermediaries to filter this jumped-up micro-content to big media organisations – an example being Scoopt.com, 'the citizen journalist's photo agency, selling mobile phone and digital camera photos to the press and media'. Others simply not interested in established media now have many opportunities to create their own forms of distribution, or contribute to alternative media forms such as the Korean cetizen.org site, where the cell-phone-user-in-the-street can, and does, upload photos (Hjorth 2006). Here the citizen-journalist begins to blur into the figure of activism, another area where camera phones have extended the importance of cellular telephony and mobile media.

Another side to this hyper-individualisation of camera phones is the intimate turn of news. The locus and matrix of news appears to move from the profes-sionalised routines and forms of circulation and production of newsrooms to the micro-arenas of personal life with their rules of relevance and tiny audiences defined by the individual, and their immediate friends, colleagues, family, and networks. Putting this very nicely, Daisuke and Ito segue from their discussion of camera phones as a technology of the everyday to noting that the photos are generated as 'photos of everday moments and events that are newsworthy only to an individual and her intimates':

> In Japanese, 'material' for news and stories is called 'neta'. The term has strong journalist associations, but also gets used to describe material that can become the topic of conversation among friends or family. Camera phones provide a new tool for making these everyday neta not just verbally but also visually shareable. As the mundane is elevated to a photographic object, the everyday is now the site of potential news and visual archiving.
>
> (Daisuke and Ito 2003)

This reworking of the everyday through the camera phone results, in turn, in a shift in the way news is produced and consumed for larger audiences, in the wider public sphere. The everyday, small acts of media consumption become also unstable, potentially bigger, and more significant interventions into what is col-lectively regarded as the news. Daisuke and Ito propose a 'broad spectrum of everyday and mass photojournalism using camera phones' where 'what counts as newsworthy, noteworthy and photo-worthy' stretches from quotidian, almost inadvertent snaps of moments never to be shared, through 'intimately news-worthy moments' to be shared with spouse, lover, family, or friend, or as 'micro-content uploaded to blogs and online journals', to larger audience activity such as sending 'camera phone photos to major news outlets' or, presumably, widely read or A-list moblogs. These themes of new media as pervasive and intimate are recurring ones, not only with the blogs but, especially given the salience of the visual here, the phenomenon of webcams and camgirls (and boys).[2]

As well as heralding the reconstruction of news, there has been much emphasis on how cell phone cameras not only inhabit a changed place (the here of the everyday), but also rearticulate photography in terms of the temporal – something familiar from the reception of digital photography. Camera phones, it is often asserted, are about the 'power of now' (Wilhelm et al. 2004: 1406). A photo from a camera phone can be immediately viewed, looked at by the phone photographer, or shown to others. Rather than being a somewhat distinct, or even formal part of the recording, documentation, and remembering of an event or ritual, the camera phone often becomes part of the event itself. Camera phones are perceived to offer a sense of immediacy, lessening the time elapsed between the time when the photo was taken and the time it is reviewed:

> One important capability of the *keitai* camera is being able to view the photographed image on the spot. In that sense, the photo can be experienced immediately, an advantage digital cameras share with *puri-kura* (instant sticker photo booths) and instant cameras. Users can check the images, and if they didn't turn out well, they can retake the photo right away.
>
> (Kato et al. 2005: 305)

In this discourse about the shift in personal time the camera phone represents, we can observe also a crucial realignment in social function and cultural practice. The camera phone's anchoring, were it ontologically possible, in the 'now', or at least the sense in which it is taken to signify, or at least be a better approximation for, the present, is most often linked to the vernacular theorisation of the device as an instrument for sociability. Digital cameras, especially those from a camera phone, are in the now, because they are about sharing. The indispensable innovations in cultural technologies of sharing here include the screen (for displaying photos) and the data storage, retrieval, and manipulation systems. With the storage and display facilities available, camera phones are already being used as a photo album, and of course the sharing, showing, and talk around photo albums are an important form of sociality. In her 2003 study of young Italian camera phone users, Barbara Scifo reasons:

> That a camera-phone – unlike the traditional mobile phone – can be seen as a social, collective resource in 'face-to-face' interaction with one's peer group is evidenced by other modes of use as well. Not only are camera-phones frequently shared and swapped, thus passing from the owner to someone who does not yet have one and is curious to its photographic possibilities, but above all, their use represents an opportunity for play and entertainment within a group of peers.
>
> (Scifo 2005: 366)

Scifo's point is well made but I would point to the fact that, contrary perhaps to dominant assumptions about use in Western countries, the cell phone and its extensions have long been something to be shared and exchanged, something deeply based in structures and routines of sociality as well as notions of the local (Larsson 2002). There are salient examples in much youth cultural practices with cell phones, but especially text messaging (as accounts of SMS as gift exchange showed; Taylor and Harper 2002). There are also antecedents in early, shared ownership of cell phones in the 1980s by a group of office workers or employees in an organisation – before a strong sense emerged of the indivisibility obtaining between an individual and her cell phone. Here I would certainly concur with Scifo's summation of the mutually constitutive relationships between personal and collective uses of camera phones:

> the camera-phone is not only an increasingly personal technology (being deeply set within the subject, his or her universe and relationships) but also a collective technology, a resource for 'face-to-face' sociality, entertainment and communicative exchanges within contexts of local interaction and principally within a group of peers.
>
> (2005: 367)

The camera phone, then, is emerging as highly significant for the crucial remaking of place and context (sometimes called relocalisation) in which technologies and cell phone culture now take part.

Indeed camera phones offer a new take, as it were, on sharing of digital cameras, because of their inherent capabilities for distributing photos over telecommunications and Internet. Not only are camera phones likely to be available in a given situation, they are potentially now 'always on': 'The *keitai* camera represents not only an ever-present image-capture device but also an ever-present image-sharing and transmission device' (Kato et al. 2005). One way that photos, videos, and other data can be sent from a cell phone is via the multimedia messaging (MMS) protocol. As we have seen in chapter 4, MMS was conceived as the successor technology to the popular SMS and extending its capabilities – hopefully also allowing the adding of greater 'value' to messaging products and services, and so greater productivity. While MMS has been critiqued, not least for the complex menu and configuration it required in its first incarnations (Jenson 2005; Scifo 2005: 367) it has also slowly been adopted.

There is a small but growing number of studies of MMS. Scifo, for instance, shows that:

> notwithstanding the number of MMS messages that are being exchanged at present between those starting to use this new process of communication, there are already clear signals concerning the spread of a precise culture of communication and the birth of a new language.
>
> (2005: 367)

She notes the association thus of sending MMS with playful, positive emotions and on special occasions; also that communicating with images is 'closely and almost exclusively linked to one's network of strong relationships' (2005: 367). This finding is echoed by a Japanese study, which found:

> Couples and close groups of female friends have the highest volume of image transmission; among male friends and less intimate relations, images are rarely transmitted, although they may be shared from the handset when people are physically co-present . . . visual sharing is most prevalent among 'full-time intimate communities'.
>
> (Kato et al. 2005: 306)

As well as patterns emerging about the sorts of interactions and networks involved in sharing of camera phone images, there are also early indications of the sorts of cultural forms and genres that are evolving. Scifo, for instance, argues that the first forms of MMS relate to representation, witnessing and narrating situations, and distinguishes between three main types of messages, namely performative, informative, and problem-solving. The theorisation of the forms, types, and genres of MMS is pursued in a thoroughgoing way with Ling et al.'s pilot study of twenty-five Norwegian users. Ling, Julsrud, and Yttri also report MMS being perceived as being fun (with humorous messages as an example), as well as identified genres such as 'almost like a post card', as documentation (for travelling sales representatives, for instance) or quasi-typical documentation (to give the receiver at least a sense of what something looks like), of paparazzi or news reporting, and finally of the need for care in sending pictures given the pitfalls of breaching privacy or sending the wrong picture to one or more unintended recipients. They also canvass whether it will be easier to misinterpret MMS communication than is the case with textual SMS communications, and, if so, whether this will give impetus to SMS/MMS 'developing as communications technologies that need to "hang together" in the eyes of the reader/receiver' (Ling, Julsrud, and Yttri 2005: 99; cf. Ling and Julsrud 2005).

While MMS is akin to the planned if not ordained direction of development in which telecommunications companies would wish camera phones to go, the intensive activity and cultural ferment is coming from the direction of Internet cultures. The easy exchange of digital photos through email, file-transfer programs, or the web, and by memory sticks, disks, cables, or wireless protocols (such as Bluetooth), now allows images to be easily shared, manipulated, displayed, or printed. A now popular way of sharing digital photos is online photosharing sites, where users can post their photos online, organised by keywords or tags, for the public or just friends, to view or save. Perhaps the most well known of these sites is flickr (http://www.flickr.com/). Because of the still comparatively low resolution, images taken by camera phone are more clearly viewed on digital screens, whether on a hand-held device or a computer screen. Camera phone images can be uploaded to a photosharing site from a computer, or directly from a cell phone (whether using a web browser, MMS, or email). Photosharing sites clearly build on over a decade's audience and user expectations of web culture – and the now taken-for-granted notion that we can easily find information, text, images, or multimedia material about a person through consulting a website.

In their incorporation into photo-sharing practices across convergent Internet and cell phone cultures, camera phones are set to play their part in an enormously important development in digital culture, the area of what has been called 'social software'. Social software is a development in networked, online software, especially that based on the Internet, which builds on the cultures of use established with chat in particular. Social software attempts to learn from the perceived problems of chat (especially the forerunner technology Internet Relay Chat), namely about how to enter a public space to meet new people but how to avoid unwanted, undesirable, or harassing strangers. Examples of social software are the Friendsters or the Orkut software. Users need to be invited to join the social group by another 'friend'. They can customise their profile to indicate whether they are interested in friendship, love, networking, or a mix of relationships. They can then access their friends' friends, or make their friends available to others. Social software provides a semi-open, regulated way of making new friendships and other relationships, by mobilising trust.

There is much else to say about camera phones, but it is worth concluding with considerations of how this type of photography has uniquely contributed to digital photography's general reworking of the phenomenology, aesthetics, and questions of value of the image. Such speculations have their pretexts in the technical characteristics of camera phones. For the first few years of their life, for instance, camera phones have suffered from obvious limitations compared to other types of cameras. The quality of their lenses is inferior to that of analog and digital cameras, as they are made from plastic rather than glass. So far resolution has been relatively poor, compared to the standard quickly established by digital cameras. Other early problems included limited storage capability, relatively short battery life, and lack of control over exposure, focus, and lens size, compared to fuller-featured digital and analogue cameras. Yet much photo theorising and investigation of cell phone cameras has taken such things as givens, and explored how cell phone photography frames the world. For instance, inspired by Susan Sontag's notion that photographs have produced a new practice of mediated vision – 'looking with photographs' (Sontag 1977) – Kato et al. claim that:

> The experience of seeing people and objects framed with a small camera and viewed on *keitai* monitor may result in a new way of seeing things. In our everyday lives the convenience of taking, storing, and viewing photos on a *keitai* handset is part of the recording of the social and cultural context in

which we find ourselves or the recalling of the situation in which the recording took place.

(Kato et al. 2005: 307)

They discuss the traits of this 'new type of photography': small, compact, and light photographs; ease of transmission from the handset; focus once again being important to 'decide what to fit inside the small rectangular frame'; immediate judgement required on whether to save, delete, send (or use as wallpaper) (2005: 307). They make another intriguing point also:

> when we look with *keitai*, our vision captures the scene inside the rectangular frame, but at the same time our attention is drawn to the surroundings (outside the frame) more than it is with the conventional photograph. These photos stimulate the imagination by conjuring absence cited by the image in the frame. Further, they are reflections of individual viewpoints and subjectivity that provide insight on the attention and interests of the person who took them.

(2005: 307)

I am not sure if I am entirely convinced about the proposal of camera phones as ushering in a 'new type of photography'. Rather I am inclined to see camera phones as occupying a dynamic and contingent niche in a rapidly changing scene of digital photography, image circulation, and visual culture. From 2004–5, for instance, camera phone models have steadily emerged with higher resolution, better storage, and memory card capability, with cell phone manufacturers hopeful that the 'quality migration from the camera industry has begun' (Nokia's head of imaging business, Juha Putkiranta, quoted in Steinbock 2005: 185). From the other direction, digital cameras are now available with Wi-Fi networking capabilities. Thus I suspect that theories of the aesthetics and cultural dynamics of cell phone photography are rather precarious at this historical moment.

Moblogging

I now wish to shift to another set of technologies and practices of mobility in which imaging has been pivotal: mobile blogging or moblogging, as it has become known. Blogging is a set of practices and technologies that have built and now considerably expanded Internet cultures and technologies (for a good introduction see Bruns and Jacobs 2006). Not long after their inception, cell phones and mobile and wireless technologies started to be used for mobile blogging. Moblogging is a handy concrete instance of the coming together of the Internet and the cell phone (a topic that I take up at length in chapter 9), and technologies of the image have been prominent in this.

I would like to approach the beginnings of moblogging by looking at a very interesting pre-history: that of University of Toronto engineering professor Steve Mann's use of wearable computing as a roving reporter.[3] Mann tells of his interest in wearable computing in the early 1970s, describing a system he devised:

> A 'photographer's assistant' system comprising my late 1970s wearable computer (pictured here with 1980 display). I integrated the computer into a welded-steel frame worn on my shoulders (note belt around my waist which directed much of the weight onto my hips). Power converter hung over one shoulder. Antennae (originally 3, later reduced to 2), operating at different frequencies, allowed simultaneous transmission and reception of computer data, voice, or video. This system allowed for complete interaction while walking around doing other things.
>
> (Mann 1997)

Later he devised his WearComp2 device, to which he added a radar location device (long before the days of Global Positioning System satellites), and in the late 1980s presented this wearable radar device to the Royal Canadian Institute of the Blind.[4] Mann also designed audio capabilities for the device – 'audio wearables' – and communications channels including a modem, to send and receive, via radio, voice and data and also video (via a different path) (1997). In addition, he designed a technology called the 'aremac' (camera spelled backwards) that allowed his remotely located assistant to see what he was seeing (that is, experience his point-of-view) (1997). In later 'generations' of this technology, Mann distributed components in clothing, then as conductive threads in clothing. Many other inventions followed, notably in 1994 a wireless wearcam (Mann 1996a; Woolford 2003; see also his 'lookpaintings', Mann 1996b). On his homepage, Mann himself relates his wireless webcam experiment to a range of concepts, including moblogs (wearcam.org). Before I leave Mann's work, I would like to note briefly his pioneering contribution to the use of mobile image devices in the service of civil rights and human rights activism.

Mann proposed a wearable photographic device for human rights workers to take photos and videos in dangerous situations and transmit these as evidence, without being the target of violence for using traditional cameras (Mann and Guerra 2001). His 'domewear' product range offered 'conspicuously concealed cameras as a deterrence against crime' (www.wearcam.org/domewear/). Mann coined the term 'sousveillance', or 'watchful vigilance from underneath' (Mann n.d.) referring to the idea of turning surveillance technologies against those people and apparatuses of control that customarily deployed them, so encouraging activists, citizens, and others to watch and record the watchers – a technologically mediated practice of bearing witness. Sousveillance was quickly picked up by the activist community, as well as artists and writers, with 24 December declared World Sousveillance Day.

Mann's Wearcam technology may have prefigured moblogging, but in any case it certainly preceded it by a number of years. Stuart Woodward's text posts from his cell phone to a livejournal server on 4 January 2001 are often cited as one of the first instances of moblogging (Ito 2003). David Davies is credited with one of the first SMS posts and blogs ('SMSblog – Wherever I am, you'll know!'), on 1 March 2001 (www.smsblog.manilasites.com). Innovations in text blogging followed, but it was the possibilities of networking camera phones that really triggered excitement. By the end of 2002, a number of people, including Ito and Woodward, had posted images directly from their phones to their blogs (these images are still available). The term 'moblogging' was coined in 2002, for which Adam Greenfield is credited (Ito 2002):

> (That's pronounced 'mo,' as in 'mobile.') Take a look at HipTop Nation for a compelling glance at the future-becoming-present in real time: this is what happens when you fuse digital cameras and text-entry functionality with a way to publish it to the Web, for better and worse.
>
> (Greenfield 2002a)

Hiptop Nation was a communal moblog started in April 2002 by Mike Popovic (2002), a beta-tester of T-Mobile Sidekick, the fashionable phone discussed in chapter 7. Moblogging using audio and video was also trialled. Moblogging via the wireless access protocol on mobiles also emerged, with technologies such as wapblogger, a wap interface to weblog tools such as Blogger and Livejournal. By the end of 2002, the new trend in weblogs had received admiring if quizzical notices in mainstream old media (Perrone 2002).

Early accounts of moblogging swung between an aesthetic of the mobile found object and reporting on the microscopic texture of daily life on the one hand, to utopian vision of transfigured citizens and community on the other – a tension picked up in the *Guardian* article: 'So far, most moblogs seem to be limited to pictures of friends at parties and text messages during long journeys. But does anyone except your nearest and dearest really want to know what sandwich you ate for lunch?' (Perrone 2002). Such a rationale was perfectly fine for some mobloggers, who saw the moblog as a practice for supporting and intensifying sociability in daily life, and for creating new possibilities for the small interactive audiences and communities sustained, if not created, by blogging:

> If we can protect our privacy and trust data networks, then we might find that some of our daily activities would be enhanced by sharing them, both with our circle of friends around the Web, and the people nearby with like minds. Each of our moblogs, our mobile information profiles and archives, could

search people in the area for compatible data. Think of it as a Web search on the real world. The results would be constant, part of conversation, tracked by your moblog.

(Hall 2002)

Moblogging could be something new because it had the characteristics of what began to be called 'locative media' (canvassed in chapter 10). With its locative media potential, moblogging promised both to extend but also to intensify blogging itself. For some, however, moblogging held far more utopian, or dystopian, possibilities. There were quite a number afire with this possibility memorably captured by Howard Rheingold's conjuring of 'the power of the mobile many': 'Smart mobs emerge when communication and computing technologies amplify human talents for cooperation. The impacts of smart mob technology already appear to be both beneficial and destructive' (Rheingold n.d.).

What was interesting, however, was the speed at which moblogging experiments and the meanings beginning to be attached to the technology were quickly inflected by the commercial. Greenfield, for instance, exhorted cellular service providers, in these terms:

Help your customers understand this. Offer them a gently branded space where they can share their stories, let a community accrete around it. Let users' allegiance develop to that community, which will be a lot realer and deeper than their entirely notional loyalty to a brand. I guarantee you it will be the stickiest thing since asphalt in August, because it will take a lot more than a competitor's superficially sexy phone to wean people away from real relationships they've built and nurtured. (Extra credit if you can somehow make the postings location-specific, and thus tie the digital back to the lived experience of the city.)

Get the UI [user interface] right, get to market first, and even when your competitors imitate you as they surely will, you'll be able to maintain your dominance. Because if you get it right, you will be offering, through your brand and your phones, access to a genuine, organic, lively, unscripted colloquy: an always-on party where people will meet and fight and fall in love.

(Greenfield 2002b)

The first international moblogging conference was organised by Greenfield and held in Tokyo in July 2003, and had a strong focus on the commercial possibilities of moblogging. I will return to the story of commerce and moblogging later on, but for the moment I look at a rather ordinary case of inventing moblogging in everday life: in the travails of a taxi blogger.

Cabbie flaneur

As moblogging gathered momentum in 2003 a blogging taxi-driver started to come to public notice: Sydney-based Adrian Neylan and his blog 'Man of Lettuce: A Cabbie's Spray' (Neylan 2006). Neylan commenced blogging in December 2003, but his rise to mainstream media prominence came in mid-2004. On 14 July 2004 Neylan announced a new purchase:

> Over the last few days I've invested heavily in a new mobile phone. The latest on the market with a 1 megapixel camera. I've been waiting 2 months for this model . . . This phone also has all the whistles and bells . . . Connectivity is my current dilemma. Once conquered however, I'll be up and running, posting stories and the like, from the cab in real time.

The first mobile post came the next day. However, Neylan was not impressed with the ease of use and quality of his cell phone camera, and discussing a later post and image with his interlocutors he felt he should be able to do better: 'With an increasing readership, and the blog to get national attention soon, I figure this is a reasonable position to take. Maybe I'm just being precious, I dunno'. Two days later he devised a bracket to steady the camera. The image posted depicts a fleet of rather blurry looking cabs. Man of Lettuce's first efforts at sending an image remotely came at the end of July 2004, with a picture of one of Sydney's best-known taxi-driver haunts, all-night Café Hernandez, in Kings Cross. More phone videos followed, including some in report-to-camera format, as befitted a fast-rising citizen journalist. In September 2004, a national lifestyle and light entertainment programme featured 'Adrian, the blogging cabbie':

> Adrian the cabbie is what you'd call a mobile publisher. He drives around in his cab, seeing a city in action and asking his passengers all sorts of questions which he then adds to his blog. A far cry from the days when the only conversation you'd get from a cabbie was, 'Mate, I can't break a 50!' But the meter's running, so let's jump in with Adrian, the blogging cabbie.
>
> (Mondo Thingo 2004)

The programme featured some snatches of dialogue, and Neyland explaining his *modus operandi*:

> ADRIAN: Those couple of passengers I picked up earlier, I've just done a quick thumbnail of what they thought would happen and just put it straight online via the mobile phone. And here it is with an image of a city scene . . . For me, because obviously in the taxi I see things around about town which I

just have to capture, things which aren't there five minutes later or an hour later.

(Mondo Thingo 2004)

The resonance of Cab Blog may lie in the figure of the taxidriver as an antipodean everyman. Taxi-drivers are renowned as (having no choice but to be) lending a sympathetic ear to their customers. As all people from many walks of life and social circumstances take cabs, cabbies oversee and observe all manner of things. They meet all sorts of people, and, like hairdressers, are able to engage them with their guard down, in a conversational mode, as it were. For this reason, the cabbie is an important cultural figure, a repository of common knowledge, popular opinion, and street wisdom. The cabbie is often cited as a barometer of the public mood. Once Neylan's reputation spread in the blogosphere, and in print and television media, this role, and the authority it carries, was recognised when he was invited to participate in a public debate on national television. (He was also invited to lodge the blog in the National Library of Australia electronic archives). As the recognisable figure of cabbie, Neylan's Man of Lettuce blog played a mediating role in representing the new technology and practice of blogging to audiences that were not familiar with it.

The Cab Blog was fit-for-purpose for introducing moblogging to wider audiences in another respect. There has been a strong association between cell phones and another twentieth-century technology of mobility, the car, as we saw in chapter 2. Moblogging made it possible to blog from a car; and a cab is a special type of car: one that perhaps collects more interesting and unpredictable textual, visual, and auditory information than other cars moving in a city in the patterns of their everyday lives. A cab is a type of moving theatre, perhaps, or a microcosm of the larger world, with some familiar, recurring characters, and some strangers – and so not surprising perhaps that rich multimedia data about a cab driver's journeys might be collected, and be of interest to audiences wider than the blogger's intimates.

What we see in this case study is typical of much of the early practice of moblogging, which very much involved the technological, social, and cultural skills and disposition of the *bricôleur*. Or, to frame the pioneering moblogger in a different way, what cultural theorist John Fiske called 'the art of making do' (Fiske 1989), something that David Marshall feels is central to new media cultures (Marshall 2005). Moblogging is still preoccupied, not surprisingly, with cobbling together the various bits of hardware, software, transmission channels, protocols, filters, scripts, and translators into kludges[5] that made it possible to post from a cell phone to the Internet.

Life = blog

From the Cab Blog case, and the early development of moblogging, I now wish to return to the question of how commerce has grasped, domesticated, and appropriated moblogging. As I suggested above, there have been different visions of moblogging. One vision of moblogging sees its technocultures as a way to organise, retrieve, and network datascapes and mediaflows of everyday life. On this view, moblogging allows those who so wish to know, find out, or locate the nomad-blogger in space. It also serves the restless blogger as a method for staying connected to the invisible skeins of community and networks, through the frequent sending of packets of data, embodying texts, words, images, sounds, and moving images of everyday.

As I have suggested, for much of the short history of moblogging it has been a kludge-practice in the interstices of networks, operating at the ragged interfaces of the Internet and cell phone culture. Much of the interest shown in moblogging has been by computer programmers, and those Internet enthusiasts or service providers interested – for reasons of profit or otherwise – in devising workarounds and applications to enable cell phones to send SMS and MMS (store-and-forward technologies) to email addresses on the Internet, to then post to weblogs. While various types of cell phones were favoured for their utility in moblogging – especially new camera phones with relatively high-resolution image capabilities, such as one megapixel – and cell phone manufacturers and network providers were doubtless pleased about the phenomenon of moblogging bringing them unforeseen business, they were not quick to embrace the phenomenon.

Nokia has been one of the first and few cell phone manufacturers (or network operators) explicitly to grasp and engage with moblogging. In 2004, it released its Lifeblog product, described as a 'mobile phone and PC application solution that keeps an organized multimedia diary of the items you collect with your mobile phone' (Nokia 2004b; see www.nokia.com/lifeblog). Nokia explained that:

> Blogging is all about communication – we are interested in other people's lives, but at the same time we want to share our own experiences and thoughts with the others. Having a multimedia diary of your life, is a unique starting point for sharing the items that make up your life memories.
>
> (Nokia 2004c)

One of the Lifeblogs Nokia displayed on its site as an exemplar was lifeblog.ani-na.net, chronicling the daily life of a model. In August 2004 Nokia announced a collaboration with Six Apart (well-known for its popular TypePad software) to offer greater functionality for Lifeblog. According to Nokia's Christian Lindholm (one of the Nokians we met in chapter 3):

> Nokia Lifeblog is further evolving into a great tool for life sharing. Thanks to the collaboration with Six Apart, a shaper in the blog community, users will be able to upload multimedia like photos, videos, text messages, and multimedia messages to their TypePad account.
>
> (Nokia 2004b)

With the release of the Nokia 7710 in November 2004, Nokia added image editing functions such as crop, zoom, rotate, and flip, as well as the possibility for users to write or draw on top of images they have taken with the photo, or just to draw their own picture (Nokia 2004a).

Nokia avoids the term 'moblogging', rarely using this word, perhaps because it is not widely recognised outside those well versed in digital culture. Instead Nokia talks about 'mobile blogging' or just 'blogging'. Note here, for instance, the emphasis on 'sharing', whether 'mobile sharing' or 'life sharing'. On his own blog, designer Christian Lindholm talks about the everyday things he does with Lifeblog and describes his cell phone as a 'life recorder' (Lindholm 2004). Thus he recognises the growing importance of the exchange of personal and personalised images, audio, messages, and video over the Internet, but increasingly too over the cell phone.

It is not clear to me yet what the take-up of Nokia's Lifeblog has been, and to what uses it has been put, and whether their particular commercial domestication of blogging is having any influence. However, as it has been promoted thus far, Nokia's Lifeblog is a quite sophisticated and insightful take, as well as an obviously self-interested take, on the mobile image.

Mobile imaging worlds

> I think that 'Moblogging' like 'Blogging' isn't really something that technically new. It is the popularization and the impact of many people doing it that is exciting to me. Blogging can be said to be just online diaries. Moblogging is just mail-to-web. Moblogging is just an extension of wearable computing. Fine. Call it whatever you like, but let's do it, make it widely available and have fun and change the world.
>
> (Ito 2003)

More so than blogging itself, moblogging is still taking shape. In this chapter, I have only sketched the outlines of a history of moblogging, and have omitted many important technical innovations and well as canny social and cultural uses. Thus far, it is 'an initial gadget' (in Latour's terms; cf. chapter 4) that has interested many groups of people, and so is proceeding. What is also occurring is how the project is transformed 'every time a new group becomes interested in the project' (Latour 1996). This is evident in the case of Nokia's Lifeblog. It is evident too in the instance of particular moblogs, such as Cab Blog, in which the meanings of moblogging take shape. It is also apparent in the many other experiments with moblogging, mobile and wireless devices, locative media, global positioning system (GPS), and the many other devices with which cell phones and mobile technologies can now articulate and connect.

If moblogging as a technology and part of cell phone culture is still under construction (actually this is the condition of all technology always, as living rather than frozen or black-boxed things), this is perforce the case with phones and telecommunicative devices in their new role as image machines. With the proportion of new phones shipping with cameras still rising, phone photographers are hypothetically almost an identical set to cell phone users as a whole. We lack reliable figures, however, on how widely camera phones are being used, and need more studies and debates on how, why, and where, and for what, they matter to people. Despite this, photography is now here to stay in cell phone culture, and there are signs that it is set to play an important role in cultural formations more generally.

9 The third screen: mobile Internet and television

In our vision, the Internet will go mobile, just as voice communications has done.

(Nokia 2000)

Advertisers refer to cell phones as the third screen, in addition to television and computers . . . As it becomes harder and harder to advertise on television, people are looking for new ways to reach people.

(Caumont 2005)

[F]ar from leaving behind the golden age of television, we are still living through it. Broadcasting is about to discover democracy. Increasingly it will be the consumers who dictate what appears on screen . . . this revolution will change far more than news . . . the power of the consumer to choose what, when and where they watch could blow apart everything we are used to.

(Hall 2005)

The coming together of photography and telephony in the form of the camera phone is only one part of the merging of formerly distinct communications platforms, technologies, audiences, and cultures in which cell phones and mobile technologies are being fervidly embraced, if not fetishised. In this chapter I turn to mobile's remediation (Bolter and Grusin 1999) and reconfiguring of features of the enormously important areas of television and Internet, and their respective cultures.

First, I reprise the case of Wireless Access Protocol (WAP), an early attempt in the 1990s to design Internet use for the cell phone. I contrast WAP, secondly, with the case of the Japanese i-mode protocol. Thirdly, I examine the lucrative area of premium rate SMS and MMS where television broadcasters, Internet content producers and service providers, and multimedia providers are all vying to use the cell phone and new, affiliated, mobile devices as a platform for new forms of media culture. From messaging's integration into television cultures, we move to mobile television itself – and the cell phone's bid for what remains the media heartland.

Wireless Access Protocol

> The Internet and its content have become an everyday source of information,
> entertainment and services for millions and millions of people around
> the world. Today, however, there is one fundamental drawback with the
> Internet: the fact that it is restricted to a location, typically the office or
> the home – in the same way that making a phone call used to be only a few
> years ago . . . The key enabler of the Mobile Internet is [WAP].
>
> (Nokia 2000)

With the growing popularity of cell phones, firmly established and growing for
voice communications, as well as the subcultural popularity of text messaging
discussed in chapter 4, handset manufacturers and network operators were considering what next. The other technology growing even more quickly during the
1990s was the Internet. An attractive direction for commercial development was
clearly the cross-over of the cell phone and the Internet.

Cell phone operators and manufacturers, like other telcos, had been steadily
working on data services, first trying to meet the needs, and attract the custom, of
business users. The Internet took telcos by surprise. Rather than coming from the
steady development of data telecommunications standards and protocols such as
the Integrated Services Digital Network we encountered in chapter 4, the widespread take-up of data services received its impetus from the decentralised and
open culture of technology and standards development of the Internet (Abbate
1999; Mueller 2002). In their response to this phenomenon, the cell phone
companies wished to draw upon the unfolding capabilities and opportunities they
felt the Internet symbolised. In doing so, their emphasis was twofold: to ensure a
business model to make revenue from customers accessing and using the Internet
over their cell phones, and to create a controllable and manageable space.

There had been a history of unsuccessful attempts to devise proprietary standards for data services on cell phones and mobile devices, so in mid-1997 a process
started to specify WAP. In December that year Nokia, Ericsson, Motorola, and
Phone.com (formerly called, rather hubristically, 'Unwired Planet') formed the
WAP Forum, with the primary goal of bringing together 'companies from all
segments of the wireless industry value chain to ensure product interoperability
and growth of the market for wireless data' (Nokia 2000). Its designers aspired for
WAP to work across the different protocols, networks, and devices of mobile
phones and wireless technologies.

To achieve this, WAP specifies how a cell phone will communicate with a
server typically operating in the mobile phone network. At the heart of the first
version of WAP lay its own language, Wireless Markup Language (WML), which
specified how web pages would be presented, or marked up, on a mobile or
wireless device. As a strategy to minimise the delays in Internet connection

detested by users, WAP was predicated on the cell phone needing only minimum processing and software requirement on the mobile phone. At the time of its invention, this was, and still remains, an important desideratum as mobile devices are relatively small not only in size but also in computing capacity, memory, and power compared to a desktop or laptop computer, or even, perhaps, a portable digital assistant. Instead of residing in the phone, the intelligence and applications were designed to reside in the WAP gateways and network services. Owing to its size, the cell phone is only able to support a very small (or micro) browser. For this reason, WAP is optimised for tiny screens, low bandwidth connections, and simple software and services.[1]

According to Nokia, the WAP Forum 'developed the de-facto world standard for wireless information and telephony services on digital mobile phones and other wireless terminals' (Nokia 2000). However, this is greatly to overstate the case. One of the difficulties faced early on was that developing websites and services for WAP required mastery of a new and specialised language (the previously mentioned Wireless Markup Language), rather than simply using or building upon the existing language widely used on the Internet (namely Hypertext Markup Language or HMTL, used for website design). This new markup language proved a barrier to consumer acceptance of WAP in some places, such as Japan (as we shall see shortly when we turn to i-mode).

While WAP was being assembled, there was also design and developmental work proceeding in another realm – the still distinct land of Internet technology and its communities of designers and users. The Internet protocol was originally developed and envisaged for connecting stationary devices: typically mainframe computers, services, or desktop computers plugged into an electricity source and network connection. The idea that people might have laptop computers, hand-held computing devices, or phones, and wish to browse the web or use other Internet services while they and their devices were located in different places or even in motion posed considerable challenges. Despite these developments in Internet protocols, especially with a new version IPv6,[2] from the perspective of the Internet technical and service provider community it was recognised that mobility of connections was something that cellular mobile networks, and their evolving data standards, had certainly had more success in achieving. Thus as well as the underlying Internet protocol, there was a clear need for those involved in technologies using this such as the World Wide Web to consider the convergence of Internet and mobile technologies. Accordingly in late 1998 the World Wide Web Consortium (W3C) and the WAP Forum released a white paper which identified areas of future co-operation, expressing a desire to 'find common solutions that will address mobile requirements . . . focus on achieving the seamless integration of mobile devices into the Web' (W3C 1998).

Returning to our discussion of WAP, however, we need note that for the first few years of its life the technology was not particularly well used and indeed has been widely derided as a flop. Part of the problem is that the beginnings of WAP lay in the period of the mid to late 1990s when the Internet really was becoming highly commercialised, and when there seemed few limits to the boom. Cell phone and consumer electronics designer and theorist Scott Jenson explains this through the idea of 'legacy vision':

> Legacy Vision is the approach we all take when first considering how to use a new technology: it gives us our initial use. This approach is very understandable: we look backwards at what we are doing, our current legacy, and apply the new technology in a manner to make this existing problem better.
>
> (Jenson 2005: 307)

For Jenson, WAP is a classic case study in the lack of historical interpretation and appreciation:

> Once mobile phones had wireless data capability, the 'obvious' thing to do was to look backwards and see the web. 'The Web is hot, phones are hot, therefore web + phone has got to be better' was the manic belief in the late 1990s.
>
> (2005: 307)

Jenson regards legacy vision as a kind of 'default thinking' that bedevils technology design and product conceptualisation. Another element is the resort to the jargon of the holy grail of 'easy to use User Interface', when it is unclear what this actually means. Analysing the imprecision of the concept of user interface, Jensen proposes the notion of 'design syntax', for the want of which WAP foundered:

> Design Syntax issues were most acutely seen in the Mobile Industry during the early days of WAP. There were significant problems ranging from screen legibility, scrolling screens, hidden buttons, complex navigation, and technical reliability. These issues were largely discussed by most industry insiders yet seem likely to be a major reason for the lack of consumer acceptance.
>
> (2005: 310)

WAP became the by-word for a technology 'failure'. In chapter 4, I used the history of text messaging to problematise such notions of technology 'success' and 'failure'. For his part, Jenson is also interested in seeing WAP's difficulties in enlisting large numbers of users early on as providing an opportunity for enlargement of our conversations, musing that such analysis can promote a 'broader discussion of the mobile space, creating not absolute truth but a richer landscape to discuss and argue', putting us in a 'much stronger position to discuss future products' (2005: 325). I would agree: for one thing, WAP services were a forerunner of what by 2005 had become a new small screen culture.

While I am not able to discuss early WAP offerings fully here, I would note that most of these services were explicitly conceived as commercial in orientation. Indeed, they were an integral part of the discursive and ideological shift of moving from e-commerce to m-commerce. Mostly, early WAP services involved transactions conceived in a narrow sense such as finding basic information on services or direction, making simple purchases, booking tickets, or checking schedules (for examples see Marcussen 2003). Clearly WAP differed quite markedly from the veritable explosion of media forms, genres, software, production, and cultures of use we can observe on the Internet in the period from the late 1990s to the middle of the first decade of the twenty-first century. WAP was largely a space imagined and even colonised by the mobile phone manufacturers, who envisaged and dictated tightly bound relationships with suppliers and third-party content producers (even at the level of code itself). In its early implementations, WAP clearly did not become a site for the development of peer-to-peer file-sharing of music or pictures (in the way that Napster did), nor did people use it extensively for chat, or for engaging in consumption of website culture, or for social software. Apart from newspapers and other news sources, neither was WAP replete with media companies seeking to develop audiences for so-called rich content. Despite this, technology is not a static object. In response to the perceived failure of WAP, for instance, the WAP Forum developed WAP 2.0, which is much more firmly based on directions in mainstream Internet protocols, languages, and standards, rather than setting out to make developers comply with a new specialised language.[3] An early instance of WAP 2 was the Lonely Planet's travel guide for mobiles, an interesting case of mobiles as locative media (something we encounter in depth in chapter 10).

i-mode

The oft-cited counter-example to the 'failure' of WAP is the phenomenal 'success' of another mobile data service, i-mode. This is a service developed by the dominant Japanese carrier NTT DoCoMo. It is a packet-switched network that works over the mobile phone network. Not a protocol or standard as such, rather it represents an integrated approach to online wireless services described with some justification as an 'ecosystem' (Natsuno 2003b). Those responsible for i-mode forged close relationships between networks (owned by DoCoMo) and the other crucial elements such as handsets, gateways, servers (with the billing systems), portals, and content. The central idea was to make the relationship between customer and content as simple as possible, allowing easy purchase of product or service as well as unobtrusive but effective systems for payment and collection of revenue. DoCoMo forged relationships with content providers, and encouraged them to develop products. The really significant innovation encapsulated in i-mode was the development of audiences and payment systems for content over mobile phones:

> i-mode is probably one of the most successful examples of a business built on subscription-based content. This success is based on the micropayment scheme, which is derived from a telecommunications model. Telephone calls have always been charged in 10-yen units and can just as easily be charged in packet units. DoCoMo built on this existing structure and took the position of agent for the content providers. Users pay for content together with their monthly i-mode fees, the service provider passes these payments on to the content provider, and the content provider in turn pays a commission to the service provider.
>
> (Kohiyama 2005: 68)

It is worth reflecting on the global context in which i-mode was conceived. As the Internet became very popular during the 1990s, there was a panoply of different approaches towards commercialisation of services, communication practices, and content. While some of these were successful, most obviously the use of the Internet for purchasing goods and services, users were not especially keen on paying for online content (such as newspapers or even video, images or audio). Perhaps this was an expectation of the medium, with the Internet developing quite differently in its economics and price structures from the mobile phone. The telecommunications industry featured widespread, sophisticated, and secure systems for measuring, pricing, and billing aspects of services, something that developed further with the advent of competition and 'intelligent' digital networks. As we have seen, from their inception cell phone calls (and other services) were tariffed, and the user sent a bill, just as they would be for a fixed line phone service. New services such as text messages were also charged, though pricing packages varied. The genius of the i-mode was to invoke some of the expectations and conventions of the evolving Internet, but to do so on a business model that drew upon the reformed world of telecommunications (Funk 2001). The i-mode system is also an early example of something that did not become commonplace in other countries until at least 2002–3, namely use of the mobile phone for purchase of content.

This said, one needs to understand that although the idea of 'mobile Internet' conjures up the image of the world of computer screen based Internet shrunk to pocket size, the reality of both services and uses is quite different. As Kohiyama wrote in 2005, the 'primary use of the *keitai* Internet is for transmitting e-mail; Web access is a growing but still relatively small share of *keitai* Internet traffic' (68). Notably, the i-mode's success was 'built on the existing practices of mobile messaging that were well established in the youth market at the time of its launch' (69). How i-mode works can be grasped by considering the case of ringtones:

> To deliver a choice of ringtones to subscribers requires more than a content provider's making the melodies available on its server. Manufacturers have to produce mobile phones designed to play back melodies, and a telecommunications provider has to set up a network to distribute them. Only then it is possible for a subscriber to choose the opening bars of Beethoven's Fifth or of 'Domo Arigato, Mr. Roboto' to personalize his/her phone. For the business to be successful, moreover, there must be a way to inform the subscriber about it in an easy-to-understand way, a portal function to lead the subscriber to the server with the service, and a billing mechanism for collecting a usage free from the subscriber.
>
> (Natsuno 2003b: 4–5)

As well as offering a secure and neat system for handling micropayments and offering consumers branded content, an important factor in the establishment and growth of i-mode was its attractiveness to content developers. I-mode was based on a simplified version of the web language (namely compact-HTML, or c-HTML). The developers of i-mode were at pains to benefit from the fact that HTML was already well known, rather than introducing a new language as WAP's proponents did (Natsuno 2003b: 21) (Fig. 9.1).

I-mode has been launched in a number of countries around the world including the Netherlands (April 2002), Taiwan (June 2002), and Australia (late 2004). The rise of i-mode and its franchising overseas has been accompanied by an intriguing discourse on its characteristics and 'Japaneseness', on how these national, cultural factors might condition adoption of the technology in other countries. Here we may approach from another angle the problem of design and culture that we encountered in relation to Nokia's global instantiations in chapter 3 and in following the contours of text messaging technology in chapter 4. One view put by competitors in other countries is that i-mode is a distinctively Japanese phenomenon that travels well when exported to other countries. This has been adroitly rejected by Natsuno (Natsuno 2003b: 156). Not surprisingly given his pride in i-mode, Natsuno argues zealously for its widespread applicability:

> Walkman, PlayStation, personal computers, Internet, cell phones . . . audio and video equipment, game machines, and other digital devices have spread without regard to national differences. I-mode is a service that only the Japanese appreciate, they tell me. But it is hard to find any other case in which the oft-touted uniqueness of the Japanese market made any difference at all.
>
> (Natsuno 2003b: 155)

Figure 9.1 Kimono Keitai.

Before we leave our discussion of i-mode, I wish briefly to canvass another issue that very much does go to the heart of the cultural politics of cell phones. Not only does i-mode principally encompass a limited range of services, but its architecture and model, at least in their present implementations, are quite circumscribed. As Harmeet Sawhney has convincingly argued, the openness of i-mode as a platform differs quite considerably from the Internet, and rather more resembles that prescient and intriguing Gallic *dirigiste* precursor, minitel. (Minitel was a videotext system launched by France Télécom in the early 1980s, eventually adopted by 20 per cent of French households. Originally, France Télécom, then still the French Post Office, wished to run the whole system on its own, but eventually moved to an open system allowing any service provider to offer minitel; see Flichy 1991 and 2002.) I-mode offers clarity of services and financial arrangements to its customers as well as its backers, such as telcos and content providers, but it does so at the cost of only allowing access to certain types of Internet services and content – and these being mostly commercial offerings. There is an argument, then, that i-mode merely offers a cut-down, highly commercialised, and, in effect, enclosed instantiation of online cultural domains, quite in contrast to the rather more open realms of the global public Internet, upon which large claims have been predicated such as the creative commons.

In response to such claims, others have pointed out that the i-mode platform and its characteristics do indeed offer support for emerging forms of cultural citizenship and the creative consumer-as-producer. For one thing, i-mode-equipped mobiles can access the wider Internet, and they are certainly not the 'walled gardens' in which many mobile and Internet companies around the world have sought to corral their customers (Funk 2001: 183ff.). For another, it has also been noted that there is a vibrant and burgeoning culture of tens of thousands of do-it-yourself i-mode sites, that are something of a counterpart to their equivalents in the public Internet (Hjorth 2005).

Multimedia after short messaging

So far I have looked at the construction of the mobile Internet, and how quite diverse technologies gathered under this rubric are being gathered together and shaped. Of course the Internet is a comparatively recent historical phenomenon in its mass take-up and is still achieving cultural centrality. A technology that has enjoyed enormous popularity and great cultural importance (if contested prestige) is television.

As I noted in chapter 4, mobile messaging has become big business for telecommunications carriers because of the extraordinary volumes of traffic and so revenue it generated. SMS also developed in other surprising ways, with a range of new cultural intermediaries seeking to commodify ('commoditise') it. Many applications have been developed in the past two to three years that are quite mundane: SMS for alerts, news, parking meters, ticketing, and so on. In many countries around the world mobile carriers are seeking to position MMS (multimedia services) as the successor to SMS, supported by heavy marketing for consumer adoption of new cell phones with picture and video capacity. Premium rate services have developed as a back channel or return path for broadcast media, especially television (for a full discussion of premium rate SMS/MMS, see Goggin and Spurgeon 2005 and 2006).

These sorts of SMS and MMS services were quickly established because of the familiarity of users with mobile text message culture. Take, for instance, the case of mobile devices being used in conjunction with television. Kasesniemi discusses the early form of SMS chat being screened on TV (2003: 176–8), something now quite commonplace, especially with music video shows and the like. However, the best illustration of the intricate fitting of mobile messaging into the repertoire, programs, conventions, and audiences of television is the case of voting and downloads for the *Big Brother* series, and, rather spectacularly, the *Idol* show (Steinbock 2005: 209–11). The marketing of *Idol* reveals much about the enlisting of users and audiences for both cell phones and television – in particularly the pre-teen and teen market of boys but especially girls, something I will explore in the following case study of the Australian version of *Idol*.

The first series of *Australian Idol* was immediately popular when it screened through 2003. Audience participation through SMS (for example, voting) and MMS (downloads) was an integral part of the program. The 2004 series was even more widely watched and discussed. This was due to the unlikely emergence of the winner, Casey Donovan, a young woman whose body, dress, and attitude did not fit the usual mainstream music industry requirements. However, there was a strong alignment between Donovan and one of the most important audience demographics, namely cell phone wielding young teenage and pre-teen girls.

In an article entitled 'At last, girls find a way to break free', redoubtable conservative columnist Miranda Devine declared:

> Casey, with her dreadlocks, face-jewellery, grunge and not exactly waif-like frame, is the antithesis of the . . . role model presented as the ideal to young women and girls. She is beautiful in a much more earthy way, and her self-confidence and poise seemed to grow in front of our eyes, as week after week her worth was validated by the text message votes of hundreds of thousands of strangers.
>
> Technology has taken some of the power of creating cultural ideals out of the hands of middle-aged, usually male, executives who run newspapers, advertising agencies, television channels and movie production houses, and placed it in the hands of those countless, anonymous girls who voted for the shy Bankstown 16-year-old with the diva voice.
>
> (Devine 2004)

Another columnist, Richard Neville, spied a cultural seachange that harked back to the counter-cultural heydays of the 1960s (and the celebrated musical of that time, *Hair*):

> *Australia Idol* is not *Hair*. And yet, there is something about the triumph of *Idol* that reaffirms the values of mateship, courage and mutual support that were at core of *Hair* . . . *Idol* showcases an under-recognised mood of optimism and confidence among our youth, perhaps emboldened by the rising tides of the urban tribes . . . Women spanning the generation of my daughters, aged 15 and 21, are having a ball. It's not just the shopping, the plethora of extreme sport options, the cheap tickets to Shanghai, the brutal wit of *South Park* and the shiny array of mobile communication tools. It's the fun they have working together, even when they're working hard. For all its faults, *Australian Idol* is celebration of cultural democracy; a reminder that between the cracks of commerce and cant, the light can still shine through.
>
> (Neville 2004)

As we have seen, there is great fascination with young people's take-up of cell phones. The example of *Idol* illustrates the potential of such juvenation not only in the new modes of cultural consumption inset in mobile telecommunication networks but also in the rejuvenation of television itself. Here cell phone culture is important for contemporary media culture and its relationship to political culture and the public sphere (McKee 2005). Of course, where television sits in relation to public spheres, identity, consumption, and citizenship is a long and noisy debate. The fusing of cell phone and television, then, has all manner of implications, something to which I will now turn.

The dawn of mobile television

There has been much debate about changing technologies, audiences, formats, programs, advertising, and business models with transformations in television from a number of perspectives. One set of concerns relates to the fuzzy and contested concept of interactivity, which has been much talked about in television for at least a decade (see for instance Jensen and Toscan 1999) but has proven very slow to materialise until the advent of the Internet, mobiles, and digital television. Another related discussion turns on changes in audiences, especially in understanding new media audiences (Ang 1996; Balnaves, O'Regan, and Sternberg 2002; Ross and Nightingale 2003; Seiter 1999). A third debate relates to how we understand television as a cultural form in the wake of the changes from Internet and other new media (Owen 1999; Noam, Groebel, and Gerbarg 2004; Wilson 2003). Bound up with this, fourthly, there is the problematic of how the political economy of the television industry, its ownership, control structures, programming and professional routines, are shifting as new media have provided impetus for corporate change. A fifth theme concerns changes to viewing habits and audience expectations associated with the advent of video recorders, DVD players and recorders, and personal video recorders allowing recording and time-shifting of programs – famously TiVo, the cultural implications of which were proposed by John Fiske (2000). Discussion of changes to cultural policy and regulation, especially public interest objectives such as support for certain types of desirable but not commercially viable content (children's programming, national content, and so on) forms a sixth strand. Finally, but not exhaustively, a seventh debate concerns the challenges faced in public sector broadcasting (Sussman 2003; Syvertsen 2003; Tracey 1998), and the possibilities for renewal and innovation new online and mobile technologies offer the project (Martin 2003). I offer this thumbnail sketch because these themes attempt to describe the shifting scene in which mobile television is arriving.

Video and television, of course, were something that influenced the design of the third-generation cellular phone system. I will discuss the vicissitudes of 3G at greater length in chapter 10, but what has emerged since the early, utopian visions of this technology is that the broadcasting of television over 3G is not so straightforward as it might be wished. A threshold technical difficulty is that 3G networks in their present incarnation will find problems dealing with the 'huge bandwidth that modern streaming Internet applications, such as TV, require' (Sieber and Weck 2004). A more subtle yet profound hurdle lies in the very different provenances of broadcast and telecommunications, especially as these have been played out and shaped in decisive regulatory and policy decisions:

> Mobile network operators . . . do not wish to see broadcasters providing telecom services to telecom customers. Similarly, broadcasters fear the loss of existing spectrum allocations as the analogue shutdown approaches, with the completion of the transition to DVB [digital video broadcasting]. Against such deep-rooted concerns, the prospect of some kind of convergence of new 3rd generation (3G) mobile networks and digital broadcast networks is remote.
>
> (Tuttlebee et al. 2003)

Despite these deep-seated obstacles, there are forces that have begun to change this, evident in at least two developments.

As we have just noticed, first, with the integration of mobile messaging into international television program formats and new forms of audience interactivity and expectations, cell phones truly have begun to be involved in significant changes to television culture. While well received by users, the industrial and cultural implications of these developments are not clear. One view is that such technologies and their use provide a way for a rapprochement between broadcasting and telecommunications, but not a merger:

> SMS voting in live TV shows is creating new revenues for both the mobile operators and the broadcasters. This is an indicator of the potential for real mutual benefits, without the need for 'convergence', if ways can be found for the two industries not to *converge*, but rather to *interwork* – each protecting and safeguarding its own independence and assets.
>
> (Tuttlebee et al. 2003)

Nonetheless from at least 2003 onwards, television broadcasters, producers, and program makers joined with advertisers and cell phone companies to announce various packages of television content being made available for viewing on handsets (especially 3G handsets).

What had also emerged since with the design of 3G networks and the initial euphoria surrounding the sale of licences was the scope and impact of the increasingly intertwined production and consumption cycles of the Internet. There had been some early recognition that developments the Internet represented were changing broadcasting:

> Traditional broadcasting assumes a model where radio and television use

autonomous technologies, systems and equipment for transmission and reception. Today, the Internet especially has widened the scope of broadcasting to include webcasting and networked multimedia services. Broadcasters are becoming increasingly 'agnostic' about the delivery mechanism and have to publish their content via whatever channels to whatever devices that are required to reach their viewers and listeners.

(Engström 2000)

The growing experience of users of broadband Internet, and the cultural possibilities this afforded, especially with peer-to-peer networks downloading and exchanging audio and music files (made famous by Napster, Grokster, Kazaa, and others) but also do-it-yourself construction of television schedules and programs made possible by programs such as BitTorrent. What also emerged from 2001 onwards was the growth of wireless, broadband Internet access through Wi-Fi-enabled laptops. Actually the advantages of combining 3G with developments in digital television and radio broadcasting had been recognised from early on (Horn, Keller, and Niebert 1999).

In 2005, mobile television trials were held in a number of countries around the world. The technology being tested was a form of digital broadcasting direct to battery-powered cell phone or mobile device handset. One standard that enables this is called Digital Video Broadcasting – Handheld (DVB-H), one of the family of open digital television standards developed by an industry consortium that includes standards for digital terrestrial television (DVB-T).[4] Key to these DVB-H mobile television standards are features designed to cope with the low power capacities of these small, light, and portable battery-operated cell phone devices as well as the particular environments in which they are used:

> DVB-H can offer a downstream channel at a high data-rate which will be an enhancement to the mobile telecommunications network, accessible by most of the typical terminals. Therefore, DVB-H creates a bridge between the classical broadcast systems and the world of cellular radio networks.
>
> (Kornfeld and Reimers 2005)

In 2002 four main requirements of the DVB-H system were agreed: broadcast services for portable and mobile usage with 'acceptable quality'; a typical user environment, and so geographic coverage, as mobile radio; access to service while moving in a vehicle at high speed (as well as imperceptible handover when moving from one cell to another); as much compatibility with existing digital terrestrial television (DVB-T), to allow sharing of network and transmission equipment (Kornfeld and Reimers 2005). A further set of technical issues to be addressed involves the growing interdependence of telecommunications, broadcast, and Internet networks. As of late 2005, a suite of standards were adopted for the transmission (in technical terms, datacast) of digital television using Internet protocol (so-called 'IP' or 'Internet' television) but via hand-held mobile devices.

There are other possible standards to deliver multimedia content. As well as the Japanese standard ISDB-T, there is also the possibility of adapting the digital radio (Digital Audio Broadcasting or DAB) standard for multimedia delivery. It has been argued, for example, that the digital radio standards are a better alternative because they were designed for mobile radio receivers from the outset, whereas the DVB-H standards involve adopting standards for cell phones that were originally conceived for stationary or portable reception using a roof top antenna (Sieber and Weck 2004). Another perspective emphasises the different but potentially complementary roles of 3G compared to digital radio and television (Kozamernik 2004).

The implications of such technical shifts are complicated and still not clear. What is key is that core telecommunications networks, including mobile cellular ones, are shifting worldwide from the traditional circuit-switched paradigm to a packet-switched paradigm, based on the Internet protocol. How this fundamental change plays out in the interaction between telecommunications and broadcasting is being explored. Viewers are accustomed to a certain level of resolution, reliability, and quality of service, cultural expectations that have their well-worked-out technical correlates in television broadcasting systems.[5]

One new set of social and cultural possibilities that is being constructed in tandem with these technical and industrial developments relates to personalisation, something that has thus far been less salient in the cell phone television debates. From a commercial perspective, there has been a slow-dawning realisation that the sexiness of cell phone operators and their platforms is not so much the whizz-bangery and utopian flavour often predicated upon their services. Rather cell phone companies are extremely desirable because of something that has intense appeal to the actuarial imagination. Cell phone companies typically have millions of customers and have very well developed and secure systems for billing them individually, and gathering data on their use of and preferences for services: 'Mobile operators fully recognize the value of their assets – both their knowledge of the end user and their highly developed, and evolving, transaction-based billing mechanisms . . . The world is becoming increasingly personalized, and the mobile network's abilities to communicate with, and bill, individual customers are very valuable assets' (Tuttlebee et al. 2003). A striking example of this pretty boring but extremely effective attribute of cell phone operators is found in how SMS has been used to authenticate personal identity of account holders in online banking transactions. With frauds such as 'phishing', or unsolicited emails being sent to people to entrap them into entering their personal details into a fake website, the blight of spam and problems with Internet security, there have been extremely serious issues for online banking and other electronic commerce transactions. A number of banks worldwide have chosen to redesign their online banking by requiring customers to authenticate their identity with a unique code sent to their cell phone via SMS, each time they wish to log on to their account. Whereas the Internet was first designed for other purposes, certainly not commerce and trade for its first two decades, but then has become indispensable, telecommunications networks have long had very robust characteristics (owing to their circuit-switched nature, but also as a result of the superior encryption and security capabilities flowing from second-generation digital cellular networks).

Desperately seeking audiences

Having established some of the features of the technical, industrial, and political economy landscape of mobile television, I will now briefly discuss some of the offerings. One area in which the cell phone operators lack experience is cultural content. From the early 1990s telcos have partnered with pay television operators, but with the intensification of the commercial Internet they also developed myriad arrangements with media and entertainment industries and the newer interactive multimedia and Internet industries. Such developments have become more commonplace since 2000 as cell phone operators have sought to 'grow' their markets and find new forms of revenue. As cell phone users have slowly become audiences to entertainment, news, and information, so those who have specialised in shaping and servicing such viewers and readers have come to the fore, such as broadcasters.

There is little independent, publicly available, reliable research to gauge how audiences and users are consuming mobile television. The only research I am aware of at this stage is that conducted by mobile and media companies themselves. Some of the findings of this research is on the Nokia TV forum website, reporting on the various mobile television trials that have been held. The central message of these trials is that consumers do want mobile television, at the right price. Take, for instance, the findings from the three-month Finnish trial held in March–June 2005:

> 'Consumers also want to watch TV programs on their mobile'
> Results announced today from one of the world's first commercial mobile TV pilots in Helsinki, Finland reveal the popularity and willingness to pay for mobile TV services, underlining the potential of this exciting new mobile application.
>
> (Nokia 2005a)

There are obvious problems with interpreting this research, given its positioning to support mobile television. Other industry research conducted by consultancy organisations, the details of which are also not in the public domain, has directly contradicted the proposition that there is significant interest among consumers in mobile television, with one widely reported survey finding that 'most people have no desire to watch television on mobile phones' (Tryhorn 2005), two other surveys suggesting that 'most of us are not insatiable TV junkies' (Benady 2005), and a good deal of sceptical media coverage recalling that the industry previously 'championed mobile web-browsing, picture-messaging and video telephony as the answer [for new avenues for growth]' (*The Economist* 2005a).

Notwithstanding the patent limitations of Nokia's Finnish trial, some of the reported findings certainly accent themes in the discourse on the new technology:

> pilot participants not only wanted to watch familiar program offerings, but they would also welcome mobile TV content that is suitable for short and occasional viewing. Familiar programs available through national Finnish television channels proved to be the most popular followed by sports and news channels (CNN, BBC World, Euronews). The Ice Hockey World cup games, the San Marino and Monaco Formula One as well as the UEFA Champions League match between Liverpool and AC Milan were among the top 10 programs viewed during the pilot. In general, mobile TV users spent approximately 20 minutes a day watching mobile TV, although more active users watched between 30 to 40 minutes per session. Participants also watched mobile TV at different times than traditional TV peak hours. Mobile TV was most popular while travelling on public transport to relax or to keep up to date with the latest news although it also proved popular at home for entertainment and complementing participants' main TV watching.
>
> (Nokia 2005a)

Such patterns of use and consumer really are unfolding at the present time. At the threshold of this social and cultural shaping of mobile television is scepticism about its prospects, not least given that with the screen quality available at present its appearance and texture is markedly different from the viewing experience expected by most:

> Compelling might not be the first word that springs to mind as Sky News's weather report smudges its way across a Sony Ericsson mobile, but then John Logie Baird's moving silhouette that kick-started the whole business back in 1924 wouldn't have been described as 'must-see TV'. Demonstrating Sky's new TV service on Vodafone 3G network in a black cab certainly proves that you can stream TV onto upmarket mobiles; but the burning question . . . is what and for how long people will watch.
>
> (Timms 2005b)

In the quest of establishing its legitimate claims to audiences, cell phone television takes as totemic the need to attract younger audiences:

> Getting TV onto mobiles matters so much to broadcasters because it offers the tantalising prospect of beefing up their younger audiences, the 16–34-year-olds, who are turning off mainstream TV in their droves. Like their older generation, weaned on the flickering, sub-broadcaster quality of VHS, younger mobile users aren't likely to put picture quality atop of their mobile wish lists. As Sky's chief operating officer, Richard Freudenstein, told analysts this morning, it's the ability to consume what they want when they want that is the big attractor rather than whether picture quality and drop-out mars their interrupted viewing.
>
> (Timms 2005a)

Nokia has been one of the handset manufacturers heavily promoting mobile television. Their dedicated website offers a mobile TV forum ('where you write the script for the future of mobile TV'). It also features a primer on the benefits for different parties (Nokia 2005a, 2005b, 2005c). One of the first Western cell phone companies to launch a cell television service was US carrier Sprint's MobiTV service in late 2003. MobiTV streams television programming directly to phones with either a low-frame or a high-frame rate option. Channels include well-known news and entertainment services available on satellite or cable television around the world (such as CNN, Discovery Channel, the Weather Channel, C-Net, and so on).

Television broadcasters have shown growing interest in the possibilities of mobile broadcasting. In September 2005, for instance, the established British commercial broadcaster ITV launched a mobile service so viewers might:

- enjoy highlights and made-for-mobile footage from your favourite shows
- get the latest on ITV's soaps and dramas and keep up to date with showbiz news and gossip
- get up to date news, sport and weather
- have the opportunity to win fantastic prizes on exclusive competitions
- purchase the latest games, ringtones and wallpapers so you can customise your mobile
- find out what's on TV and plan your viewing with a complete TV guide on your mobile.

(ITV 2005)

The service took two forms. First, there was a mobile website (using WAP) which contained the content, that users could access and download. Second, there was a subscription service called 'ITV Mobizines'. An application is downloaded to the phone, and two daily updates are then sent at 7.30 a.m. and 4 p.m. daily, and the user can browse the chosen Mobizine at leisure, whether news, entertainment, fun, what's on, or the TV guide. The TV guide offers SMS reminders for the user's favourite programs. Mobizine subscribers also remain able to browse the ITV mobile (WAP) site. Essentially here ITV mobile uses mobile messaging and mobile Internet technologies as part of an integrated 'portal' to offer customised, tariffed services drawing upon, modifying, and repackaging its existing broadcast, print, and website content. So highlights of programs, gossip and extra information, weather and news are staples. When ITV Mobile launched, however, it also offered special episodes of top-rating programs: 'These could include parallel storylines that link television episodes of the show. From next year, the broadcaster will also start to commission programmes specifically to be viewed on mobile devices' (Gibson 2005).

The British public broadcasters BBC and Channel 4 have also experimented with extending their broadcast to cell phone customers. Proud of its innovative offerings in interactive digital television, in November 2005 the BBC launched its first cell phone video game, based on the spy drama *Spooks*. Interestingly, though, the BBC positioned this in the context of the popularity of games, rather than cell phones per se, with the executive producer at BBCi speaking of the need for the public broadcaster to 'define a public service role for video games' (*Guardian* 2005a).

Channel 4 has staked much on its digital strategy to assist, including the 2005 launch of a new channel, More4 (Robinson 2005b). Channel 4's positioning is deliberately aimed to contrast with its traditionalist, conservative confrère the BBC: 'It's a highbrow offering infused with a populist touch . . . "It's a really important channel for us," says [Andy] Duncan [Channel 4 CEO]. "In my mind it's a 'little-sister' public service channel" ' (Robinson 2005b). Adjacent to an image of Big Brother stars on a cell phone, Channel 4 mobile promises:

> Wherever you are, keep up-to-date with Channel 4's mobile site, where you can access the latest video clips and exclusive mobi-soaps from Channel 4 shows, from Hollyoaks to Lost. You also have reviews and news from the world of music, film and entertainment at your fingertips.
>
> (Channel 4 2005)

Again, the core of the service revolves around a WAP site. It is supplemented by various SMS services, including news alerts, 'TexTips4Lovers', cricket alerts, and, somewhat more creative, 'daily texts from the Hollyoaks characters with exclusive insight into what's really going on'. The use of cell phones as an integral part, or at least available channel or mode, for television is signalled clearly in the website of Channel 4 program 'Totally Frank', about the trials and tribulations of a girl-band. The website offers an introduction to the series, the option of catching up on 3-minute catch-up videos of past episodes and sneak previews of the next ones, extra information and photos on the band and cast, an 'episode blog' (written in the voice of the characters), a photo gallery, a forum, and a mobile episode:

> Get extra mini-episodes of Totally Frank – never before seen on telly – direct to your mobile! There's a special 'mobi soap' for each episode on T4, so you can stay one step ahead of your mates by finding out how the girls came up with their name, get the dirt on make-ups and break-ups, and even witness a saucy snog!
>
> (Totally Frank 2005)

Short for 'mobile episode', mobisodes are very brief, designed for the limitations of attention span and environment of the cell phone users:

> The scene veers abruptly from seduction to murder. In one of the shortest, smallest television premieres ever, a woman deftly snaps her lover's neck, then steal his identity to access secret government data. The miniature version of the TV show '24' lasts just 60 seconds, and it unfolds on a two-inch cell phone screen.
>
> (Noguchi 2005)

The mobisode mentioned here has been adapted from the Fox series '24', and offered by Wireless. Much was made of the fact that Fox's '24: Conspiracy' 'has its own cast and writers . . . Fox concluded that it had to develop original programming with closer shots and short scripts' (Noguchi 2005).

Orange launched a TV-over-mobile service in May 2005, expanding its coverage to eighteen channels later in the year. Sport featured heavily, as it had earlier with pay television, and digital and interactive television, because of the particular characteristics that work well with 'live' events. So, for instance, in October 2005 Orange announced it was adding live coverage of the international cricket. The coverage will be streamed to handsets (in particular Nokia's 6630, 6680, and N70 series phones), to subscribers to Orange's 3G TV services costing £10 per month for 1 gigabyte of data, or about twenty hours' viewing (Keegan 2005; Timms 2005c). With other sorts of programming, live streaming is not such a drawcard. Thus Orange also offers content in one of the early boom areas of mobile media innovation, namely music video television.[6] It has funded a late-night music service on ITV1, Orange Playlist, 'which features musical guests interviewed about their music tastes, [and which will] generate interactive content for mobile phone handsets and the Internet' (Timms 2005c).

If the broadcasters have been relatively conservative in pitching for the eyeballs of the 'third screen' of cell phone (not to mention ears and thumbs), for their part the 3G network operators are starting to recapture their post-auction enthusiasm and seriously to offer 'live' television. Hutchison, the company most associated with 3G around the world, has been reticent to discuss publicly what proportion of their business derives from consumers being prepared to pay for video downloads (as opposed to discounted voice services or text or relatively well-accepted services such as ringtones). Certainly Hutchinson is hoping mobile television will become a lucrative revenue stream. In 2005 the Italian 3 company launched a reality mobile TV channel, 'See Me TV', based on a peer-to-peer, micropayment model (Wray 2005). In October 2005 the British 3 venture announced it would sell airtime on its network to advertisers, apparently a world first (Wray 2005).

As this survey shows, there is growing interest in mobile television among broadcasters and cell phone manufacturers and network operators in Europe and North America – and there are pockets of intense interest and early adoption elsewhere, notably in South Korea, seen as the 'test-bed' of 3G and mobile television as it has been for broadband Internet. Not all the corporate desire is motivated by an urge to refresh and reform television, of course: fixed-line telcos as much as mobiles are also getting involved in mobile television to ensure they can offer the 'quadruple play' of TV, broadband Internet, telephony, and mobile, and compete with their cable TV network competition (*The Economist* 2005b). Such defensive, competitive strategies aside, there are two broadly but not mutually exclusive approaches I can see in all this. While some are experimenting with broadcasting television directly to cell phones and mobile devices (as part of developments in digital radio and television broadcasting), others are cleaving to the safer ground of modified or dedicated made-for-mobile content purchased and delivered through premium mobile services, via mobile Internet (whether WAP or i-mode), or through 3G networks.

Having approached mobile television from the broadcaster or telco angle, it is worth considering the perspective of content and cultural producers, including new intermediaries. One of the most powerful of these comes, in many ways, from the television production community. The Dutch-founded producer Endemol is famous for its *Big Brother* program format, with its successful adaptations worldwide. *Big Brother* is often seen as synonymous with 'reality TV', and there has been much public and academic debate regarding this. However, what may well be more enduring about *Big Brother* is the way that it has generated new genres and modes of understanding television across different media and delivery platforms (television, magazine, newspaper, word-of-mouth, Internet, and cell phone). It is fitting that Endemol is now owned by the Spanish carrier Telefonica. Endemol produces specific programming for cell phones (such as comedy clips for three operators), and in late 2005 announced two TV channels specifically targeted to mobile television: a comedy channel and an extreme reality channel featuring the ' "bizarrest and weirdest" video clips' (Timms 2005a).

As the mobile television balloon was rising in late 2005, serious competition was not far off – from a company with a proven track record in mobile media. The spectacular and iconic digital successor to the Sony Walkman has not, of course, been any of Sony's MP3 players (Belson 2004), or other MP3 or other digital music technology; it has been Apple Mackintosh's computer iPod device, first released in 2001. With its sleek design aesthetic, software functionality and compatibility, and relative ease of use, the iPod has been taken up by millions of users despite its relatively high price. During 2004, Apple conducted a mass marketing campaign for the iPod, taking it beyond the digiterati, including iPod giveaways tie-in with a range of household consumer goods. Not surprisingly there has been a considerable public discourse about the curious customs of iPod users with their distinctive 'earbud' headphones, listening to music in all sorts of public places (on the iPod, see Bull 2005; also the detailed *Wikipedia* entry, 2005b, and the growing popular literature such as D. Jones 2005; Kahney 2005; and, from the business perspective, Young and Simon 2005).

One of the most intriguing things about the iPod, that distinguishes it from predecessors such as the Walkman, is its imbrication in online cultures and economy. As well as its ability to store and play audio from CDs or the Internet, the iPod has given rise to the phenomenon of 'podcasting', or the downloading of radio programs to the iPod (the iTunes programs allows the user to select a radio program for regular feeds and updates to be 'podcast'). Once radio stations saw the potential of podcasting, many mainstream broadcasters quickly moved to leave substantial amounts of programming online (such as recent or notable programs), so users can download to play at their leisure. In October 2005, Apple chief executive officer Steve Jobs unveiled the new video iPod, allowing users to download video for playback. Apple appeared to have doubts about whether there would be a market for portable video, Jobs calling the video iPod the 'best music player we've ever made' (Timms 2005d) and the video capability a 'bonus' (Johnson and Gibson 2005).

Radical consumption and 'the great cultural unifier'

As is plain from my discussion so far, mobile television is at an early stage of formation, with various ideas of what it might be and who might be interested in watching or interacting with it, and producing cultural content and forms for it, being played out. In this sense mobile television truly is in the process of becoming – rather than having achieved or reached a more-or-less accepted identity – a 'black box', whose details do not concern most of its viewers or users. Although it is early days, I would like to conclude by noting what I think are two important ways in which the discourse on mobile television is contributing to overarching media and cultural meanings and debates. What I would point to here are the narratives of use and significance put into circulation by those shaping the technology, and seeking to persuade and enlist users.

The first of these ways in which mobile television is being discussed is a radical intensification and extension of new modes of consumption and the pivotal force and agency of the figure of the consumer. So, for instance, an important discursive moment in the construction of mobile television occurred in and around the September 2005 biennial Cambridge Convention of the Royal Television Society, grappling with the theme of 'TV is dead'. Mobiles were hailed as the 'small-screen future':

> John Pluthero . . . who is executive director of Cable & Wireless UK, delivered a powerful piece of crystal ball-gazing on how television will be delivered in the future: forget the television set in the corner of the living room and think of broadband computers and 3G mobile phones. The 3G handsets . . . are destined to become like mini-TVs, according to the TV futurologists. It is a development which Richard Freudenstein, Sky's chief operating officer, speaking at the convention, seized upon, saying the broadcaster would offer key news and sports channels 24 hours a day on mobile phones from next year. Teenagers, he said, wanted choice, accessibility, convenience and control over their viewing.
>
> (Culf 2005)

Pluthero ferociously criticised television's lack of real innovation:

> What drives me to the depths of despair is that TV's ideas of interactivity is [asking viewers] to text in votes. I'm just a bit worried that the broadcasters will be a bit Marks & Spencer-ish about [industry changes], and keep making St Michael jumpers while their customers get old and drop dead . . . It's 50 years since they created the soap opera . . . They've been short of creative ideas every since.
>
> (Robinson 2005b)

The Schumpeterian 'creative destruction' associated with digital technologies is palpable here.

The second way in which mobile television is being discussed is keyed into larger debates about the relationship between media – specifically the privileged claims made for television as a forum for society-wide conversations that matter – and culture. If the viewer is once again pronounced dead to make way for, indeed give birth to, the consumer, what becomes of the cultural role of television?

A representative version of the new myth is nicely put in a British op-ed piece, authored by Tony Hall. Hall previously headed BBC news but at the time of

writing was chief executive of an institution regarded as the epitome of traditional culture, the Royal Opera House. Hall opens with a sally on those who
decry contemporary television as a fallen medium, arguing to the contrary that
the present developments stand to extend the golden age by radically changing
it. Temper democratic, agent the consumer: 'Broadcasting is about to discover
democracy. Increasingly it will be consumers who dictate what appears on
screen. Far from narrowing the choice of programming, I believe this can
broaden and enrich it' (Hall 2005). For Hall this is portended in the cell phone
equipped citizen journalist in the aftermath of the July 2005 London Tube
bombings:

> What made the coverage so compelling were the informal ways of gathering
> information: emails, texts, pictures and snips of video from mobile phones.
> The half-lit images of the smoke-filled tunnels were unforgettable. The story
> unfolded not through the polished phrases of traditional broadcasters, but
> through the eyes of ordinary people caught up in the horror.
>
> (Hall 2005)

Drawing on these developments in new-gathering and circulation, Hall posits a
thoroughgoing revolution of which the iPod is the emblem:

> The balance of power between the broadcasters and the audience is shifting,
> brought about by the new ways we can both record and receive informa-
> tion. You can see it reflected in those jerky images on the news, but you
> can also sense it when you look at the iPod. Right now it is for listening,
> but before long something very similar will also be a means of viewing.
> Then the power of the consumer to choose what, when and where they
> watch could blow apart everything we are used to. When we all own
> television iPods, we will also be able to dictate where we watch, and
> demand the ability to download both current and archived material to suit
> the mood of the moment.
>
> (2005)

For Hall, the vision is borne out by what cultural theorists would call 'lived
experience':

> For me this vision of the future centres on the train I take to work. I have a
> long commute, and I can't wait to use it to watch the programmes I missed
> last night. I already cherry-pick programmes to hear on the BBC radio player
> via the website. When the BBC applies the same logic to television . . . it will
> truly be extraordinary. For people like me who don't have a huge amount of
> time and who really want to watch television, but have so far been limited

because we can rarely catch the programmes we like, it means a complete change in our viewing habits.

(2005)

One is tempted to dub this vision of the mobile television revolution as an 'ideology of the cell phone' (Sarikakis and Thussu 2005). Certainly similar themes and assumptions regularly crop up in discourse on mobile television, as they have in digital technologies discourses for at least twenty years. What presents itself more insistently and clearly, and at an earlier stage, however, is the problematic of what constitutes a culture. That is, a common culture. Hall ends his opinion piece with a note of caution:

> As we all become more discriminating, more specialised in what we watch, choosing niche channels, the question becomes: what will bring us together? One thing that makes this country special is our diversity. But the more divided we become in the way we use media, the job of communicating the common ground between us becomes much, much harder . . . The big journalistic or editorial question that broadcasters have to face in the next 5 to 10 years is how to reflect this variety of cultures. How do we avoid stereotypes, caricature or cultural ghettos? . . . Back in that mythical golden age, television was the great cultural unifier in Britain. In some sense it still is: I find it fascinating that Big Brother draws strong nationwide audiences by showing us a group of people who sometimes get along, but more often don't. Can television still somehow bring us together in the multi-channel future? This time the answer will have to come not from the broadcasters, but from the consumers.

(2005)

This is a question also posed elsewhere by commentator Will Hutton, in reflecting on the vast potential of Xboxes, iPods, and other devices for consumers to choose what, when and where they consume entertainment and information. The plaintive question that Hutton raises is reminiscent of the early work of Raymond Williams (1958 and 1961): 'Britain's broadcast culture, and with it our wider culture, will change dramatically, weakening public values and experiences held in common – as it has already begun to do' (Hutton 2005).

We are a long way from Raymond Williams now, though much of his work, especially his pioneering 1974 book on television, still affords resources for making sense of these new developments. Certainly I am surprised that the current problematic of mobile television is still being framed in terms of the threat to common culture. Perhaps the persistence of such unifying rhetorics underlines that we are still in the process to understanding how we connect through media – if not constitute through media – communities, audiences, and publics. What is at the centre of debates about convergent technologies and cultures are questions of how we make use of these new technologies and networks to fashion shared as well as individual spaces in our lives, relationships, and ideas. Thus far, however, the developments surrounding and discourses characterising mobile television have tended to obscure these developments and struggles in social relations and cultural politics – something that I think merits considered and urgent attention.

10 Next gen mobile: 3G, 4G and the return of location

Rarely does an individual or an organization have an opportunity to create something of broad utility that will enrich the daily lives of everybody. Alexander Graham Bell with his invention of the telephone in 1876, and the various people who subsequently developed it for general use, perceived such an opportunity and exploited it for the great benefit of society. Today there stands before us an opportunity of equal magnitude – PICTUREPHONE service . . . I predict that before the turn of the century Picturephone will similarly displace today's means of communication . . . Picturephone . . . may in fact help solve many social problems, particularly those pertaining to life in the big city. Bringing Picturephone into general use I see as one of the most exciting opportunities for the wise use of modern technology.

(Molnar 1969)

We'll be wearing wristwatch-style mobile phones, beer-can sized low orbiting satellites will enable easy communication anywhere in the world, and voice-and-image telephone link-ups around the world will introduce comprehensive business and family communications.

(Gibbs 1990)

Just five years ago, the reality of 'mobile data' meant little more to real-world users than sending text messages or struggling to browse share prices and weather reports via a slow connection . . . Today, however, customers are experiencing their first real taste of faster, user-friendly multimedia on the move . . . Hand in hand with the accelerating rollout of high-speed 3G/UMTS cellular networks, the end-user experience continues to improve . . . becoming steadily more in tune with the needs of real customers.

(UMTS Forum 2005b)

The prospects for mobile television and even mobile Internet as cultural forms are still unclear, bound up as they are in all manner of different logics involved in the reinvention of media at this time. Ancient dreams of the potency of word and image reappear, as too does the idea of means of communications rendering itself nigh invisible to bring together humans over time. Such ambiguous yet culturally pervasive and recurrent myths shape our ideas about technology (Mosco 2004).

In the making of mobile television, we see various deeply held views about the functions and meanings of this broadcast medium in our society being sifted through, something that might be grasped as an opportunity for reflection. For its part, and after some anticipation, the Internet has many intersections with television, and the future of both is becoming intertwined. Significantly, the Internet any-to-any potential challenges the broadcast model in its classic phase, and points to new possibilities for the relationship between broadcasting and cultural institutions on the one hand, and viewers, users, audiences, and publics on the other hand. A notable form of new media culture that has emerged in the Internet revolves around the peer-to-peer (p2) technologies. We could see the telephone as an *ur*-p2p, and there is something of this conceit in the social shaping of the subject of this chapter: third-generation and fourth-generation cellular systems.

Greatly anticipated in the late 1990s at the time not only of the dot.com bubble but also of its speculative sibling, the telco crash, 3G was widely believed to herald a fundamental shift in telecommunications and media, realising a long-cherished dream of being able to see as well as hear a person while one conversed with such a distant interlocutor. In this chapter I describe the development, design, and deployment of 3G and 4G mobiles, and consider what their implications are for cell phone culture. First, I review the development of 3G mobile, including a discussion of the debacle concerning inflated prices initially paid for these licences. Secondly, I look at the emerging take-up and use of 3G, in particular looking at locative mobiles and media. Thirdly, I consider the design of 4G mobiles, and what sorts of cultural consumption are being inscribed in this technology – even prior to the deployment and consumer use of these services.

The development of 3G mobiles

The Europeans were keen to continue their collaborative scientific, technical, and standards-setting work in the 'pre-market' technology to build on the lessons they had learnt from the fragmentation of first-generation mobiles. As the chronicler of GSM says, 'UMTS is built on the GSM footprint and plans to repeat the GSM success' (Hillebrand 2001a). As GSM was being launched the Europeans had already commenced standardisation work for its successor, next-generation network through the European Telecommunications Standards Institute (Korhonen 2001: 9). In the late 1980s the European Commission program, Research into Advanced Communications in Europe (RACE), recognised that before GSM would be commercially introduced 'a new generation of mobile technology would be necessary to cater for the perceived challenges of the 21st century' (da Silva et al. 2001: 116). At this stage two broad types of mobile communication were envisaged: universal mobile telecommunications system (UMTS), aiming to provide voice communications; and low to medium rate data services but with near complete geographical coverage and a very high rata data service in 'hotspot' areas (da Silva et al. 2001: 116). At the project's completion in 1992 it was estimated UTMS take-up would be 50 per cent of the European market by 2005. Collaborative work continued within the European Community on UMTS. Key decisions on allocation of new frequency spectrum to support such services was taken in the same year at the World Administrative Radio Conference. By the mid-1990s UTMS was conceived as a 'multi-function, multi-service, multi-application digital system that would use end-of-the century technology to support universal roaming and offer broadband multimedia services with up to 2 Mb/s throughput' (da Silva et al. 2001: 121–2).

By the end of the decade, a vision had emerged and was widely shared of UMTS, and 3G in general, as a 'truly new generation of services' (2001: 129). Da Silva et al.'s view can stand as representative of key actors in the system's design:

> [3G] has the potential to allow higher transmission bandwidth and allowing for a better efficiency in radio spectrum usage . . . Although the exact profile of the new applications remains largely untested, the following characteristics are relevant for the new service generation:
>
> - The possibility to convey data with a large bandwidth enables the *wireless transmission of a vast range of content forms* such as high quality audio, still and moving pictures, large data streams including access to the Internet. A vast range of multimedia services . . . is at reach.
> - . . . *a truly global access capability* . . .
> - . . . *a personalised service profile* . . .
> - *Location determination* of 3G terminals will become a key feature of the new services . . .
> - Integrating *smart cards* in 3G terminals . . .
>
> These new dimensions clearly qualify 3G as a key element in realising the Information Society.
>
> (2001: 129; authors' emphasis)

Such visions of 3G are akin to a grand narrative, with its emphasis on a new multimedia interactive paradigm of mobile communications. However, even at its inception it was evident that 3G was not so much a paradigm shift away from the two previous major cellular systems (analogue first-generation and digital second-generation). Rather an evolutionary view did make considerable sense, understanding 3G as essentially an extension of 2G capabilities . . . UTMS does not strictly represent a major technological breakthrough because GSM already provides many services that were not originally expected to evolve until a later stage of development. Furthermore, upgraded or 2.5G variants of GSM will coexist with UMTS for an extended period. However, UMTS will eventually result in the provision of more sophisticated services that require greater bandwidth – effectively multimedia on the move.

(Curwen 2002: 9)

One important difference between 2G and 3G networks is that the latter are packet-switched networks (as we know, the principle upon which the Internet operates), rather than the circuit-switched networks of 2G cellular systems and traditional telecommunications. Notably, as is evident in the discussion of mobile television also, all telecommunications networks are now shifting to packet-switching, as dramatised in the rapid rise of Voice over Internet Protocol (VoIP).

The decidedly utopian register of the discourse about the identity of 3G, and how it marked a radical break and supercession of existing mobile networks, of course plays an important ideological function. Our contemporary notions of utopian often are predicated on the salvific properties of technology; conversely, our societies' grappling with novel technologies nearly always rhapsodises their beneficent even magical qualities. This not only provides symbolic resolution for social contradictions, it obscures and represents key ideas and narratives about what is occurring in the social world at a historical moment. So, returning to the development of 3G, we see that the European Commission funded research into the new technologies, as did the United States, Japan, and Korea, all keen to build on their investments in their existing, chosen 2G networks, as well as gaining leverage in what standard would prevail globally. Korhonen highlights an important shift in the social and political shaping of telecommunications that 3G represents:

In all, the 3G development work has shown that development of the new systems is nowadays done more and more within the telecommunications industry itself. The companies join to form consortia, which then produce specification proposals for the official standardization organizations for a formal approval. This results in a faster specification development process, as these companies often have more available resources than intergovernmental organizations. Also, the standards may be of higher quality (or at least more suitable for the actual implementation) when they have been written by the actual end-users. On the other hand, this also means that the standardization process is easily dominated by a few big telecommunications companies and their interests.

(Korhonen 2001: 10–11)

As well as research and development conducted by individual private companies, especially the equipment vendors and network providers, they also joined together in collaborative ventures among potential competitors.[1] One of these is the UMTS Forum ('promoting the global success of third generation mobile') which describes itself as:

> an open, international body for promoting the global uptake of UMTS third generation (3G) mobile systems and services. The UMTS Forum recognises the importance of all players – including new entrants – in the mobile value chain . . . The UMTS Forum serves the interests of all its members through educational and promotional activities in its role as the voice of the 3G mobile market.
>
> (UMTS 2005a)

Among its objectives are 'to express a strong, unified industry voice promoting UMTS and WCDMA technology through lobbying and promotional actions globally' (2005a).

As well as the UMTS Forum, key players in 3G joined the Partnership Project for the standardisation of a Third Generation Mobile Communications System (3GPP), created in December 1998 (Korhonen 2001: 10–17; Rosenbrock and Andersen 2001). The 3GPP's original aim was to develop global specifications for a 3G system, based on the evolved GSM network, and the Universal Terrestrial Radio Access (UTRA) radio interface. Its scope was subsequently amended to include the maintenance and development of GSM specifications including the 2.5G radio technologies (such as EDGE and GPRS) that had extended the network (www.3gpp.org).

Despite the aspirations of 3GPP to achieve a unified approach, another major 3G standardisation collaboration was founded and dubbed the 3GPP2 (www.3gpp2.org). Comprised of the leading North American, Korean, Chinese, and Japanese standards development organisations, the 3GPP2 aims to develop the alternative cdma2000 system and also to be backwards compatible with North American 2G systems, namely IS-95 backed by operators Qualcomm, Lucent, and Motorola. The cdma2000 project is important in the USA because here 3G needs often to use spectrum already allocated to 2G, so compatibility between the two generation systems is important (Kurhonen 2001: 17–19; cdma2000 is explained in Holma and Toskala 2000). Like UMTS's emergence from and compatibility with GSM, so too are there economic, technical, and regulatory factors that make it more likely that cdma2000 will built upon CDMA in those countries. That said, cmda2000 faces a battle with the other main 3G systems W-CDMA, for instance in Canada and Japan. It has, however, been adopted by one of the early pioneers of 3G, namely South Korea.

The cdma2000 system will also be important in South America, because of the 'path dependence' and popularity of various countries' choice of 2G CDMA (Curwen 2002: 47–8). How this will play out, however, is debated. Hillebrand writes with a sense of almost palpable horror contemplating South America's fate in eschewing GSM: 'With the adoption of AMPS 800 MHz in the late 1980s throughout the continent, the North American evolution model was set in the region . . . Dominated by mostly North American suppliers, the continent was entirely aligned with the US and condemned to live without GSM' (Hillebrand 2001b: 540). He hails the 2000 decision of Brazil (pushed by the joint forces of Alcatel, Nokia, and Siemens) as the biggest market in South America to align itself with the GSM/UMTS model, predicting the corollary will be that the 'wide adoption of GSM and its evolution to third generation UMTS in the continent is not considered a question of "if" anymore, but only a question of "when" ' (Hillebrand 2001b: 540).[2]

Before I leave this discussion of the technologies involved in 3G, it is important to note the role of satellites. The invention and launch of satellites in the 1960s, the era when space travel became a reality, fuelled visions of the communicative cornucopia that would unfold. Satellites were a technology, you might recall, that was invented by a scientist later to become famous for his science fiction and popular commentary, namely Arthur C. Clarke. The possibilities of satellites for digital communication and mobile communication emerged from the 1970s through to the 1990s (Howell 1986; Pelton 1995; Miller, Vucectic, and Berry 1993; Ohmori, Wakana, and Kawase 1998). I vividly remember being contacted by a US-based satellite provider in the mid-1990s to talk about how to launch their services into the Australian market. Then satellite services were being touted as the solution for profitably meeting the needs of consumers living in rural and remote areas, without incurring the costs of extending terrestrial networks and infrastructure into sparsely populated areas. One of the most famous ventures at this time was Teledesic, a joint partnership in which Bill Gates was famously involved. Teledesic had the grand vision of offering 'Internet-in-the-sky', ubiquitous, fast, and high-bandwidth voice and data services regardless of location. The problem with satellite mobile services at this time was at least twofold: first, the handsets were bulky, heavy, and expensive; and the voice calls were spectacularly costly. In the face of these difficulties, companies typically assured investors and consumers that costs of calls and terminal equipment would rapidly fall once satellite mobiles started to be taken up. Things look rather different a few years on, as Curwen concludes in his thoughtful treatment:

> Expensive new satellite services were always perceived as somewhat risky, but the reality is that their prospects have declined at an astonishing rate. It is less than a decade since such services were widely seen as the obvious answer to meeting the problem of 'go-anywhere' communications. However, in the space of a few years the reduced size, weight and cost of cellular handsets and

the implementation of global standards for cellular networks, combined with a big reduction in wireless tariffs, have combined to destroy much of the rationale for satellite provision. This conclusion is very strongly held in relation to voice telephony whereas prospects for broadband networks, when they eventually come on stream, remain for now the subject of considerable disagreement.

(Curwen 2002: 38–9)

While those involved in the technical and regulatory shaping of 3G genuinely had utopian visions for the technology, when it came to a crucial moment in the implementation of the system the interests of capital charged off in another direction. In Europe various national governments offered licences for sale. About half of the governments chose auctions as their method for doing so, while the others used comparative bidding (Niepold 2001: 141). Price varied very widely indeed. In some countries telecommunications companies paid a very high price for licences, by historical standards.[3] This 3G 'bubble' burst quite quickly, with serious implications for the evolution of the technology. One consequence was that quite a number of aspirant 3G carriers had outlaid enormous sums of money that needed to be recouped, making it likely that the early offerings of 3G services would be quite expensive. Another consequence was that many carriers reacted by taking a conservation response to the development of 3G services. With consumers showing unexpected interest in 2.5G services, especially SMS as we have seen, carriers sought to extend the capabilities and so life of these networks, putting off the day when they would have to spend substantial sums of money investing in and marketing the as yet unknown to consumers 3G platform and its possibilities.

Video calling

The idea of being able to see moving images of people while communicating with them over the phone has a long genesis. In his tracing of the evolution of video phone, Carson notes that the 'first public demonstration of the television as an adjunct to the telephone took place on April 7, 1927, when Herbert Hoover, then Secretary of Commerce, and other officials in Washington, D.C., spoke "face-to-face" with Walter S. Gifford, President of AT & T and other Bell System officials in New York City' (Carson 1977: 283). Serious research into commercial video telephone service did not commence until the mid-1950s:

The time was right – technology was beginning to catch up with the concept. The transistor had been invented, and inexpensive and reliable camera and display tubes were becoming available. Only then did video telephone service seem possible as an economic venture.

(1977: 284)

Video telephone sets were displayed at the New York World's Fair, and some 700 curious visitors to the exhibit were researched for their reaction. A commercial picturephone trial between New York, Chicago and Washington, DC, commenced on 25 June 1964, with further trials, including respectively of videoconference and satellite video telephony services (1997: 284–91). Writing about this, Carson hopefully declared that 'a new "see-as-you-talk" telephone, long a dream of telephone people, is nearing the day when it will be a standard service' (1977: 283).

As it transpired, video telephony was not enthusiastically welcomed by users in the late 1960s and 1970s, and was not commercially offered on any widespread basis until ISDN networks were implemented in the 1980s and 1990s. Video-conferencing did become quite common at this time as a way of conducting meetings, conferences, or seminars, used mostly by large business or institutional users (though with a few very interesting community applications, such as its use by the indigenous Warlpiri people through their Tanami network in the Western Desert of Australia; Toyne 1994). With the development of the Internet and its associated technologies in the early 1990s it become possible and increasingly frequent for users to videoconference or have video communications using the Internet and desk-based computers. The difficulty here was dedicated bandwidth, with quality of interactive video often quite poor and unreliable, although the situation improved considerably with widespread availability of broadband networks from the late 1990s onwards.

Despite such setbacks, and the length of time taken to realise the dream of video communication, the techno-optimist discourse regarding telecommunica-tions contains some relatively stable themes across some decades and across Western cultures. Here are some Australian press forecasts on video calling that call up the fantasy of anywhere-anytime video communication:

> As if the aggravation of mobile phones is not already enough, users of the fashion accessories may soon be staring into them for live video communication.
>
> (Storey 1996)

> Calling Mum live by videophone from an African desert trek, faxing docu-ments to a business contact sitting on the Ghan train to Alice Springs or finding a Tibetan restaurant on the Internet using your mobile phone screen . . . Mobile phones are advancing way beyond being simply a wire-less version of the kitchen telephone.
>
> (Webb 1998)

With 3G networks in the early 2000s, mobile video calling became a possibility (Camarillo and Garcia-Martin 2004; Myers 2004). It was certainly promoted heavily around the world by 3G providers (Klenk 2005), especially by Hutchinson and its partners, as ushering in, or making possible, new patterns of communication. In 2003–4, for instance, Hutchinson advertised its '3' service in Australia, featuring images of families able to communicate while apart – for instance, fathers away on business able to see their children while saying goodnight to them.

While video calling has been an attractive feature for some users and particular demographics, it still is not widely used, and there are few studies of how it is being adopted. However, it does seem clear that it has not been much of a drawcard to attract new users in the early phase of 3G, as this report of the Japanese experience of 3G suggests:

> The first country which introduced 3G on a large commercial scale was Japan. In 2005 about 40% of subscribers use 3G networks only, and 2G is on the way out in Japan. It is expected that during 2006 the transition from 2G to 3G will be largely completed in Japan, and upgrades to the next 3.5G stage with 3 Mbit/s data rates is underway.
>
> The successful 3G introduction in Japan shows that video telephony is not a killer application for 3G networks after all. Actually, the real-life usage of video telephony on 3G networks is only a very very small fraction of all services. On the other hand, downloading of music finds very strong demand by customers. Music downloads were pioneered by KDDI with the EZchakuuta and the Chaku Uta Full services.
>
> (*Wikipedia* 2005)

The art of location

Theories in the 1990s of cyberculture were dominated by the lure of the 'virtual', the concept of 'cyberspace', and the idea that online communications abolished place. From their inception, cell phones had an overlapping yet distinctly different relationship to concepts of space and place. Earlier users of cell phones, as we have noticed, were intrigued about the new places in which these wireless technologies could be used, as indicated by the catch-cry of 'I'm here' to accentuate, in a shifting mobile deixis, the matrix of place. This attention to place in the reception of cell phones in 1980s and 1990s cultural and use imaginaries widened in its ramifications and possibilities in the early 2000s, especially with the roll-out of 2.5 and 3G networks and the vernacular theorisation of mobile media. What makes this new instantiation of place possible with extended 2G as well as 3G cellular networks are a range of technologies that are able to map and mark location.

Location services are an important new concept in 3G networks, though positioning technologies have been around for some time.[4] There are broadly three ways of locating a handset or other user equipment with cellular networks (see discussion in Korhonen 2001: 355–65, which I rely upon here). The first method takes advantage of the cellular radio design, which allows the user's handset to be identified as being within a particular cell. Clearly the limitation of this approach is that cells can vary from micro- or pico- cells of several hundred metres across to several kilometres (or more in flat countryside). The second method is called 'observed time difference of arrival' involving measuring the time taken from signals from the handset to two or more network base station transmitters. If the exact position of the transmitters is known, it is possible to calculate the relative time difference to the handset, and so estimate its location with varying degrees of accuracy depending on a number of complicating factors. The third way of locating a cell phone relies upon the Global Positioning System (GPS), a constellation of intermediate circular orbit satellites that allow calculation of position based on propagation delays of different transmissions. Developed for and initially dedicated to military use, the first GPS satellite was launched in 1978. Civilian use was hampered by 'selective availability', reducing its accuracy to no more than 100 metres (*Wikipedia* 2005a), until this restriction was phased out from 2000 by order of President Bill Clinton. GPS and other satellite information and imagery is now so commonly available that it has fed the new appetite for locating oneself found in Google Earth (' "For anyone who has ever dreamed of flying . . ." – *NY Times* . . . It's a globe that sits inside your PC. You point and zoom to anyplace on the planet that you want to explore'). Attracting much attention upon launch in 2005, Google Earth allows household users to download an application that will provide images of locations on earth, with the ability to zoom down to an image of a home (such as one's own). There are at least two ways to figure location with 3G equipment when relying upon GPS, either with full GPS receiver based in the handset or using a simplified GPS receiver in the handset (Wisniewski 2005).

Location-based services are of intense interest to the cell phone, wireless, and mobiles industries. They already began to develop in earnest before the arrival of 3G networks. A significant factor in the development of location-based services was the US Federal Communications Commission's requirement that, first, mobile operators ensure users could dial emergency services (famously 911 in the USA, first offered by AT & T in 1965; and 112 elsewhere in the world) and, second, additional information on their location be relayed to the relevant police, fire, and ambulance service (the latter requirement was called wireless Enhanced 911 (E911) (FCC 2005a). In phase I of the FCC's E911 rules wireless carriers were obliged to provide emergency services dispatchers with the telephone number of an emergency caller and the location of the cell site or base station transmitting the call. Under the phase II rules, commenced in 2001, the requirement upon wireless carriers is to provide the emergency caller's location to within 50–150 metres accuracy. In June 2005, the FCC required interconnected voice over Internet protocol providers to provide enhanced 911 service

(FCC 2005b), again reiterating its view that consumers using telephony services, whether via mobile, wireless, or Internet means, should continue to expect to enjoy emergency service calling. Other jurisdictions such as Europe also require wireless operators to provide enhanced emergency calling with cell phones and are extending such requirements into voice over Internet protocol also.

These moves by regulators and government policymakers to stipulate location information for emergency calling have provided additional impetus for cell phone operators to develop location technologies and capabilities, that can then provide a basis for commercial offerings also. The commercial perspective on locational services stems from the possibilities that flow from being able to locate the customer in space, but also, by virtue of this, better to map and understand what they are doing in a particular place and at a particular time, and so articulate and enmesh product and service offerings into this context: 'Location-based services provide customers with a possibility to get information based on their location . . . Location services are added value services that depend on a mobile user's geographic position' (Fraunholz, Unnithan, and Jung 2005: 131).

There are a number of location-based services aimed at firms or industrial users, such as tracking of delivery trucks or fleet management, remote diagnostics of power systems as well as information support, scheduling, data entry and form filling systems, and other resource management systems, for employees in the field (2005: 146–8). Much excitement concerning location-based services, however, has been associated with the potential of the wireless device to gather and transmit its location, and make available services in the vicinity:

> Weather forecasts, tourist attractions, landmarks, restaurants, gas stations, repair shops, ATM locations, theatres, public transportation options (including schedules) are some examples of information provision filtered to the user location.
>
> (Fraunholz et al. 2005: 144–5)

The commercial fantasy of such locational services tends to go something like this widely circulated release on a 3G system to be implemented in 2004–5:

> Imagine your mobile phone telling you of hotels, restaurants and other services in your immediate vicinity no matter whether you're in an underground shopping mall or on a remote hilltop in the Alpujarras.
>
> (3G newsroom 2004)

As it happens, such services have been slow to eventuate.

Tourism and travel services are an obvious area where location-based 3G cell phone services could be popular. In 2004 China Unicom commercially launched a position location service that provides its subscribers with access to information and services based on their proximity (claiming accuracy within 5–50 metres), including traffic, entertainment, and emergency services. The same year Japan's KDDI offered the EZ Naviwalk service that includes map search, train and traffic information, 'my spot', current position emails, and interactive services (www.3gtoday.com). A lucrative seam of location-based services comes from the use of already available geographical and place-based information from street directories and maps (extended with Geographical Information Systems technologies) and phone directories. Phone directories, for instance, were once taken for granted as an integral part of a national telephone service. They are now regarded as extremely profitable businesses in their own right, and tend to be operated as separate businesses (if not sold off completely). The popularity of Internet-based electronic phone directories (CD-Rom directories never really were taken up by the household user) is now extended by the facility many of these offer to combine a phone number search with map details and street directories of the desired location (not to mention the possibility of combining phone and street directories searches with Internet search engine enquiries). Phone directory businesses are now forming joint ventures or even merging with street directory businesses. The behemoth search engine Google launched a version of its Google Local for mobile in late 2005: 'Combining directions, maps, and satellite imagery, Google Local for mobile is a free download that lets you find local hangouts and businesses across town or across the country – right from your phone' (http://www.google.com/glm/index.html). For its part, Hutchinson quite early on sought agreements with leading owners of digital map and geographical information, as well as newer developers of software, platforms, messaging applications, and tools to deliver location-based services (for example see Hutchinson 3G UK's 2002 announcement).

An area of activity in the construction of place in media that overlaps with these commercial imaginings, and also provides a counterpoint to them, goes under the tag of 'locative arts' or 'locative media'. There is now a substantial body of work and practice by new media artists concerning mobile and wireless technologies and the cultural shaping and implication of location. Leading locative art theorist Drew Hemment claims that:

> Artists are responding to the technical possibilities of location-aware, networked media by asking what can be experienced now that could not be experienced before, in some cases producing more-or-less conventional artistic representations using location data, in others playing with the possibilities of the media itself. The exploratory movements of locative media lead to a convergence of geographical and data space, reversing the trend towards digital content being viewed as placeless, only encountered in the amorphous and other space of the internet.
>
> (Hemment 2004)

The use of the telephone to generate art has a long history. One of the first (though possibly apocryphal) instances often cited is Lazlo Moholy-Nagy, in Adriana de Souza e Silva's words, 'one of the first artists to create a telepresence work' (de Souza e Silva 2004), There is the well-known tale of how Moholy-Nagy experimented with the telephone to communicate directions for the making of enamel tiles:

> In 1922, I ordered by telephone from a sign factory five paintings in porcelain enamel. I had the factory's color chart before me and I sketched my paintings on graph paper. At the other end of the telephone, the factory supervisor had the same kind of paper, divided into squares. He took down the dictated shapes in the correct position. (It was like playing chess by correspondence.) One of the pictures was delivered in three different sizes, so that I could study the subtle differences in the color relations caused by the enlargement and reduction.
>
> (Moholy-Nagy 1947: 79, cited in Kac 1992)

In 1969, an exhibition called 'Art by Telephone' was held at the Chicago Museum of Contemporary Art that partly repeated the premise of Moholy-Nagy's earlier work, followed by an intensification of interest with the new possibilities in tele-communications with intelligent network services and convergence through the 1980s and 1990s (as evidenced in Chandler and Neumark 2005; Sommerer and Mignonneau 1998; de Souza e Silva 2004). With telephones becoming much more than just voice telephony, through advanced telecommunications networks and then developments in cellular phones (through acceptance of communicative and cultural practices in social settings as well as popular culture), artistic work expanded. There are now many instances of cell phone art such as *Dialtones: A Telesymphony*, a 2001 Austrian event using audience members' cell phones to download and then play ringtones (Levin et al. 2004); or *Japanese Whispers*, a 2000 Tokyo project in which '[c]ellphones are laid in a circle and calls are initiated from one phone to another in a variety of patterns with differing results' (Haque 2000); or projects that move beyond audio and telephony properties of mobiles to play with new features, such as blu_box, which uses the connective possibilities of the Bluetooth protocol (which connects cell phones to each other, and other devices, at short range) to prototype new network gaming possibilities (Wetherall and Stukoff 2005).[5]

One group of artists whose work explores the construction of location is the UK-based Blast Theory. Blast Theory has now devised three projects that use location-based technologies, exploring urban settings, and converging online and mobile technologies. In introducing its 2001–5 game *Can You See Me Now?*, Blast Theory explains that its starting point is:

the near ubiquity of handheld electronic devices in many developed countries. Blast Theory are [*sic*] fascinated by the penetration of the mobile phone into the hands of poorer users, rural users, teenagers and other demographics usually excluded from new technologies . . . The advent of 3G (third generation mobile telephony) brings constant internet access, location based services and massive bandwidth into this equation. *Can You See Me Now?* is a part of a sequence of works (Uncle Roy All Around You and I Like Frank have followed) that attempt to establish a cultural space on these devices. While the telecoms industry remains focused on revenue streams in order to repay the huge debts incurred by buying 3G licenses and rolling out the networks, Blast Theory in collaboration with the Mixed Reality Lab are looking to identify the wider repercussions of this communication infrastructure.

(Blast Theory 2005)

In *Can You See Me Now?* players from around the world play online in a virtual city alongside Blast Theory's runners in a 'real' cityscape. The runners carry GPS-equipped hand-held computers, showing the position of players in the game and guiding the runners in tracking them down. When players log on to join the game, they are asked the question: 'Is there someone you haven't seen for a long time that you still think of? The runners communicate with each other via walkie-talkies, the audio of which is streamed to the online players. When the runners successfully find and 'see' an online player, a picture of the empty terrain of the locale where this occurs is uploaded to the game. At this point, the online players hear their last words telling them that the runner has seen the person they first mentioned when entering the game.

For Blast Theory the game is about exploring ideas of absence and presence using the 'overlap of a real city and a virtual city' (Blast Theory 2005), as an example of the sorts of 'hybrid space' that have emerged. It is also about questions of relationship and desire:

In what ways can we talk about intimacy in the electronic realm? In Britain the Internet is regularly characterized in the media as a space in which paedophiles 'groom' unsuspecting children and teenagers. Against this back drop can we establish a more subtle understanding of the nuances of online relationships . . . public declarations [of runners and players] coexist with the private moments that appear marginal to the casual observer.

(Blast Theory 2005)

Blast Theory's next project moved from GPS technology to explicit engagement with cell phone technology. Premiered in London in June 2003, 'Uncle Roy All Around You' is also played online as well as on the streets of a city, and 'investigates some of the social changes brought about by ubiquitous mobile devices, persistent access to a network and location aware technologies' (Blast Theory 2004b). Street players buy a ticket to enter, and are given a unique code to enter into their hand-held device, and have sixty minutes to find and meet Uncle Roy, from whom they receive various messages. Their device shows a map with names and positions of online players. Online players are also on a mission to find Uncle Roy, and they can view the avatars of street players as they seek him out. Online players can message the street players to direct them, who, if they choose to respond, can only do so by recording audio replies. Blast Theory's follow up, 'I Like Frank', also pivoted on the search (indeed quest) narrative. Again using their distinctive mix of street and online activity, players were invited to search for Frank over a sixty-minute period in the streets of Adelaide, Australia, in March 2004 (Blast Theory 2004a). Online players could open location-specific photos of the city, but then needed to message a street player to retrieve a hidden postcard or answer a question. 'I Like Frank' used messages sent to players, but also video calls.[6]

In her discussion of mobile art, including Blast Theory, de Souza e Silva claims that:

> Mobility brought new artistic meanings to the telephone interface: bringing phones into the city space, releasing them from a fixed place, transforming them into collective/social mediums and ludic devices . . . Mobile and pervasive technologies help us to be aware of the physical space in which we live. Digital technologies in the 1990s were mostly criticized for creating sociability in a virtual space that was disconnected from our reality, placing users in a simulated and 'unreal' world. Mobile technologies bring these multiuser and playful experiences to physical spaces, encouraging users to go out on the streets and bringing new meanings to familiar spaces.
>
> (de Souza e Silva 2004)

There are many other projects underway at present exploring the potential of 3G cell phone as locative media, such as the Dutch Waag Society for Old and New Media Game Frequency 1550, in which 'students are transported to the medieval Amsterdam of 1550 via a medium that's familiar to this age group: the mobile phone' (Waag 2005). In collaboration with the carrier KPN, the game uses 3G phones and network to allow students to compete in finding answers to questions about the old city of Amsterdam, for a history class excursion and assignment.

Another broad category of projects exploring mobiles and online technologies and location revolves around public art and public spaces, especially through projecting images onto buildings, and other ways of creating and transforming public digital displays. In a 2001 project called *Blinkenlights* the Chaos Computer Club arranged lamps behind the windows of an eight-storey building in Berlin's Alexanderplatz, which were controlled by computer that could be directed by the viewer using a cell phone or the Internet (http://www.blinkenlights.de/; for discussion see de Souza e Silva 2004). The use of texting projected onto screens as a method of viewer or audience interactivity is a motif of various projects: the Norwegian group Re-public (http://www.intermedia.uio.no/republic/); the events of the London-based Cybersalon group (http://www.cybersalon.org/info.html). A cultural event of the 2003 World Summit on the Information Society at Geneva, the *Hello World!* project allowed people to email or SMS messages, which were recorded by webcams and projected by laserbeam 'onto a mountain overlooking Ipanema Beach in Rio de Janeiro, onto the UN building in New York City, onto the most prominent building in downtown Mumbai or onto a 140 metre tall water fountain in Geneva' (http://helloworldproject.com). The Japanese *Amodal Suspension* project receives SMS, encoding them as sequences of flashlights with twenty giant searchlights in the sky (http://www.amodal.net/intro.html).[7] SMS writing in public places is given a literal twist with Joshua Kinberg's clever activist project, *Bikes Against Bush*:

> an interactive protest/performance occurring simultaneously online and on the streets of NYC during the Republican National Convention. Using a wireless Internet enabled bicycle outfitted with a custom-designed printing device, the Bikes Against Bush bicycle can print text messages sent from web users directly onto the streets of Manhattan in water-soluble chalk.
>
> (Kinberg 2004)[8]

As I hope this brief sample indicates, locative arts and media are a broadly and diversely constructed field, in which a range of mobiles and wireless technologies are marshalled. It is the case, however, that 3G plays a particular role, holding promise to recast location, its construction and politics in new and significant ways. Although I have not highlighted it here, I suspect there are many underlying assumptions and connections between the sorts of projects I have presented as more commercial in focus and those I have seen as more self-consciously artistic or political. Certainly research and cultural funding bodies, as well as industry parties, designers, and technology agents themselves, have seen strong affinities between the realms of commerce and the aesthetic, a much-debated topic of course. As well as accentuating tensions in the politics of cell phones, artistic and activist avant-gardes, much like in the medium of the Internet, are also increasingly dependent on everyday connection and habitation in and through mobile networks.

Fourth-generation mobiles

By 2006, there has already been quite some discussion and excitement about the prospect of fourth-generation (4G) networks. Just as it was hoped that 3G networks would be a paradigm shift, moving mobile communications far beyond their 2G predecessors, so the aspirations for 4G are already quite spectacular – if marked thus far by a lack of detail and concrete planning. Korhonen suggests one should approach 4G by thinking about what the deficits in 3G are.

A key problem is that 3G only affords a maximum of 2Mbps on its current specifications with the real effective rate being about 384 kps. To make interactive video telephony of high quality a reality this is not adequate: 'Live high-precision video requires about 2Mbps. More bandwidth is needed to deliver that kind of service to handsets' (Korhonen 2001: 473). In Japan, NTT DoCoMo has been testing wireless devices with a possible 100 Mbps speed while mobile and 1Gps while stationary, emphasising that 4G will mark a break from 3G:

> Japanese officials stress that 4G should not be seen as an evolution from 3G, but rather as a brand new technology. This research effort was started in 2001 and has caused controversy in other parts of the world, where companies perhaps feel they should reap the benefits of 3G before too much funding, time, and media attention are spent on the next generation.
>
> (Karlson et al. 2003: 162)

Another problem relates to the communications ecologies in which 3G operates. 3G cellular networks are becoming just one among a number of high data capacity portable technologies, including wireless laptop computers (using Wi-Fi or in the future Wi-Max); wireless local area networks; digital radio broadcasting; digital video broadcasting; bluetooth networks; and asynchronous technologies such as podcasting that have been very much co-produced by users and technology specialists. As well as these networks, there are also the computing and network capabilities being designed and engineered into all sorts of everyday devices not previously seen as communication and media technologies, such as fridges, groceries, books, kitchens, heating and cooling technologies, and homes. There is also the growing use of Radio Frequency Identification (RFID) technologies, small wireless devices which can be embedded in all sorts of everyday objects to be communicated with by a network. (For instance, RFID tags could be placed in every book in a library, and then these could be 'pinged' to find out their location. Or product lines in a supermarket could communicate to a central server and database when they were about to run out and needed restocking.) With this proliferation of networks, technologies, and addressable and connectable devices, one dream for 4G is actually quite an old one: convergence, especially through the agency of the Internet protocol as a common layer. Korhonen imagines:

> The 4G technology will provide for a collection of different kinds of multiple access networks in which a user can gain a portal to the Internet (or whatever the entity) by the most appropriate means. This will be a departure from a

one-network-can-do-anything approach. The networks must cooperate seam-
lessly. The user will not have to know which network provides the services.
The smart device can analyze its environment and choose the best available
service provider and technology.

(Korhonen 2001: 473–5; see also Hecker et al. 2005)

Some theorists of 4G have also suggested that it will be characterised by a focus on
the user (for example, Frattasi et al. 2005). This may well be the case, but in these
early stages this is reminiscent of another myth associated with new technologies
– namely, that this time, finally, the technologies and those that design and
arm them will be able to discern what users want, and consummate their desire
(on the user and 3G, see Vincent 2004).

11 Conclusion: mobiles as media

My starting point in this book has been to consider the cell phone and mobile technologies from a cultural standpoint. For those routinely engaged in cultural research, theory, and studies, the desire to embark upon such a study may be relatively uncontentious, and the resulting process or product hopefully a more-or-less useful contribution to knowledge. For many others, however, the very notion of cell phone or mobile culture is still something odd, a contradiction in terms, or simply indulgent. There is a very strong sense that cell phone culture, as a species of popular culture, is very much regarded as low, vulgar culture of the multitudes. While the fact is that it has instrumental uses and meets certain needs, it threatens rather than complements, extends, reconfigures or replaces proper, high culture (actually middlebrow culture, really). There is an important role here for cultural studies, as with sociology, anthropology, and other disciplines, to reclaim the sense of rich wonder and importance of the ways that people do make meaning in their everyday lives, and to make sense of how cell phone culture fits into the broad culture field and its relations to the social.

When I received a government grant to research this topic, the award was welcomed by many academic, non-government organisation and industry colleagues, but was attacked by a prominent conservative commentator as a scandalous waste of money. I was happy enough to shrug off this cheap shot, not least because it was prompted by something of a set-piece, the annual 'find-the-looniest-arts-research-grant-to-pillory' hunt by the tabloid paper in my city. As it turned out, however, the attack on the idea of taking cell phone culture seriously was part of what became a larger and far more serious attack on humanities research generally – a sustained assault taken seriously by the Minister responsible for university research funding raising genuine questions about academic independence and scholarly standards. Now I tell this story not principally to even the score (though there's that too) but to tease out a strange, persistent contradiction about how the cultural dimension of information and communications technologies – particularly mobile technologies – is regarded.

On the one hand, cell phones, Internet, and other new digital technologies are prized because of the possibilities for economic development and wealth creation they bring. After all, these are produced by some of the biggest industries on the planet, numbering among them the largest global corporations, and potentially making huge contributions to civil society and polity as well as the economic well-being of individuals and nations. It would be logical to think that research into such technologies would be welcomed and encouraged. On the other hand, social and cultural approaches to information and communications technologies are often not desired or supported. This is despite the fact that society's under-standing of the most pressing economic, not to mention philosophical or ethical issues, in information and communications technologies – trust, privacy, con-sumer expectations and desires, what content is attractive, cultures of use – would benefit from intensive investigation and wide debate of their cultural dimensions.

I am reminded here of a meeting with a well-informed telecommunications analyst for a major stockbroking firm and discussing consumer take-up of mobile services. We shared great curiosity and interest in telecommunications, but mutual incomprehension also. There was a yawning gulf between his emphasis on price as the prime, if not overriding, reason consumers might adopt or ignore certain services, and my interest in how cultural and social concerns motivated their purchasing choices, what they used the technology for, and what it meant to them in particular situations. In response to such talking past one another that is well entrenched and institutionalised in mobile technologies, an aim of this study has been to try to find ways to connect the different facets of cell phone culture, knitting together the different sides of this phenomenon as revealed by the work of arenas often regarded as separate or at least not often crossing. In this spirit I wish to conclude with some thoughts about what I hold significant for cell phone culture and mobile media's present and futures, and for those who inhabit them (willingly or otherwise), take an interest in them, or study them.

Speaking of mobiles

In the course of this book, I have discussed various conceptions and representa-tions about cell phones and mobile technologies, that have certainly shaped cell phone culture, and are widely and passionately held. The most striking of these are those that fall under the label of moral panics, but there are many others I have not touched upon that often recur – such as the addictiveness cell phones engender. There is certainly a Manichean view held by many of the ills versus the wonders of such technology, with little middle ground. It underscores that there are very deep, structuring myths about technology that are not going to go away anytime soon. The much discredited, yet hydra-headed notion of technological determinism is very much alive here, as we see in the idea that the cell phone has the 'good' power to increase dramatically our productivity and social capital, become our life-recorder, or help us powerfully organise a rally. The flip-side of this is the belief that mobile technologies are powerfully 'bad', inciting us to riot, affray, excessive sociability or solipsism, or crimes against grammar or cultural values.

Scholars and critics by virtue of our professions have a reflex response to paint in shades of grey, add tonality, and plead that things are not so simple. However, there are important concerns at stake here, that I for one am curious to find better methods to promote genuine public debate and consideration. There are, for instance, important ethical issues regarding the appropriate use of communication devices – take the case of the vast data- and image-capturing capabilities now made possible with camera, smart-phones, and other mobile media devices. In the emerging ideas, uses, and cultural practices associated with these, in the case of moblogging for instance, there are visions of recording, annotating, and sharing all sorts of personal and collective information. The debate regarding camera phones has been waylaid to a great extent by fears they will be used to take photos of vulnerable children for nefarious purposes. This has obscured much-needed, wide, and thoroughgoing debate about if or how we should regulate mobile imaging.

Where discussions of the social and cultural implications of mobile media are occurring, the principles in these are often proceeding unaware of the actual and developing cultures of use of such devices. A controversial example is the case of erotica and pornography ('adult' content or entertainment) over mobile media devices. We know from studies of Internet use that a wide cross-section of people consume pornography and do not believe it is harmful; yet this sort of understanding of patterns of consumption and beliefs of users is not entering the policy and regulatory arena. Rather, decisions shaping key aspects of mobile technologies are predicated on long-held and problematic assumptions about public attitudes, and also on the nervousness of the larger corporations offering mobile services that are keen to avoid taking risks and incurring 'brand damage' as a result. There is a traditional and very useful role that those studying and analysing social and cultural aspects of mobile media can play, and that is to communicate their knowledge and perspectives to inform and open up spaces for discussion.

Mobile designs

The importance of design has been manifest in cell phone culture, all the more critically perhaps because these communication devices have become not only mediators of much conversation and exchange but also bearers of many meanings, to do with identity, fashion, belonging, and the symbols and images that mark out collective and overarching aspects of our cultures. Design is a meeting place for ideas and practices to do with aesthetic considerations, functionality, economics, and signs, as well as engineering and marketing. Design is also the hinge between production and consumption; it is a space of translation between desires of those building and offering the technology, and those who might possibly find themselves drawn to, reflecting, using, or having such things.

Given the near chaotic, teeming field of possible shapes and directions that cell phones and mobile technologies might take, the turns they might make, the connections between design and cultural reflection will become all the thicker, and need to do so. It is no surprise that there is a lively, dense literature and body of practice on design in mobiles, and that there is much more to do still to keep open design as a site of potentiality in which all sorts of visions of use and consumption can be inscribed.

The user is dead, long live the user

In contemporary study and theory of the cell phone and mobile media, but also in corporate and management practice and philosophy, we encounter time and time again the fetish of the user. The invocation of the user is a much-needed exhortation to those deeply involved in commercial enterprise, doctrinally guided by shareholder value and management imperatives; a reminder that the meaning of technology is not in the gift of industry, ultimately. Rather technology needs to be received, completed, supplemented and found wanting, by the user.

The question of what the user wants is, like all such ponderings of desire, an interrogative that cannot be answered straightforwardly. Certainly the various representatives of the user need to be proliferated as much as possible, and inserted in the interstices of the production process. There are processes, structures, and techniques that are tried and tested to consult with, involve, join, employ, partner with, and be directed by users – and these are not used enough.

There are deeper questions, however, about what the rhetoric of the user signifies. The full implications of conceptualising the user-as-producer are only now being registered. The achievements of productive, creative users in their active, everyday appropriation and domestication of technology have not been registered in the annals of mobile technology, yet do we really need such documentation and reckoning. Among other things, such diverse cultural histories and accounts of use and consumption are needed to articulate better into multilayered mediascapes and flows of mobile culture in the present conjuncture. With the new technologies and cultural forms shaping the intersection of cell phones, audio and visual cultures, and Internet cultures – from customisation of devices, to everyday image recording, through moblogging, to peer-to-peer networks, email and messaging, and web cultures – mobile media networks, like the Internet, offer support, indeed clamour, for the user.

Media politics

The coming into being of mobile media is the next phase of what convergence has entailed: a long, complicated, unpredictable transformation of media and the cultural realm, since at least the early 1980s. The lessons from the 'information superhighway' talk of the early to mid 1990s and then the dot.com and telco crash later in that decade concerned the sheer massive scale of media changes, the twists and turns these could take, and yet also the intimate implications of all these in the conduct and bounds of daily life. Though much has been brought together, sorted out, compared, harmonised, or left as it is across media industries, I think that internationally we all are still in the process of comprehending how the distinct forms of, say, television and radio broadcasting, newspapers and magazines, cinema and music, Internet and telecommunications, computers and mobile technologies will go together. Hence, under the banner of mobile media, there are already and will continue to be crucial struggles over pivotal issues such as: what cultural forms will survive and be supported; how audiences will be imagined and served; how the new publics will be understood; in whose interest will policies be arbitrated; and, crucially, who will be involved in these arenas and decisions that will shape mobile media.

One of the pressing concerns goes directly to questions of cultural citizenship and democracy because, while the user is still much talked about, very few users are taken notice of, let alone involved, in media organisations or institutions, government or regulatory policymaking. Indeed the large and powerful mobile companies naturally work hard in the interests of their own shareholders to shape the outcomes they believe are favourable, and – though it varies across jurisdictions, depending on the democratic traditions of national or regional systems of governance – show little inclination to consult genuinely or share critical decisions over technology shaping and policy with citizens or household customers.

There is much hope vested in a new, shifting dynamic between production and consumption, where the balance is tipping, unpredictably and excitingly, in favour of the latter. Much more attention has been paid by scholars and by marketers over the past decade or more to the consumer (the relative of the user). What this has shown, as in the cases of text messaging or the innovation of disability cultures, is that consumers, through the accretion of their accidental, everyday innovations, do have considerable power to shape technologies. Further, new media technologies, forms, and cultures rely on the consumer in ways that were not possible, or required before; quite a number of the convergent mobile media technologies, such as smart phones, moblogging, or mobile Internet, rely on very active, informed, and knowledgeable consumers. There has been a groundswell of optimistic, even millenarian rhetoric about this new agency. Indeed, the assertive noisiness of individual consumers should be celebrated, but it remains unclear how multitudes of users will come together to steer change in their own interests.

Open mobile

A pressing question regarding the future of cell phones as they metamorphise irrevocably into mobile media revolves around openness, something – not straightforwardly, not unproblematically – that is critical to the exercise of cultural agency. If mobile media technologies and platforms are becoming integral to our culture, how do we ensure that all voices, identities, and people may avail themselves of these conduits and means of cultural production, consumption, and exchange, should they wish to do so? These considerations have become more complex, intractable, and hotly debated as traditional media forms have transformed over the past two decades, so I am not overly sanguine about how we can also find some consensus around equality, access, diversity, and cultural maintenance and expression when grappling with new media cultures.

I suppose that I reflect upon the inheritance of almost a century of telecommunications, and the accepted forms of governance that accumulated around these in which each nation was paramount (true, with a few clearly establishing their colonial and imperial reach into telegraph and telephone, and dominating the others), and structures of international co-ordination and co-operation were established. The national telecommunications carrier played a pre-eminent role in serving the user, employing the worker, building the industry, and providing universal service across the country's territory. There are different sorts of telecommunications culture, but the 'telco' culture I have mentioned in the course of this book relates to the way that telecommunications came to be regarded during its classic, PTT admin phase, with its apogee in the deliberate, well-documented, carefully organised technical yet intense political decision making of the International Telecommunications Union. The first such international body, and a forerunner to the United Nations, such telecommunications fora structured the participation of citizens through the putative representation of the technical and administrative personnel of the government agencies (or private monopolies in the case of the USA and to some extent Canada) that were responsible for delivering services to what were then termed subscribers.

With competitive markets established in most jurisdictions, the setting of international rules on telecommunications' place in free (though clearly not fair) trade in goods and services, and the widespread privatisation of former monopoly network operators, a new vision for telecommunications has not really emerged. And given that the cell phone came on the scene, certainly in its accelerating diffusion, from the mid-1980s onwards, as a creation of more-or-less competitive markets, the older heritage of telecommunications, crumbling as it was, has not offered a cultural or political rationale. Yet there are real issues to be confronted: for instance, if cultural material is to be carried via SMS/MMS, who decides what content is appropriate and what is not? How is access of cultural producers to networks to be safeguarded, against the countervailing property rights of network operators who feel they are entitled to a return on their investment? How open are mobile media platforms to carrying different applications, or allowing different software or applications, or permitting devices to be modified for the users own preferences or purposes? Should WAP, i-mode, portals (or other 'walled gardens'), and other online mobile protocols and configurations allow the user freedoms like the public Internet, or indeed to access the Internet, or content be freely available over television or radio sets?

I am now veering, of course, into thinking about the politics of mobile code and technologies from the perspective of computers, Internet, and other digital culture, to see what resources could be suitable for developing notions of how mobile media can be kept open for cultural activity. For instance, there is the idea of creative or open commons, much discussed and inspiring different, concrete and viable models for democratic, economically sustainable cultural exchange (as represented in the 'Creative Commons' licence, for instance). In 2005, discussion was beginning about the notion of a 'mobile commons', and while this holds promise it will need considerable elaboration to make compelling sense of the way that mobile media are developing.

In pondering all this, I am keenly aware that cell phone culture is certainly now a far larger, more radically diverse, collection of meanings, practices, and technologies than it was in the 1980s, the first decade when such telephony became commercial and publicly available. There are many ways to map the vectors of the development of mobile technologies, but schematically at least it is a movement from voice telephony to media broadly conceived. As is evident from my account, there is much we do not know or understand about the pre- and early history of the cell phone, and much work to do here. The additional challenge we face now, however, and one I certainly felt in writing this book in the midst of a technology infiltrating into and reworking all sorts of old and media forms, is the need to bring together a broad knowledge of communications, cultural and media history and theory to follow the cell phone's metamorphosis into media *par excellence*. Not only to follow, however, but also to participate actively and knowingly in the opening up and shaping of such media and technology.

Notes

2 Making voice portable

1 Apparently D. H. Ring devised the idea of cellular radio in a Bell Laboratories technical memorandum entitled 'Mobile telephony – wide area coverage', dated 11 December 1947 (Farley 2005).

2 One of those integrally involved in the European second-generation GSM digital system, Hillebrand records that the support of hand-helds as a mandatory requirement of the GSM system only occurred in June 1985. However, 'for a long time it remained unclear, whether the basic technology choices would really allow the building of small and cheap hand-helds with a low power consumption' (Hillebrand 2001e: 273).

3 The subscriber identity module (SIM) is a smart card that stores the relevant details of the phone subscriber and network, allowing these to be transferred to, and used by, a different handset.

4 For further discussion of the history of cell phones in Australia, see Goggin 2006.

3 Cool phone

1 On Nokia I rely in particular on two thorough studies: Martti Häikö's *Nokia: The Inside Story* (2002), an English abridgement and translation from the Finnish of his three-volume official corporate history (Häikö 2001); and Dan Steinbock's *The Nokia Revolution* (2001b).

2 Good information, modification software, manuals, and illustrations related to these and other early Finnish phones can be found at the 'Finnish Made PMR, Trunking and Cellular (NMT) Phone Amateur Radio Conversion' website: http://oh3tr.ele.tut.fi/english/modifications.html.

3 In a later study, Steinbock notes the similarities between Motorola's humanistic 'people values' of the mid-1980s and the late 1990s 'Nokia Way', surmising that the former's values 'became benchmarks for Motorola's Nordic rivals, including Nokia, as they engaged in internationalisation efforts of their own' (Steinbock 2003: 214).

4 For my understanding of Vodafone corporate development, I am indebted to Trevor Merriden's lively 2003 study of the corporation through the figure of CEO Chris Gent, and also Peter Curwen's succinct, useful case study focusing on the firm's reorganisation in the 1997–2001 period (Curwen 2002: 162–93).

5 Those involved in a web of interlocking share holdings and directorships included French mobile operator Vivendi (through CEO Jean-Marie Messier) and the Hong

Kong conglomerate Hutchinson Whampoa (owned by billionaire Li Ka-Shing). Hutchinson held a 44 per cent stake in Orange at that time (see Merriden 2003: 49–64 for discussion), but also held stock in Vodafone (Doward 2001).

6 Given the Orange mythology of simplicity, it is interesting that by 2005 observers were discerning a jaded company no longer having distinctive brand connotations:

> 'The problem is, Orange is all over the place,' says one leading agency chief. 'There's nothing to hold on to, no core strategy. It's almost impossible to say what the brand stands for any more. It's a real shame, because Orange used to be the best case study for a brand launch we'd ever seen . . . you find that there's still some cool left over from that original campaign even though it's over ten years old.'
>
> (Armstrong 2005)

7 Vodafone had also been negotiating with Formula One racing team Jordan, who in 2003 sued the phone company for breaking a verbal agreement when it signed with Ferrari instead (Blackstock 2003).

8 Bird formed a partnership with French defence communications technology Sagem and later with Korean and Taiwanese manufacturers and designers for components (Spurgeon and Keane 2005).

4 Txt msg

1 As well as these issues that Hillebrand chronicles, he also notes the complacent attitude in the ISDN community, as many 'saw the GSM service as a small service compared to ISDN and did not co-operate intensively' (2001e: 273). This was reinforced by the rhythms and assumptions of the traditional telecommunications culture with its enshrining of the standards setting, and so much of the technology shaping process, in the International Telecommunications Union (ITU): 'The market needs of GSM had no weight in the definition of such timetables' (2001c: 273). A delegate with an electronics background involved in the design of GSM remarks that 'we were modelling GSM on ISDN, but there were no textbooks on ISDN then – the knowledge was mainly in the PTTs [post-telegraph-telephone administrations; that is, the government-owned national carriers]' (Cox 2001: 287).

2 Another GSM standards participant, Kevin Holley, remembers that:

> During 1988 interest also increased in the cell broadcast service. The basic concept was to make text available to all phones in a particular area when they are idle (i.e. not in any kind of call). The text could be general information or 'teasers' which encourage users to make revenue-generating phone calls . . . it was envisaged that a whole range of information could be made available to users, however as the service proceeded to market it hit problems with handset implementation and investment by network operators.
>
> (Holley 2001: 418)

3 Regarding 'immediate display messages', Holley surmises that these 'caught the imagination of the more technically aware teenagers, who call them "flash text" ' (2001: 420).

4 Unicode is a common character code standard defined in 1992 that seeks to be universal in covering all major written languages, across all computer platforms and programs (see http://www.unicode.org/).

5   Discussing mobiles in Italy, Leopoldina Fortunati cites the case of SMS as evidence for her contention that the 'impossibility of sustained communication over long periods . . . has led to a new cultural interest in brevitas (the Latin virtue of brevity), and, paradoxically, has reconciled many people to writing who would not otherwise have done so' (Fortunati 2002a: 44). She is interested in the way that the cell phone 'frustrates users' attempts to communicate', and that the 'mobile phone does not seem a very communicative instrument' (43).

5 Cellular disability

1   This chapter is very much based on an earlier piece co-written with Christopher Newell, whom I thank for allowing me to rework and incorporate it in this book. The earlier version was published in A.P. Kavoori and N. Arceneaux's 2006 collection *Cultural Dialectics and the Cell Phone*.

6 Mobile panic

1   The place of the beach in settler Australian culture is well known, and it has also played an important role in the early days of cultural studies, most flamboyantly in John Fiske's 'Surfalism and sandiotics: the Beach in Oz popular culture' (Fiske 1983).

7 Intimate connections

1   Walker and Wright note that security 'was perceived by some in the first days of GSM as an unnecessary expense' (2001: 385). Whereas the focus initially was on securing the user's communications and data against eavesdropping, authentication of the user identity (and avoidance of fraud) later became a much more important consideration and rationale.
2   That encryption in GSM was a precursor to a loosening up of encryption is very interesting. The debate, especially in the USA, revolves around balancing the right of a citizen to secure the privacy of personal conversations and transactions versus the countervailing need of the state's security and law enforcement agencies reasonably to intercept communications. In the mid to late 1990s debates on the availability of encryption of Internet technology to citizens in general was a cause célèbre when the US government wished to legislate to restrict this, as in the debate over the so-called 'clipper chip' (see Gurak 1997).
3   Made prominent with the advent of the Internet, a 'celebrity sex tape is a home video of sex acts, as performed by a celebrity and his or her partner, which finds Internet and/or bootleg distribution and is made available to an audience for which it was not intended' (*Wikipedia* 2006a).

8 On mobile photography

1   Quoted in Fukutomi 2003 as cited in Okada 2005.
2   My thanks to Larissa Hjorth for this observation.
3   My attention was drawn to this by Joi Ito's chronology of milestones in moblogging, part of his handy 'Moblogging, Blogmapping and Moblogmapping related resources' (Ito 2003).
4   Because of its then limited capabilities WearCompu2 was not widely adopted, but

in 1997 Mann expressed a desire to revive this 'BlindVision' project of the 1980s (see Mann 1997).

5 In computing parlance a kludge is a 'machine, system, or program that has been improvised or "bodged" together; a hastily improvised and poorly thought-out solution to a fault or "bug" ' (OED). Though, as another source points out, a kludge is 'a method of solving a problem . . . that is inefficient, inelegant, or even unfathomable, but which nevertheless works' (*Wikipedia* 2006b).

9 The third screen

1 WAP is a layered architecture, consisting of a series of 'stacks'. In this regard it resembles the way the World Wide Web language and protocols run across the various Internet protocols and devices. However, in the original WAP specifications there was no direct correspondence between WAP and Internet protocols, so translation between a WAP-enabled handset and Internet server had to be achieved via a WAP gateway.

2 It was possible to find a solution to staying connected with the Internet Protocol version 4 (still current at the time of writing), but a better technical arrangement was created as part of Internet Protocol version 6, now being steadily implemented (see http://www.ipv6.org).

3 Rather than WML, WAP 2 uses a markup language called XHTML Mobile Profile (XHTML-MP), based on XHTML Basic, a W3C standard (for an accessible discussion on the design implications of this see Worthington 2005).

4 The Digital Video Broadcasting (DVB) project is 'an industry-led consortium of over 270 broadcasters, manufacturers, network operators, software developers, regulatory bodies and others in over 35 countries committed to designing global standards for the global delivery of digital television and data services' (http://www.dvb.org). The family of DVB standards are handled by a Joint Technical Committee of the Centre for Electrotechnical Standards (CENELEC), the European Broadcasting Union (EBU), and the European Telecommunications Standards Institute (ETSI), which latter publishes the standards.

5 Writing in 2003, Tuttlebee et al. note that the 'case for IP in a broadcast network – with constant bit-rate streams requiring guaranteed QoS [quality of service] – is still under evaluation . . . implementation in broadcast networks is unlikely to be universal and is probably some years off'. While technology development has been very rapid in mobile television, this assessment still holds much of its veracity in early 2006.

6 In November 2005, the music video for vocalist James Blunt's new single 'Goodbye My Lover' premiered on 3's mobile service was available for download to their customers, a trend apparently started by Robbie Williams's 'Misunderstood' in 2004 (Gibson 2005). Major label EMI's digital media director commented that she 'can't see a single campaign going forward that doesn't have a mobile element to it, from the lowliest act to the biggest global superstar' (Gibson 2005).

10 Next gen mobile

1 The enthusiastic reader may consult a number of detailed accounts of the byzantine 3G standards endeavours, not least the surprisingly entertaining participant treatments in Hillebrand 2001b.

2 I have focused here on the two major 3G systems, which are both broadly Wideband

CDMA in nature. There are several other proposals for a 3G standard. The holy grail of the one, unified 3G standard was sought by the International Telecommunication Union (ITU) but it ended up instead defining an 'umbrella specification' of all 3G systems 'for both technical and political reasons' (Korhonen 2001: 14). Called IMT-2000, the ITU states it will provide the 'framework for worldwide wireless access by linking the diverse systems of terrestrial and/or satellite based networks . . . [and] will exploit the potential synergy between digital mobile telecommunications technologies and systems for fixed and mobile wireless access systems' (http://www.itu.int/home/imt.html).

3 For details of 3G licensing in Western Europe and elsewhere in the world, including tables of successful bidders and the prices paid, see Curwen 2002: 55–127.

4 Fraunholz et al. divide positioning technologies into a number of different classification systems: 'sign-post systems' (determining location based on a landmark or beacon); wave-based positioning systems (using propagation properties of waves to determine position of a mobile object relative to one or more reference sites); 'dead reckoning systems' (relying on several vehicle-mounted sensors to determine a mobile object's movements); 'self-positioning systems' (where position in determined in the mobile object itself (2005: 134–5). They make the point that for the best possible positioning systems, a number of these methods will be combined.

5 Two helpful websites on mobile arts are: Dr Reinhold Grether's 'directory to mobile art and locative media' http://www.netzwissenschaft.de/mob.htm; and Golan Levin's (of *Dialtone* fame) 'Informal Catalogue of Mobile Phone Performances, Installations and Artworks', http://www.flong.com/telesymphony/related/>.

6 The development of Blast Theory's 'I Like Frank' is discussed at http://www.amutualfriend.co.uk/html/frank_about.html.

7 See also a project with an innovative way collaboratively to generate captions for photos on public display, which raises interesting questions for how mobiles fit into developments in public spheres and public discourse (Ananny, Biddick, and Strohecker 2003).

8 In August 2004 Kinberg was arrested while describing the *Bikes Against Bush* project in a media interview (Farivar 2004). He was held in jail overnight with a number of cyclists arrested by police in a sweep during the Republican National Convention. Kinberg's case was finally dismissed in January 2005.

Bibliography

Abbate, J. (1999) *Inventing the Internet*, Cambridge, MA: MIT Press.

Abberley, P. (1992) 'Counting us out: a discussion of the OPCS surveys', *Disability, Handicap and Society*, 7: 139–55.

Adams-Spink, G. (2003) 'UK debut for "blind mobile" ', *BBC News*, 21 November, http://news.bbc. co.uk/1/hi/technology/3226314.stm (accessed 1 August 2005).

Agar, J. (2003) *Constant Touch: A Global History of the Mobile Phone*, Cambridge: Icon Books.

Akwagyiram, A. (2005) 'Does "happy slapping" exist?', *BBC News*, 12 May, http://news.bbc.co.uk/1/hi/uk/4539913.stm.

Albrecht, G.L., Seelman, K.D. and Bury, M. (eds) (2001) *Handbook of Disability Studies*, London and Thousand Oaks, CA: Sage.

Alder, G. (2003) 'Squidgygate revisited', *nth position*, http://www.nthposition.com/squidgygate.php (accessed 28 December 2005).

Ali-Yrkkö, J. and Hermans, R. (2004) 'Nokia: a giant in the Finnish innovation system', in G. Schienstock (ed.), *Embracing the Knowledge Economy: The Dynamic Transformation of the Finnish Innovation System*, Cheltenham: Edward Elgar, pp. 106–27.

Ali-Yrkkö, J., Paija, L., Reilly, C. and Ylä-Anttila, P. (2000) *Nokia: A Big Company in a Small Country*, Helsinki: The Research Institute of the Finnish Economy (ETLA).

Ali-Yrkkö, J., Paija, L., Rouvinen, P. and Ylä-Anttila, P. (2004) 'Nokia: an extended company with local and global operations', in P.N. Gooderham and O. Nordhaug (eds), *International Management: Cross-boundary Challenges*, Oxford and Maiden, MA: Blackwell, pp. 399–411.

Altman, B.M. (2001) 'Disability definitions, models, classification schemes, and applications', in G.L. Albrecht, K.D. Seelman and M. Bury (eds), *Handbook of Disability Studies*, Thousand Oaks, CA: Sage, pp. 97–122.

American National Standards Institute (ANSI) (2001) *Method of Measurement of Compatibility between Wireless Communication Devices and Hearing Aids, C63.19*, Washington, DC: ANSI.

America Online (AOL) and MCI (2004) 'America Online and MCI enable deaf and hard-of-hearing individuals to receive incoming calls anywhere, anytime using their own, unique phone number', media release, 13 December, http://www.timewarner.com/corp/newsroom/pr/0,20812,1007089,00.html (accessed 24 June 2005).

Andrews, D.L. and Jackson, S.J. (eds) (2001) *Sport Stars: Cultural Politics of Sporting Celebrity*, London and New York: Routledge.

Ang, I. (ed.) (1996) *Living Room Wars: Rethinking Media Audiences for a Postmodern World*, London: Routledge.

Ang, I. et al. (eds) (1997) *Planet Diana: Cultural Studies and Global Mourning*, Sydney: Research Centre in Intercommunal Studies, University of Western Sydney.

Ananny, M., Biddick, K. and Strohecker, C. (2003) 'Constructing public discourse with ethnographic/SMS "texts"', in L. Chittaro (ed.), *Mobile HCI 2003*, Berlin and Heidelberg: Springer. Available at http://citeseer.ist.psu.edu/anannyoz03constructing.html.

Araki, K. (1968) 'Fundamental problems of nation-wide mobile radio telephone system', *Rev. Electrical Communications Laboratories*, 16: 357–73.

Armstrong, S. (2005) 'Brand on the run', *Guardian.co.uk*, 5 September.

Arthur, C. (2004) 'Becks, texts and a message for us all', *Independent*, 6 April.

Atkinson, D. (1992) 'Rabbit to revive Telepoint mobile telephone system', *Guardian*, 12 October.

Attman, A., Kuuse, J., Olsson, U. and Jacobæus, C. (1977) *L.M. Ericsson 100 Years*, 3 vols, Stockholm: L. M. Ericsson.

Australian Broadcasting Corporation (ABC) (2004) 'Rumsfeld bans camera phones in Iraq', *ABC News Online*, http://www.abc.net.au/news/newsitems/s1114150.htm (accessed 8 January 2006).

Australian Bureau of Statistics (ABS) (2004) *Disability, Ageing and Carers: Summary of Findings*, Canberra: ABS.

Australian Competition and Consumer Commission (ACCC) (1998) *Competition in Data Markets: A Final Report on Whether to Declare Certain ISDN Services . . .*, Canberra: Commonwealth of Australia.

Australian Science and Technology Council (ASTEC) (1995) *Surf's Up: Alternative Futures for Full Service Networks in Australia: A Foresighting Study: Information and Communications Technology 2010*, Canberra: Australian Government Publishing Service.

Bailey, L.W. (2005) *The Enchantments of Technology*, Urbana: University of Illinois Press.

Baker, J.W. (1970) *A History of the Marconi Company*, London: Methuen.

Bakken, F. (2005) 'SMS use among deaf teens and young adults in Norway', in R. Harper, L. Palen and A. Taylor (eds), *The Inside Text: Social, Cultural and Design Perspectives on SMS*, Dordrecht: Springer, pp. 161–74.

Balnaves, M., O'Regan, T. and Sternberg, J. (eds) (2002) *Mobilising the Audience*, Brisbane: University of Queensland Press.

Barber, J. (1990) 'Telecom also-rans', letter to the editor, *Sydney Morning Herald*, 21 July.

Barendregt, B. (2005) 'The ghost in the phone and other tales of Indonesian modernity', in A. Lin (ed.), *Proceedings of International Conference on Mobile Communication and Asian Modernities, 7–8 June, City University of Hong Kong, Kowloon*. Hong Kong: City University of Hong Kong.

Barker, M. (ed.) (1984) *The Video Nasties*, London: Pluto.

Barlow, G. and Hill, A. (eds) (1997) *Video Violence and Children*, London: Hodder and Stoughton.

Barnes, C. and Mercer, G. (2003) *Disability*, Cambridge: Polity Press.

Baron, N. (2000) *Alphabet to Email: How Written English Has Evolved and Where It's Heading*, London and New York: Routledge.

Baron, N.S., Squires, L., Tench, S. and Thompson, M. (2005) 'Tethered or mobile? Use of away messages in instant messaging by American college students', in R. Ling and P.E. Pederson (eds) *Mobile Communications: Re-negotiation of the Social Sphere*, London: Springer, pp. 293–311.

Barthes, R. (1985) *The Grain of the Voice: Interviews, 1962–1980*, trans. Linda Coverdale, New York: Hill and Wang.

Beck, U. (1992) *Risk Society*, trans. M. Ritter, London: Sage.

Becker, M. (2005) 'Now Paris is burning in cell hell', *New York Daily News*, 23 February, Sports Final edition.

Bell, G. (2005) 'The age of the thumb: a cultural reading of mobile technologies from Asia', in P. Glotz and S. Bertschi (eds), *Thumb Culture: Social Trends and Mobile Phone Use*, Bielefeld: Transcript Verlag, pp. 67–88.

Belson, K. (2004) 'Teaching an old walkman some new steps', *New York Times*, 19 April.

Benady, A. (2005) 'Mixed signals over mobile TV', *MediaGuardian*, 28 November, http://media.guardian.co.uk (accessed 28 December 2005).

Berg, S., Taylor, A.S. and Harper, R. (2005) 'Gift of the gab', in R. Harper, L. Palen and A. Taylor (eds), *The Inside Text: Social, Cultural and Design Perspectives on SMS*, Dordrecht: Springer, pp. 271–85.

Berger, M.S. (1997) 'Hearing aid compatibility with wireless communications devices', in *Proceedings of the IEEE International Symposium on Electromagnetic Compatibility*, pp. 123–8.

Bernstein, J. (1984) *Three Degrees Above Zero: Bell Laboratories in the Information Age*, Cambridge: Cambridge University Press.

Berry, C., Martin, F. and Yue, A. (eds) (2003) *Mobile Cultures: New Media in Queer Asia*, Durham, NC: Duke University Press.

Best, J. (1990) *Threatened Children: Rhetoric and Concern about Child-victims*, Chicago: University of Chicago Press.

Bird, S. (2004) 'Sex-text claim could cost Beckham dear', *The Times*, 5 April.

Blackstock, C. (2003) 'A £100m deal of trouble in F1 case', *Guardian*, 18 June http://www.guardian.co.uk (accessed 13 September 2005).

Blast Theory (2004a) 'I Like Frank', http://www.blasttheory.co.uk/bt/work_ilikefrank.html (accessed 4 January 2006).

—— (2004b) 'Uncle Roy All Around You', http://www.blasttheory.co.uk/bt/work_uncleroy.html (accessed 8 November 2005).

—— (2005) 'Can You See Me Now?', http://www.blasttheory.co.uk/bt/work_cysmn.html (accessed 8 November 2005).

Blondheim, M. (1994) *News over the Wires: The Telegraph and the Flow of Public Information in America, 1844–1897*, Cambridge, MA: Harvard University Press.

Blundell, N. and Blackhall, S. (1992) *Fall of the House of Windsor*, London: Blake.

Bolter, J.D. and Grusin, R. (1999) *Remediation: Understanding New Media*, Cambridge, MA: MIT Press.

Bonner, F. (2003) *Ordinary Television: Analysing Popular TV*, London: Sage.

Bourdieu, P. with Boltanski et al. (1965) *Un Art moyen: essai sur les usages sociaux de la photo*, Paris: Les Éditions de Minuit; trans. S. Whiteside (1990), *Photography: A Middle-Brow Art?*, Cambridge: Polity Press.

Bowe, F. (2002) 'Deaf and hard of hearing Americans' instant messaging and e-mail use: a national survey', *American Annals of the Deaf*, 147: 6–10.

Boyd, B. (2003) 'Talk is a CWOT when you can txt', *Irish Times*, 11 October.

Brock, G. (2003) *The Second Information Revolution*, Cambridge, MA: Harvard University Press.

Brooks, L. (2005) 'Monsters in the making', *Guardian*, 7 June, http://www.guardian.co.uk (accessed 20 September 2005).

Brooks, S. (2004) 'Vodafone sticks with Beckham', *MediaGuardian*, 17 August, http://media.guardian.co.uk (accessed 15 September 2005).

Brown, B., Green, N. and Harper, R. (eds) (2002) *Wireless World: Social, Cultural and Interactional Issues in Mobile Communications and Computing*, London: Springer.

Bruce, R. V. (1973) *Bell: Alexander Graham Bell and the Conquest of Solitude*, Ithaca, NY and London: Cornell University Press.

Bruns, A. and Jacobs, J. (eds) (2006) *Uses of Blogs*, New York: Peter Lang.

Buckingham, D. (1996) *Moving Images: Understanding Children's Emotional Responses to Television*, Manchester: Manchester University Press.

Bull, M. (2005) *Sound Moves: iPod Culture and Urban Experience*, London: Routledge.

Burgess, A. (2004) *Cellular Phones, Public Fears, and a culture of Precaution*, New York: Cambridge University Press.

Burke, N. (2005) 'Telltale signs of the sext maniac', *Daily Telegraph* (Sydney), 2 July.

Burton, D. (2004) 'The signal gets stronger: three cell phones with speech output', *AccessWorld*, 5.4, http://www.afb.org/afbpress/pub.asp?DocID=aw050406.

—— (2005a) 'Two more approaches: a review of the LG VX 4500 cell phone from Verizon Wireless and Microsoft's Voice Command Software', *AccessWorld*, 6.3, http://www.afb.org/afbpress/pub.asp?DocID=aw060308.

—— (2005b) 'You get to choose: an overview of accessible cell phones', *AccessWorld*, 6.2, http://www.afb.org/afbpress/pub.asp?DocID=aw060206.

Burton, D. and Uslan, M. (2003) 'Answering the call: top-of-the-line cell phones, part 1', *AccessWorld*, 4.3, http://www.afb.org/afbpress/pub.asp?DocID=aw040302.

—— (2004a) 'Do cell phones equal software equal access: part 1?', *AccessWorld*, 5.1, http://www.afb.org/afbpress/pub.asp?DocID=aw040606.

—— (2004b) 'Do cell phones equal software equal access: part 2?' *AccessWorld*, 5.1, http://www.afb.org/afbpress/pub.asp?DocID=aw050106.

Burton, D., Uslan, M., Schnell, K. and Swisher, C. (2003) 'Answering the call: top-of-the-line cell phones, part 2', *AccessWorld*, 4.4, http://www.afb.org/afbpress/pub.asp?DocID=aw040404.

Burwood, E. and Le Strange, R. (1993) *Interference to Hearing Aids by the New Digital Mobile Telephone Systems, Global Systems for Mobile (GSM) Communications Standard*, Sydney: National Acoustic Laboratories.

Business Review Weekly (1989) 'Blue caller', *Business Review Weekly*, 26 May.

Bye, C. (1997) 'Fat pockets, big toys fill empty nests', *Sun-Herald* (Sydney), 14 September.

Camarillo, G. and Garcia-Martin, M.-A. (2004) *The 3G IP Multimedia Subsystem: Merging the Internet and the Cellular Worlds*, New York: John Wiley.

Cantlon, G. (1992) 'Aussies put a ring in their pocket', *Sun-Herald* (Sydney), 15 March, 115.

Carson, D.N. (1977) 'The evolution of picturephone service', in G. Shiers (ed.), *The Telephone: A Historical Anthology*, New York: Arno Press, pp. 282–91; reprinted from *Bell Laboratories Record*, 46.9 (1968).

Carvel, J. (2005) 'Thousands of pupils bullied by camera phone', *Guardian*, 7 June.

Cashmore, E. (2002) *Beckham*, Oxford: Polity Press.

Caumont, A. (2005) 'Start-up', *Washington Post*, 30 May, EO5.

Chandler, A. and Neumark, N. (2005) *At a Distance: Precursors to Art and Activism on the Internet*, Cambridge MA: MIT Press.

Channel 4 (2005) 'Mobile services', http://www.channel4.com/life/microsites/M/mobile_services/index.html (accessed 8 December 2005).

Chapman, S. and Wutzke, S. (1997) 'Not in our back yard: media coverage of community opposition to mobile phone towers: an application of Sandman's outrage model of risk perception', *Australian and New Zealand Journal of Public Health*, 21: 614–20.

Cheung, L. (2003) 'A perspective on the mobile markets in Japan and Korea', paper presented at the Digital News, Social Change and Globalization Conference, Hong Kong Baptist University, 11–12 December, http://www.trp.hku.hk/papers/2003/japan3.pdf (accessed 26 May 2005).

Clarke, R. (2004), 'An Internet primer: technology and governance', in G. Goggin (ed.), *Virtual Nation: The Internet in Australia*, Sydney: University of NSW Press, pp. 13–27.

Coates, K. and Holroyd, C. (2003) *Japan and the Internet Revolution*, Houndsmill, Basingstoke: Palgrave Macmillan.

Code Factory (2005) 'Mobile accessibility', http://www.codefactory.es/mobile_accessibility/maccessibility (accessed 24 June 2005).

Coe, L. (1993) *The Telegraph: A History of Morse's Invention and Its Predecessors in the United States*, London: McFarland.

Cohen, S. (1972) *Folk Devils and Moral Panics: The Creation of the Mods and Rockers*, London: MacGibbon and Kee.

Column 8 (1992a) 'A long story but stay with it', *Sydney Morning Herald*, 1 October.

—— (1992b) 'Those mobile phones go everywhere, *Sydney Morning Herald*, 12 September.

Constable, N. (1997) *Maid to Order in Hong Kong: Stories of Filipina Workers*, Ithaca, NY: Cornell University Press.

Courier-Mail (2005) 'Lurid text messages define affair', *Courier-Mail* (Brisbane), 29 June.

Cox, A. (2001) 'Services and services' capabilities: section 2: the years from mid-1998 to early 2001', in F. Hillebrand (ed.), *GSM and UMTS: The Creation of Global Mobile Communication*, New York: John Wiley, pp. 286–300.

Cox, K. (1999) 'Mobiles sending our kids bankrupt', *Daily Telegraph* (Sydney), 31 January.

Crace, J. (2005) 'Graham Barnfield: they thought he was an expert. He is now', *Guardian*, 7 June, http://guardian.co.uk (accessed 5 October 2005).

Critcher, C. (2003) *Moral Panics and the Media*, Buckingham: Open University Press.

Cronin, A. (2004) *Advertising Myths: The Strange Half-lives of Images and Commodities*, London: Routledge.

Crystal, D. (2000) *Who Cares about English Usage?*, 2nd edn, London: Penguin.

—— (2002) *The English Language*, London: Penguin.

—— (2003) *English as a Global Language*, 2nd edn, Cambridge and New York: Cambridge University Press.

—— (2004) *A Glossary of Netspeak and Textspeak*, Edinburgh: Edinburgh University Press.

Culf, A. (2005) 'Forget TV, mobiles are the small-screen future', *Guardian Unlimited*, www.guardian.co.uk, 22 September (accessed 8 December 2005).

Cummins, F. (2005) 'How low can they go?', 21 May, *Mirror.co.uk*, http://mirror.co.uk (accessed 15 September 2005).

Cummins F., Showbiz, and Moyes, S. (2004) 'Beckham sex sensation', 5 April, *Mirror.co.uk*, http://mirror.co.uk (accessed 15 September 2005).

Curwen, P. (2002) *The Future of Mobile Communications: Awaiting the Third Generation*, Houndsmill, Basingstoke: Palgrave Macmillan.

Daily Telegraph (1996) 'Our elderly revel in new technology', *Daily Telegraph* (Sydney), 11 November.

—— (1997) 'Work hours are on the rise', *Daily Telegraph* (Sydney), 29 September.

Daisuke, O. and Ito, M. (2003) 'Camera phones changing the definition of picture-worthy', *Japan Media Review*, 28 August, http://www.ojr.org/japan/wireless/1062208524.php (accessed 7 January 2006).

da Silva, J.S., Niepold, R., Fernandez, B., Beijer, T. and Huber, J. (2001) 'The UMTS related work of the European Commission, UMTS Task Force, UMTS Forum and GSM Association', in F. Hillebrand (ed.), *GSM and UMTS: The Creation of Global Mobile Communication*, New York: John Wiley, pp. 115–46.

Davies, J. (2001) *Diana, a Cultural History: Gender, Race, Nation, and the People's Princess*, Houndmills, Basingstoke and New York: Palgrave.

Day, J. (2004a) 'Beckham grants Vodafone voice rights', *MediaGuardian*, 14 August, http://media.guardian.co.uk (accessed 1 October 2005).

—— (2004b) 'Beckhams' PR guru left out in the cold', *MediaGuardian*, 6 August, http://media.guardian.co.uk (accessed 1 October 2005).

—— (2005) 'Oil blast fuels explosion in citizen journalism', *MediaGuardian*, 12 December, http://media.guardian.co.uk (accessed 8 January 2006).

de Sola Pool, I. (1983) *Forecasting the Telephone: A Retrospective Technology Assessment*, Norwood, NJL Ablex.

—— (ed.) (1997) *The Social Impact of the Telephone*, Cambridge MA: MIT Press.

de Souza e Silva, A. (2004) 'Art by telephone: from static to mobile interfaces', *Leonardo Electronic Almanac*, 12.10, http://mitpress2.mit.edu/e-journals/LEA/TEXT/Vol_12/lea_v12_n10.txt; also available at: http://www.flong.com/telesymphony/press/souza/ (accessed 4 January 2006).

Devine, M. (2004), 'At last, girls find a way to break free', *Sydney Morning Herald*, 24 November.

Dickson, D. (2005) 'The case for a "deficit model" of science communication', *Science and Development Network*, 27 June, http://www.scidev.net/editorials/index.cfm?fuseaction=printarticle&itemid=162&language=1 (accessed 11 January 2006).

Dietze, C. (2005) 'The smart card in mobile communications: enabler of next-generation (NG) services', in M. Pagani (ed.), *Mobile and Wireless Systems Beyond 3G*, Hershey, PA: IRM Press, pp. 221–53.

Disley, J. (2005a) 'Battered by the happy slapping cowards: ordeal of Becky, 16', *Mirror.co.uk*, 20 May, http://mirror.co.uk (accessed 20 October 2005).

—— (2005b) 'Girl, 16, is held over beating of Becky', *Mirror.co.uk*, 21 May, http://mirror.co.uk (accessed 20 October 2005).

—— (2005c) 'Slapper snappers could be charged', *Mirror.co.uk*, 20 May, http://mirror.co.uk (accessed 20 October 2005).

Donner, J. (2003) 'What mobile phones mean to Rwandan entrepeneurs', in K. Nyíri (ed.), *Mobile Democracy: Essays on Society, Self and Politics*, Vienna: Passagen Verlag, pp. 1–21.

—— (2005) 'Research approaches to mobile use in the developing world: a review of the literature', in A. Lin (ed.), *Proceedings of International Conference on Mobile communication and Asian modernities, 7–8 June, City University of Hong Kong, Kowloon*. Hong Kong: City University of Hong Kong, pp. 75–97.

Dorros, I. (ed.) (1987) *Integrated Services Digital Network: Evolving to ISDN in North America*, proceedings of the Regional Conference of the International Council for Computer Communication, ICCC-ISDN '87, Dallas, Texas, September 15–17 1987, Amsterdam and New York: Elsevier.

Doward, J. (2001) 'Weak signals from Vodafone', *Guardian*, 3 June.

Drakopoulou, S. (2006) 'Kino-phone: location, broadcast and autonomy', *Southern Review*, 38.2 (forthcoming).

du Gay, P., Hall, S., Janes, L., Mackay, H. and Negus, K. (1997) *Doing Cultural Studies: The Story of the Sony Walkman*, Milton Keynes: Open University; Thousand Oaks, CA: Sage.

du Gay, P. and Pryke, M. (eds) (2002) *Cultural Economy*, Thousand Oaks, CA: Sage.

Eastway, J. (1997) 'What Australians are doing with their money', *Sydney Morning Herald*, 26 February.

The Economist (2005a) 'Anyone for telly? TV on mobile phones', *The Economist*, 16 September.

—— (2005b) 'Television on your mobile phone: both fixed and mobile operators are getting into television', *The Economist*, 15 January.

Edmund, S. and Crutcher, M. (2005) 'Warnie hit with new text claims', *Hobart Mercury*, 28 March.

Eldridge, J., Kitzinger, J. and Williams, K. (1997) *The Mass Media and Power in Modern Britain*, Oxford: Oxford University Press.

Elgood, G. (1992) 'Callers ring mystery Diana "love tape" ', *Reuters News*, 25 August.

Elwood-Clayton, B. (2003) 'Virtual strangers: young love and texting in the Filipino archipelago of cyberspace', in K. Nyíri (ed.), *Mobile Democracy: Essays on Society, Self and Politics*, Vienna: Passagen Verlag, pp. 225–35. Online. Available at: http://21st.century.phil-inst.hu/Passagen_engl3_Ellwood.pdf (accessed 20 December 2005).

—— (2005) 'Desire and loathing in the cyber Philippines', in R. Harper, L. Palen and A. Taylor (eds), *The Inside Text: Social, Cultural and Design perspectives on SMS*, Dordrecht: Springer, pp. 195–211.

English. B. (2005a) 'Bored of the rings', *Herald Sun* (Melbourne), 11 June.

—— (2005b) 'No text please I'm Warnie', *Daily Telegraph* (Sydney), 11 June.

—— (2005c) 'Warne's SMS mate revealed', 27 June, *Herald Sun* (Melbourne), 1.

Engström, K. (2000) 'Mobile and interactivity: the saviour of digital terrestrial broadcasting', *EBU Technical Review*, 285, http://www.ebu.ch/en/technical/trev/trev_285-engstrom.pdf.

European Telecommunications Standards Institute (ETSI) (1993) *Technical Report, GSM 05.90, GSM EMC Considerations*, Sophia-Antipolis: European Telecommunications Standards Institute.

Evers, J. (2005) 'Hilton hacker sentenced to juvenile hall', *CNET News.com*, 14 September, http://news.com.com/ (accessed 7 January 2006).

Farivar, C. (2004) 'Cops put brakes on bike protest', *Wired.com*, 31 August, http://www.wired.com/news/culture/0,1284,64782,00.html (accessed 15 November 2005).

Farley, T. (2005) 'Mobile telephone history', *Privateline.com*, http://www.privateline.com/PCS/history.htm (accessed 28 December 2005).

Featherstone, M., Thrift, N. and Urry, J. (eds) (2004) 'Automobilities', special issue, *Theory, Culture & Society*, 21.4.

Federal Communications Commission (FCC) (2003) 'FCC acts to promote accessibility of digital wireless phones to individuals with hearing disabilities', media release, 10 July, http://hraunfoss.fcc.gov/edocs_public/attachmatch/DOC–236430A1.pdf (accessed 30 June 2005).

Federal Communications Commission (FCC) (2004) 'A history of pagers', http://www.fcc.gov/kidszone/history_pager.html.

—— (2005a) 'Enhanced 911 – wireless services', http://www.fcc.gov/911/enhanced/.

—— (2005b) *In the matters of IP-enabled services, e911 requirements for IP-enabled service providers . . . first report and order and notice of proposed rulemaking*, http://hraunfoss.fcc.gov/edocs_public/attachmatch/FCC–05–116A1.pdf (accessed 15 November 2005).

Finnila, R. (2005) 'Fingers do the talking', *Courier-Mail* (Brisbane), 16.

Fischer, C. (1992) *America Calling: A Social History of the Telephone to 1940*, Berkeley: University of California Press.

Fiske, J. (1983) 'Surfalism and sandiotics: the beach in Oz popular culture', *Australian Journal of Popular Culture*, 1: 120–49.

—— (1987) *Television Culture*, London and New York: Routledge.

—— (1989) *Reading the Popular*, Boston: Unwin Hyman.

—— (2000) 'Surveillance and the self: some issues for cultural studies', keynote address to the *Television: past, present and futures* conference, University of Queensland, Brisbane, 1–3 December.

Flichy, P. (1991) 'The losers win: a comparative history of two innovations: videotext and the videodisc', in J. Jouët, P. Flichy and P. Beaud (eds), *European Telematics: The Emerging Economy of Words*, Amsterdam: North Holland, pp. 73–86.

—— (2002) 'New media history', in L. Lievrouw and S. Livingstone (ed.), *The Handbook of New Media*, Thousand Oaks, CA: Sage, pp. 136–50.

Fortunati, L. (2002) 'Italy: stereotypes, true and false', in J.E. Katz and M. Aakhus (eds), *Perpetual Contact: Mobile Communication, Private Talk, Public Performance*, Cambridge: Cambridge University Press.

Fortunati, L., Katz, J.E. and Riccini, R. (eds) (2003) *Mediating the Human Body: Technology, Communication, and Fashion*, Mahwah, NJ: Lawrence Erlbaum.

Frattasi, S., Fathi, H., Fitzek, F., Katz, M. and Prasad, R. (2005) 'A pragmatic methodology to design 4G: from the user to the technology', *Lecture Notes in Computer Science*, 3420: 366–73.

Fraunholz, B., Unnithan, C. and Jung, J. (2005) 'Tracking and tracing applications of 3G for SMEs', in M. Pagani (ed.), *Mobile and Wireless Systems Beyond 3G*, Hershey, PA: IRM Press, pp. 130–54.

Frith, K.T. and Mueller, B. (2003) *Advertising and Societies: Global Issues*, New York: Peter Lang.

Fukutomi, T. (2003) *Hitto Shouhin no Butaiura (The Back Stage of Hit Products)*, Tokyo: Ascii.

Funk, J.L. (1998) 'Competition between regional standards and the success and failure of firms in the world-wide mobile communication market', *Telecommunications Policy*, 22: 419–44.

—— (2001) *The Mobile Internet: How Japan Dialed Up and the West Disconnected*, Pembroke, Bermuda: ISI Publications.

—— (2002) *Global Competition Between and Within Standards*, London: Palgrave.

Funston, A. and MacNeill, K. (1999) *Mobile Matters: Young People and Mobile Phones*, Melbourne: Communications Law Centre.

Garnet, R.W. (1985) *The Telephone Enterprise: The Evolution of the Bell System's Horizontal Structure, 1876–1909*, Baltimore: Johns Hopkins University Press.

Gerpott T.J. and Jakopin N.M. (2005) 'The degree of internationalization and the financial performance of European mobile network operators', *Telecommunications Policy*, 29: 635–61.

Gibbs, S. (1990) 'Smooth operators', *Sun-Herald* (Sydney), 29 July.

Gibson, M. (1997) 'Upwardly mobile students', *Daily Telegraph* (Sydney), 29 January.

Gibson, O. (2005) 'ITV to put top programmes on mobiles phones', *Guardian*, 7 September, www.guardian.co.uk (accessed 8 December 2005).

Gizmag (2004) 'Two new products modelled to teen lifestyle', *Gizmag*, http://www.gizmag.com.au/go/3131/ (accessed 7 January 2006).

Glotz, P. and Bertschi, S. (eds) (2005) *Thumb Culture: Social Trends and Mobile Phone Use*, Bielefeld: Transcript Verlag.

Goggin, G. (ed.) (2004) *Virtual Nation: The Internet in Australia*, Sydney: University of NSW Press.

—— (2006) 'Notes on the history of the mobile phone in Australia' *Southern Review*, 39 (forthcoming).

Goggin, G. and Newell, C. (2003) *Digital Disability: The Social Construction of Disability in New Media*, Lanham, MD: Rowman & Littlefield.

—— (2004) 'Disabled e-nation: telecommunications, disability and national policy', *Prometheus: Journal of Issues in Technological Change, Innovation, Information Economics, Communication and Science Policy*, 22: 411–22.

—— (2005a) *Disability in Australia: Exposing a Social Apartheid*, Sydney: University of NSW Press.

—— (2005b) 'Foucault on the phone: disability and the mobility of government', in S. Tremain (ed.), *Foucault and the Government of Disability*, Ann Arbor: University of Michigan Press.

—— (2005c) 'Technology and disability', special double-issue of *Disability Studies Quarterly*, 25.2 and 3, http://www.dsq-sds.org/_articles_html/2005/spring/.

—— (eds) (2006) 'Disability, identity, and interdependence', special issue of *Information, Communication & Society*.

Goggin, G. and Noonan, T. (2006) 'Blogging disability: the interface between new cultural movements and Internet technology', in A. Bruns and J. Jacobs (eds), *Uses of Blogs*, New York: Peter Lang.

Goggin, G. and Spurgeon, C. (2005) 'Mobile message services and communications policy', *Prometheus: Journal of Issues in Technological Change, Innovation, Information Economics, Communication and Science Policy*, 23: 181–93.

—— (2006) 'Premium rate culture', mss.

Goggin, G. and Thomas, J. (eds) (2006) Special issues on 'Cultures and histories of mobiles', *Southern Review*, 39, in press.

Goode, E. and Ben-Yahuda, N. (1994) *Moral Panics: The Social Construction of Deviance*, Oxford and Cambridge, MA: Blackwell.

Gottlieb, N. (2000) *Word-Processing Technology in Japan: Kanji and the Keyboard*, Richmond: Curzon.

Gottlieb, N. and McLelland, M. (eds) (2003) *Japanese Cybercultures*, London: Routledge.

—— (2002) 'Who's watching whom? Surveillance, regulation and accountability in mobile relations', in B. Brown, N. Green and R. Harper (eds), *Wireless World: Social, Cultural and Interactional Issues in Mobile Communications and Computing*, London: Springer, pp. 32–45.

Green, N., Harper, R., Murtagh, G. and Cooper, G. (2001) 'Configuring the mobile user: sociological and industry views', *Personal and Ubiquitous Computing*, 5: 146–56.

Greenfield, A. (2002a) 'Moblogging', *Adam Greenfield: Studies and Observations*, 5 November, http://www.v-2.org/displayArticle.php?article_num=59#59 (accessed 9 January 2006).

—— (2002b) 'Moblogging as, um, CRM enhancement', *Adam Greenfield: Studies and Observations*, 27 November, http://www.v-2.org/displayArticle.php?article_num=185 (accessed 9 January 2006).

Gross, L.P., Katz, J.S. and Ruby, J. (eds) (2003) *Image Ethics in the Digital Age*, Minneapolis: University of Minnesota Press.

Guardian (1992) ' "Misery" life for royal snooper who sold tape to the Sun newspaper', *Guardian*, 9 September.

—— (1993) 'Caught in the tender tap – Royal scandal', *Guardian*, 14 January, 4.

—— (2000) 'United announce £30m Vodafone sponsorship', *Guardian*, 11 February, http://football.guardian.co.uk/ (accessed 15 October 2005).

—— (2005a) 'Spooks is part of BBC game plan', *MediaGuardian*, 6 November, mediaguardian.co.uk (accessed 2 December 2005).

—— (2005b) 'Teenager bailed in "happy slapping" inquiry', *Guardian*, 20 May, http://guardian.co.uk (accessed 20 September 2005).

Gurak, L.J. (1997) *Persuasion and Privacy in Cyberspace: The Online Protests over Lotus MarketPlace and the Clipper Chip*, New Haven, CT, and London: Yale University Press.

Haddon, L. (2003) 'Domestication and mobile telephony', in J.E. Katz (ed.), *Machines That Become Us: The Social Context of Personal Communication Technology*, New Brunswick, NJ: Transaction Publishers, pp. 43–56.

—— (2004) *Information and Communication Technologies in Everyday Life: A Concise Introduction and Research Guide*, Oxford and New York: Berg.

—— (2005) 'Research questions for the evolving communications landscape', in R. Ling and P.E. Pederson (eds), *Mobile Communications: Re-negotiation of the Social Sphere*, London: Springer, pp. 7–22.

Häikö, M. (2001) *Nokia Oyj: n historia*, 3 vols, Helsinki: Edita Oyj.

—— (2002) *Nokia: The Inside Story*, trans. Olli V. Virtanen, London: Pearson Education.

Hall, J. (2002) 'From weblog to moblog', *The Feature*, 21 November, http://www.thefeature.com/article?articleid=24815&ref=7263644 (accessed 8 May 2005).

Hall, S. (1996) 'On postmodernism and articulation', in D. Morley and K.-H. Chen (eds), *Stuart Hall: Critical Dialogues in Cultural Studies*, London: Routledge.

Hall, S. et al. (1978) *Policing the Crisis: Mugging, the State, and Law and Order*, London: Macmillan.

Hall, T. (2005) 'Behold the golden age of television', *MediaGuardian*, 6 November, http://media.guardian.co.uk (accessed 7 December 2005).

Hamill, L. and Lasen, A. (eds) (2005) *Mobile World: Past, Present and Future*, London: Springer.

Hamilton, A. (1992) 'Watchdog bans Sun "Diana" phone line – ICSTIS', *The Times*, 4 September.

Hansen, J. (2001) 'The short answer: mobile messaging starts slowly in Hong Kong', *Asiaweek.com*, 27.11, 23 March, http://www.asiaweek.com/asiaweek/technology/article/0,8707,102611,00.html (accessed 25 May 2005).

Haque, U. (2000) 'Japanese whispers', http://www.octodog.com/usman/index2.html? http://www.octodog.com/usman/jw.html (accessed 6 January 2006).

Harkins, J. and Barbin, C. (2002) 'Cell phones get smart – and more accessible', *Silent News*, http://tap.gallaudet.edu/WirelessTelecom/AccessibleCell.htm (accessed 12 May 2005).

Harper, P. (2003) 'Networking the Deaf nation', *Australian Journal of Communication*, 30: 153–66.

Harper, R. (2003) 'Are mobiles good or bad for society?' in K. Nyíri (ed.), *Mobile Democracy: Essays on Society, Self and Politics*, Vienna: Passagen Verlag.

Harper, R., Palen, L. and Taylor, A. (eds) (2005) *The Inside Text: Social, Cultural and Design Perspectives on SMS*, Dordrecht: Springer.

Hartley, J. (1992) *The Politics of Pictures: The Creation of the Public in the Age of Popular Media*, London: Routledge.

—— (1996) *Popular Reality: Journalism, Modernity, Popular Culture*, London and New York: Arnold.

Head, B. (1990) 'Yuppie stockbrokers found mobile phones invaluable', *Australian Financial Review*, 8 May.

Headrick, D.R. (1991) *The Invisible Weapon: Telecommunications and International Politics, 1851–1945*, New York and Oxford: Oxford University Press.

Hecker, A., Labiod, H., Pujolle, G., Afifi, H., Serrhouchni, A. and Urien, P. (2005) 'A new access control solution for a multi-provider wireless environment', *Telecommunication Systems*, 29: 131–52.

Hellström, G. (2002) Standardization of text telephony, http://www.omnitor.se/english/standards (accessed 15 March 2002).

Hemment, D. (2004) 'Locative arts', http://www.drewhemment.com/2004/locative_arts.html (accessed 7 November 2005).

Hillebrand, F. (2001a) 'GSM's achievements', in F. Hillebrand (ed.), *GSM and UMTS: The Creation of Global Mobile Communication*, New York: John Wiley, pp. 1–10.

—— (2001b) 'GSM and UMTS acceptance in the world', in F. Hillebrand (ed.), *GSM and UMTS: The Creation of Global Mobile Communication*, New York: John Wiley, pp. 535–45.

—— (2001c) 'Services and services' capabilities: section 1: the early years . . .', in F. Hillebrand (ed.), *GSM and UMTS: The Creation of Global Mobile Communication*, New York: John Wiley, pp. 263–85.

—— (2001d) 'Short message and data services: section 1: the early years . . .', in F. Hillebrand (ed.), *GSM and UMTS: The Creation of Global Mobile Communication*, New York: John Wiley, pp. 407–16.

Hine, C. (2000) *Virtual Ethnography*, Thousand Oaks, CA: Sage.

Hjorth, L. (2005) 'Odours of mobility: Japanese cute customization in the Asia-Pacific region', *Journal of Intercultural Studies*, 26: 39–55.

—— (2006) 'Fast-forwarding present: the rise of personalization and customization in mobile technologies in Japan', *Southern Review*, 39 (in press).

Hoare, S. (2005) 'Danger: cyber torturers online', *Guardian*, 7 June, http://guardian.co.uk (accessed 15 August 2005).

Holley, K. (2001) 'Short message and data services: section 2; the development from mid-1988 to 2000', in F. Hillebrand (ed.), *GSM and UMTS: The Creation of Global Mobile Communication*, New York: John Wiley, pp. 417–24.

Holma, H. and Toskala, A. (eds) (2000) *WCDMA for UMTS: Radio Access for Third Generation Mobile Communications*, New York: John Wiley.

Honigsbaum, M. (2005) 'Concern over rise of "happy slapping" craze: fad of filming violent attacks on mobile phones spreads', *Guardian*, 26 April, http://guardian.co.uk (accessed 15 September 2005).

Horn, U., Keller, R. and Niebert, N. (1999) 'Interactive mobile streaming services: the convergence of broadcast and mobile communication', *EBU Technical Review*, 281, http://www.ebu.ch/en/technical/trev/trev_281-umts.pdf.

Hornery, A. (1995) 'Commercial reality', *Sydney Morning Herald*, 'The Guide', 20 November, 7.

Howell, W. J. (1986) *World Broadcasting in the Age of the Satellite: Comparative Systems, Policies, and Issues in Mass Telecommunication*, Norwood, NJ: Ablex.

Hubbard, G. (1965) *Cooke and Wheatstone and the Invention of the Electric Telegraph*, London: Routledge and Kegan Paul.

Hurley, F. (2003) ' "Illiterate" blast at text message kids', *Sun* (Scotland), 3 March.

Human Rights and Equal Opportunity Commission (HREOC) (2000) *Inquiry on Mobile Phone Access for Hearing Aid Users*, Sydney: HREOC, http://www.hreoc.gov.au/disability_rights/inquiries/MP_index/mp_index.html (accessed 19 July 2005).

—— (2005) *Access to Telecommunications: Status Report*, Sydney: HREOC, http://www.hreoc.gov.au/disability_rights/communications/update05.htm (accessed 19 July 2005).

Hutton, W. (2005) 'Does the BBC deserve a rise?', *MediaGuardian*, 16 October, media.guardian.co.uk (accessed 3 December 2005).

Huurdeman, A.A. (2003) *A Worldwide History of Telecommunications*, Hoboken, NJ: John Wiley.

Independent Expert Group on Mobile Phones (Stewart Report) (2000) *Mobile Phones and Health*, Didcot: National Radiological Protection Board, http://www.iegmp.org.uk/report/text.htm (accessed 19 August 2005).

International Telecommunications Union (ITU) (2005a) 'Mobile cellular, subscribers per 100 people', *World Telecommunication Indicators*, http://www.itu.int/ITU-D/ict/statistics/at_glance/cellular04.pdf (accessed 15 December 2005).

—— (2005b) 'Top mobile cellular operators: 2004', http://www.itu.int/ITU-D/ict/statistics/at_glance/topptoc_2004.html (accessed 15 December 2005).

Irwin, A. and Wynne, B. (eds) (1996) *Misunderstanding Science? The Public Reconstruction of Science and Technology*, Cambridge: Cambridge University Press.

IT Matters (2002) 'Mobile data success story diverges in RP [Republic of Philippines], Hong Kong', *IT Matters, Business World Online*, 14 January, http://itmatters.com.ph/news/news_01142002b.html (accessed 24 May 2005).

Ito, J. (2003) 'Moblogging, Blogmapping and Moblogmapping related resources', http://joiwiki.ito.com/joiwiki/index.cgi?moblog (accessed 9 January 2006).

Ito, M. (2002) 'Mobiles and the appropriation of place', *receiver magazine*, 8, www.receiver.vodafone.com.

Ito, M., Okabe, D. and Matsuda, M. (eds) (2005) *Personal, Portable, Pedestrian: Mobile Phones in Japanese Life*, Cambridge, MA: MIT Press.

ITV (2005) 'ITV mobile', http://www.itv.com/page.asp?partid=4262 (accessed 8 December 2005).

Jackson, S.J. and Andrews, D.L. (eds) (2005) *Sport, Culture and Advertising: Identities, Commodities and the Politics of Representation*, New York: Routledge.

Jagasia, M. (2004) 'The sex texts that caught out Becks', *Express*, 5 April.

Jasanoff, S. (1986) *Risk Management and Political Culture*, New York: Russell Sage Foundation.

Jenkins, H. (2005) 'Welcome to convergence culture', *Receiver*, 12, March, http://www.receiver.vodafone.com/12/articles/pdf/12_01.pdf (accessed 10 January 2006).

Jenkins, P. (1992) *Intimate Enemies: Moral Panics in Contemporary Great Britain*, New York: Aldine de Gruyter.

Jensen, J.F. and Toscan, C. (eds) (1999) *Interactive Television: TV of the Future or the Future of TV?*, Aalborg: Aalborg University Press.

Jenson, S. (2005) 'Default thinking: why consumer products fail', in R. Harper, L. Palen and A. Taylor (eds), *The Inside Text: Social, Cultural and Design Perspectives on SMS*, Dordrecht: Springer.

Johnson, B., and Gibson, O. (2005) 'The new Apple iPod: now it does video too', *Guardian Unlimited*, 13 October, www.guardian.co.uk (accessed 23 December 2005).

Johnson, R. (1986) 'The Story So Far: and for the transformations', in D. Punter (ed.), *Introduction to Contemporary Cultural Studies*, London: Longman, pp. 277–313.

Johnson, R. et al. (2004) *The Practice of Cultural Studies*, Thousand Oaks, CA: Sage.

Jolley, W. (2003) *When the Tide Comes In: Towards Accessible Telecommunications for People with Disabilities in Australia*, Sydney: Human Rights and Equal Opportunity Commission, http://www.hreoc.gov.au/disability_rights/communications/tide.htm   (accessed 20 June 2005).

Jones, A. (1998) 'Upwardly mobile', *Sun-Herald* (Sydney), 'Sunday Life', 26.

Jones, D. (2005) *iPod, Therefore I Am*, London: Bloomsbury.

Jones, S. (2005) 'Girl knocked out in "happy slap" craze', *Guardian*, 20 May, http://guardian.co.uk (accessed 20 October 2005).

Jong, K.E. and Armstrong, B.K. (1997) 'A lesson from kindergarten on mobile phones', *Australian and New Zealand Journal of Public Health*, 21: 555–7.

Joyner, K.H. et al. (1993) *Interference to Hearing Aids by the New Digital Mobile Telephone System, Global System for Mobile (GSM) Communication Standard*, Sydney: National Acoustic Laboratory.

Kac, E. (1992), 'Aspects of the aesthetics of telecommunications', in J. Grimes and G. Lorig (eds), *Siggraph Visual Proceedings*, New York: ACM, pp. 47–57. Online. Available at: http://www.ekac.org/Telecom.Paper.Siggrap.html (10 September 2005).

—— (2005) *Cult of iPod*, San Francisco: No Starch Press.

Kaiser, A. (1999) 'Express yourself: why phone makes offers something "special" for you', *Wall Street Journal*, 11 October.

Karlson, B., Bria, A., Lind, J., Lönnqvist, P. and Norlin, C. (2003) *Wireless Foresight: Scenarios of the Mobile World in 2015*, Chichester: John Wiley.

Kasesniemi, E.-L. (2003) *Mobile Messages: Young People and a New Communication Culture*, Tampere: Tampere University Press.

Kasesniemi, E.-L. and Rautiainen, P. (2002) 'Mobile culture of children and teenagers in Finland', in J.E. Katz and M. Aakhus (eds), *Perpetual Contact: Mobile Communication, Private Talk, Public Performance*, Cambridge: Cambridge University Press.

Kato, F., Okabe, D., Ito, M. and Uemoto, R. (2005) 'Uses and possibilities of the *keitai* camera', in M. Ito, D. Okabe and M. Matsuda (eds), *Personal, Portable, Pedestrian: Mobile Phones in Japanese Life*, Cambridge, MA: MIT Press, pp. 300–10.

Katz, J.E. (1999) *Connections: Social and Cultural Studies of American Life*, New Brunswick, NJ: Transaction Publishers.

—— (ed.) (2003) *Machines That Become Us: The Social Context of Personal Communication Technology*, New Brunswick, NJ: Transaction Publishers.

Katz, J.E. and Aakhus, M. (eds) (2002) *Perpetual Contact: Mobile Communication, Private Talk, Public Performance*, Cambridge: Cambridge University Press.

Kavanagh, J. (1989) 'Everybody's talkin'', *Business Review Weekly*, 2 June, 14.

Kear, A. and Steinberg, D.L. (1999) *Mourning Diana*, London and New York: Routledge.

Keegan, V. (2005) 'How to fit the world in your pocket', *Guardian*, 13 October, http://guardian.co.uk (accessed 7 December 2005).

Kelner, M. (2005) 'Arsenal hoodies leave doddery Motty confused', *Guardian*, 23 May, http://guardian.co.uk (accessed 15 September 2005).

Kelso, P. (2004) 'Bad news for brand image as Beckham denies affair', *Guardian*, 5 April, http://guardian.co.uk (accessed 2 October 2005).

Kieve, J. (1973) *The Electric Telegraph: A Social and Economic History*, Newton Abbot: David & Charles.

Kilner, K. (2005) 'The latest: not just trendy. T-Mobile Sidekicks are more than a fashion statement for the deaf community', *Web@devil*, 28 April, http://www.statepress.com/issues/2005/04/28/arts/693124?s (accessed 1 August 2005).

Kinberg, J. (2004) 'About – FAQ', http://www.bikesagainstbush.com/blog/about.php (accessed 15 November 2005).

Klenk, T. (2005) *Mobile Video Telephony – the 3G Killer Application? Technical and Marketing Aspects of Mobile Video Telephony, More than a Pure 3G Bearer Service*, Fribourg: iimt University Press.

Kohiyama, K. (2005) 'A decade in the development of mobile communications in Japan (1993–2002)', in M. Ito, D. Okabe and M. Matsuda (eds), *Personal, Portable, Pedestrian: Mobile Phones in Japanese Life*, Cambridge, MA: MIT Press, pp. 61–74.

Koivusalo, M. (1995) *Kipinästä Tuli Syttyy: suomalaisen radiopuhelinteollisuuden kehitys ja tulevaisuuden haasteet*, Espoo: Cetonia Systems.

Konkka, K. (2003) 'Indian needs – cultural end-user research in Mombai', in C. Lindholm, T. Keinonen and H. Kiljander (eds), *Mobile Usability: How Nokia Changed the Face of the Mobile Phone*, New York: McGraw-Hill.

Kopomaa, T. (2000) *The City in Your Pocket: Birth of the Mobile Information Society*, Helsinki: Gaudeamus.

Korhonen, J. (2001) *Introduction to 3G Mobile Communications*, Boston and London: Artech.

Kornfeld, M. and Reimers, U. (2005) 'DVB-H: the emerging standard for mobile data communication', *EBU Technical Review*, 301 http://www.ebu.ch/en/technical/trev/trev_301-dvb-h.pdf.

Koskinen, I., Kurvinen, E. and Lehtonen, T.-K. (2002) *Mobile Image*, Helsinki: IT Press.

Kozamernik, F. (2004) 'DAB: from digital radio towards mobile multimedia', *EBU Technical Review*, http://www.ebu.ch/en/technical/trev/trev_297-kozamernik.pdf.

Krebs, B. (2005) 'Paris Hilton hack started with old-fashioned con', *Washingtonpost.com*, 19 May, http://www.washingtonpost.com (accessed 7 January 2006).

Kunerth, J. (2005) 'Deaf culture fades', *Sun-Sentinel* (South Florida), 27 January 2005; also at http://www.deafcoffee.com/ (accessed 27 June 2005).

Lacohée, H., Wakeford, N. and Pearson, I. (2003) 'A social history of the mobile telephone with a view of its future', *BT Technology Journal* 21: 203–11.

Laird, G. (2005) 'Deaf culture fades – misleading?', *Grant W Laird Jr Blog*, http://grant-lairdjr.com/b2evolution/index.php/all/2005/02/01/p149 (accessed 1 August 2005).

Lally, E. (2002) *At Home with Computers*, Oxford and New York: Berg.

Lang, H.G. (2000) *A Phone of Our Own: The Deaf Insurrection against Ma Bell*, Washington, DC: Gallaudet University Press.

Larsson, C. (2002) 'Local use and sharing of mobile phones', in B. Brown, N. Green and R. Harper (eds), *Wireless World: Social and Interactional Aspects of the Mobile Age*, London: Springer.

Lasen, A. (2005) 'History repeating? A comparison of the launch and uses of fixed and mobile phones', in L. Hamill and A. Lasen (eds), *Mobile World: Past, Present and Future*, London: Springer.

Latour, B. (1996) *Aramis, or the Love of Technology*, trans. Catherine Porter, Cambridge MA: Harvard University Press.

LaVallee, A. (2005) 'For the deaf, instant messaging reaches out and touches', *Columbia*

News Service, 1 March, http://jscms.jrn.columbia.edu/cns/2005-03-01/lavallee-deafmessage (accessed 1 August 2005).

Lee, K. (2005) 'I am a camera', *Guardian*, 12 November, www.guardian.co.uk (accessed 8 January 2006).

Lehne, P.H. (ed.) (2004) '100th anniversary issue: perspectives in telecommunications', *Telektronikk*, 3, http://www.telenor.com/telektronikk/.

Leinbach, T.R. and Brunn, S.D. (2002) 'National innovation systems, firm strategy, and enabling mobile communications: the case of Nokia', *Tijdschrift voor Economische en Sociale Geografie*, 93: 489–508.

Levin, G. et al. (2004) 'Dialtones (a telesymphony)', http://www.flong.com/telesymphony/ (accessed 6 January 2006).

Lin, A. (2005a) 'Gendered, bilingual communication practices: mobile text-messaging among Hong Kong college students', *Fibreculture Journal*, 6 http://journal.fibreculture.org/issue6/issue6_lin.html.

—— (ed.) (2005b) *Proceedings of International Conference on Mobile Communication and Asian Modernities, 7–8 June, City University of Hong Kong, Kowloon*. Hong Kong: City University of Hong Kong.

—— (2005c) 'Romance and sexual ideologies in SMS manuals circulating among migrant workers in southern China', in A. Lin (ed.), *Proceedings of International Conference on Mobile Communication and Asian Modernities, 7–8 June, City University of Hong Kong, Kowloon*. Hong Kong: City University of Hong Kong.

Lin, A. and Lo, J. (2004) 'New youth digital literacies and mobile connectivity: text-messaging among Hong Kong college students', paper presented at the International Conference on Mobile Communication and Social Change, 18–19 October 2004, Korean Press Foundation, Seoul, South Korea.

Lindholm, C. (2004) 'Nokia Lifeblog beta is available', http://www.christianlindholm.com/christianlindholm/2004/07/nokia_lifeblog_.html (accessed 27 April 2006).

Lindholm, C. and Keinonen, T. (2003) 'Managing the design of user interfaces', in C. Lindholm, T. Keinonen and H. Kiljander (eds), *Mobile Usability: How Nokia Changed the Face of the Mobile Phone*, New York: McGraw-Hill.

Lindholm, C., Keinonen, T. and Kiljander, H. (eds) (2003) *Mobile Usability: How Nokia Changed the Face of the Mobile Phone*, New York: McGraw-Hill.

Ling, C. and Arnold, W. (1998) 'Stylish mobile phone from Nokia becomes the rage in Hong Kong', *Wall Street Journal*, 15 September.

Ling, R. (2004) *The Mobile Connection: The Cell Phone's Impact on Society*, San Francisco, CA: Morgan Kaufmann.

Ling, R. and Julsrud, T. (2005) 'The development of grounded genres in Multimedia Messaging Systems (MMS) among mobile professionals', in K. Nyíri (ed.), *A Sense of Place: The Global and the Local in Mobile Communication*, Vienna: Passagen Verlag, pp. 329–38.

Ling, R. and Pedersen, P. (eds) (2005) *Mobile Communication: Re-negotiation of the Social Sphere*, London: Springer.

Ling, R. and Yttri, B. (2002) 'Hyper-coordination via mobile phones in Norway', in J.E. Katz and M. Aakhus (eds), *Perpetual Contact: Mobile Communication, Private Talk, Public Performance*, Cambridge: Cambridge University Press, pp. 139–69.

Livingston, K. (1996) *The Wired Nation Continent: The Communication Revolution and Federating Australia*, Melbourne and New York: Oxford University Press.

London Observer Service (1993) 'It appears the chat's out of the bag; reports of conversation between Charles and Camilla adds to Royal mess', *Globe and Mail*, 14 January, A1.

Lovink, G. (2002) *Dark Fiber: Tracking Critical Internet Culture*, Cambridge, MA: MIT Press.

Lucent Bell Labs (2004) 'Lucent Bell Labs' top innovations', http://www.bell-labs.com/about/history/timeline.html (accessed 27 December 2005).

—— (2000) 'Cyberschooling and technological change: multiliteracies for new times', in M. Kalantzis and B. Cope (eds), *Multiliteracies: Literacy Learning and the Design of Social Futures*, Melbourne: Cambridge University Press.

Luke, C. (2003a) 'Critical media and cultural studies in new times', in T. Lavender, B. Tufte and D. Lemish (eds), *Global Trends in Media Education*, Cresskill, NJ: Hampton Press.

—— (2003b) 'New directions in ICT research: pedagogy, connectivity, multimodality, and interdisciplinarity', *Reading Research Quarterly*, 38: 397–403.

Lyytinen, K. and King, J.L. (2002) 'Around the cradle of the wireless revolution: the emergence and evolution of cellular telephony', *Telecommunications Policy*, 26: 97–100.

McKay, D. and Brady, C. (2005) 'Practices of place-making: globalisation and locality in the Philippines', *Asia-Pacific Viewpoint*, 46: 89–103.

McKee, A. (2005) *The Public Sphere: An Introduction*, New York: Cambridge University Press.

MacKenzie, D. and Wajcman, J. (1985) *The Social Shaping of Technology: How the Refrigerator Got Its Hum*, Milton Keynes and Philadelphia, PA: Open University Press.

—— (eds) (1999) *The Social Shaping of Technology*, 2nd edn, Buckingham, UK and Philadelphia, PA: Open University Press.

McKenzie, G. (2001) 'Virtual dating can lead to virtual dumping', *Business Edge*, 5 September, http://www.mckenzieink.ca/Mclnk2/edge_050901_dating.htm (accessed 23 May 2005).

Magid, L. (2005) 'What Paris Hilton has done for you', *CBS News*, 21 February, http://www.cbsnews.com/stories/2005/02/21/scitech/pcanswer/main675320.shtml (accessed 7 January 2005).

Mangan, L. (2004) 'Becks' texts uncensored: mind your language', *Guardian*, 6 April.

Mann, S. (1996a) 'An experiment in connectivity: look out through my glasses right now', http://wearcam.org/myview.html (accessed 9 January 2006).

—— (1996b) 'Gallery of recently transmitted lookpaintings', http://genesis.eecg.toronto.edu/orbits/gallery.html (accessed 9 January 2006).

—— (1997) 'An historical account of the "WearComp" and "WearCam" inventions developed for applications in "Personal Imaging" ', *IEEE Proceedings of the First ISWC*, October 13–14, 1997, Cambridge, MA. Online. Available at http://n1nlf-1.eecg.toronto.edu/historic/historic.html (accessed 8 January 2006).

—— (n.d.) 'Sousveillance, not just surveillance, in response to terrorism' http://www.chairetmetal.com/cm06/mann-complet.htm (accessed 1 May 2005).

Mann, S. and Guerra, R. (2001) 'The Witnessential Net', Proceedings of IEEE ISWC 2001, http://wearcam.org/iswc01/ (accessed 1 May 2005).

Manovich, L. (2001) *The Language of New Media*, Cambridge, MA: MIT Press.

Mansell, R. (ed.) (1993) *The New Telecommunications: A Political Economy of Network Evolution*, London: Sage.

Marcussen, C.H. (2003) *Early Adopters of WAP for Hotels: A Series of European Case Studies*, Centre for Regional and Tourism Research, Bornholm: Denmark, http://www.crt.dk/uk/staff/chm/wap/cases.pdf (accessed 12 January 2006).

Marshall, P.D. (1997) *Celebrity and Power: Fame in Contemporary Culture*, Minneapolis: University of Minnesota Press.

—— (2005) *New Media Cultures*, London: Arnold.

Martikainen, O. and Palmberg, C. (2005) 'The GSM standard and Nokia as an incubating element', *Innovation: Management, Policy & Practice*, 7: 61–78.

Martin, B. and Richards, E. (1995) 'Scientific knowledge, controversy and public decision-making', in S. Jasanoff, G.E. Markle, J.C. Peterson and T. Pinch (eds), *The Handbook of Science and Technology Studies*, Thousand Oaks, CA: Sage.

Martin, F. (2003) 'Net Worth: the unlikely rise of ABC Online', in G. Goggin (ed.), *Virtual Nation: The Internet in Australia*, Sydney: UNSW Press, pp. 193–208.

Martin, M. (1991) *Hello Central?: Gender, Culture, and Technology in the Formation of Telephone Systems*, Montreal: McGill-Queen's University Press.

Marvin, C. (1988) *When Old Technologies Were New: Thinking about Electric Communication in the Late Nineteenth Century*, New York: Oxford University Press.

Matsuda, M. (2005a) 'Discourses of *keitai* in Japan', in M. Ito, D. Okabe and M. Matsuda (eds), *Personal, Portable, Pedestrian: Mobile Phones in Japanese Life*, Cambridge, MA: MIT Press, pp. 19–39.

—— (2005b) 'Mobile communication and selective sociality', in M. Ito, D. Okabe and M. Matsuda (eds), *Personal, Portable, Pedestrian: Mobile Phones in Japanese Life*, Cambridge, MA: MIT Press, pp. 123–42.

Mercer, D. (1998) 'Hazards of decontextualised accounts of public perceptions of radio frequency radiation (RFR) risk', *Australian and New Zealand Journal of Public Health*, 22: 291–3.

Merriden, T. (2001) *Business the Nokia Way: Secrets of the World's Fastest Moving Company*, Oxford: Capstone.

—— (2003) *Rollercoaster: The Turbulent Life and Times of Vodafone and Chris Gent*, Oxford: Capstone.

Metts, R.L. (2000) *Disability Issues, Trends and Recommendations for the World Bank*, Washington, DC: World Bank.

Michaelis, A. R. (1965) *From Semaphore to Satellite*, Geneva: International Telecommunications Union.

Miller, D., Kitzinger, J., Williams, K. and Beharrell, P. (1998) *The Circuit of Mass Communication: Media Strategies, Representation and Audience Reception in the AIDS Crisis*, London: Sage.

Miller, D. and Slater, D. (2000) *The Internet: An Ethnographic Approach*, Oxford and New York: Berg.

Miller, M.J., Vucectic, B. and Berry, L. (eds) (1993) *Satellite Communications: Mobile and Fixed Services*, Boston: Kluwer Academic Publishers.

Millership, P. (1992) 'Exit the Duchess', *Reuters News*, 24 August.

Mirror (2005a) 'Happy slappers hit by crackdown', *Mirror.co.uk*, 27 January 2005, http://mirror.co.uk (accessed 17 October 2005).

—— (2005b) 'Kent mall bans "urban crime" hoods and baseball caps', *Mirror.co.uk*, 12 May, http://mirror.co.uk (accessed 17 October 2005).

—— (2005c) 'One in 10 kids bullied by picture phone-survey', *Mirror.co.uk*, 7 June 2005, http://mirror.co.uk (accessed 17 October 2005).

Mirror (2005d) 'Alcatel One Touch 756', 18 February 2005.

Mobile Speak (2005) 'The screen reader made for you', http://mobilespeak. codfact.com/ (accessed 24 June 2005).

Moholy-Nagy, L. (1947) *The New Vision and Abstract of an Artist*, New York: Wittenborn.

Molloy, F. (2004) 'Scene and heard', *The Age (Melbourne)*, 30 October.

Molnar, J. P. (1969) 'Picturephone service – a new way of communicating', *Bell Laboratories Record*, 47.5: 134–35. Online. Available at: http://long-lines.net/sources/BLR.htm (accessed 9 November 2005).

Mondo Thingo (2004) 'Cab blog', http://www.abc.net.au/thingo/txt/s1204582.htm (accessed 12 January 2006).

Mosco, V. (2004) *The Digital Sublime: Myth, Power, and Cyberspace*, Cambridge, MA: MIT Press.

Moyal, A. (1992) 'The gendered use of the telephone: an Australian case study', *Media, Culture and Society*, 14: 51–72.

Mueller, M. (1997) *Universal Service: Competition, Interconnection, and Monopoly in the Making of the American Telephone System*, Cambridge, MA: MIT Press; Washington, DC: The AEI Press.

—— (2002) *Ruling the Root: Internet Governance and the Taming of Cyberspace*, Cambridge, MA: MIT Press.

Mullin, J. and Henry, G. (1992) ' "Diana tape" voice named by tabloid – The Sun newspaper', *Guardian*, 26 August.

Murray, J. B. (2001) *Wireless Nation: The Frenzied Launch of the Cellular Revolution in America*, Cambridge, MA: Perseus Publishing.

Myers, D. J. (2004) *Mobile Video Telephony: For 3G Wireless Networks*, New York: McGraw-Hill Education.

National Council on Disability (NCD) (2004) *Design for Inclusion: Creating a New Marketplace*, Washington, DC: NCD, http://www.ncd.gov/newsroom/publications/2004/ publications.htm (accessed 12 May 2005).

National Statistics Office (2005) 'Press release on the 2004 survey on overseas Filipinos', Manila: National Statistics Office, http://www.census.gov.ph/data/pressrelease/ 2005/of04tx.html (accessed 11 January 2006).

National Telecom Agency Denmark (NTAD) (1994) *Interference with Hearing Aids Caused by GSM Digital Cellular Telephones and DECT Digital Cordless Telephones*, Conclusive report by the working group on GSM and DECT telephones and hearing aids, Copenhagen: NTAD.

Natsuno, T. (2003b) *The i-Mode Wireless Ecosystem*, trans. R. S. McCreery, Chichester: John Wiley.

NCH and Tesco Mobile (2005) *Putting U in the Picture: Mobile Bullying Survey 2005*, http:// www.nch.org.uk/uploads/documents/Mobile_bullying_%20report.pdf (accessed 3 September 2005).

Nelkin, D. (ed.) (1979) *Controversy: Politics of Technical Decisions*, Thousand Oaks, CA: Sage.

Nelson, R.R. and Rosenberg, N. (1993) 'Technical innovation and national systems', in

R.R. Nelson (ed.), *National Innovation Systems: A Comparative Analysis*, New York: Oxford University Press, pp. 3–21.

Neville, R. (2004) 'Crass, corny, but still a Woodstock moment for a new generation', *Sydney Morning Herald*, 23 November.

Neylan, A. (2006) *Man of Lettuce: A Cabbie's Spray*, blog, http://jafablog.typepad.com/man_of_lettuce/ (accessed 12 January 2006).

Nieminen-Sundell, R. and Väänänen-Vainio-Mattila, K. (2003) 'Usability meets sociology for richer consumer studies', in C. Lindholm, T. Keinonen and H. Kiljander (eds), *Mobile Usability: How Nokia Changed the Face of the Mobile Phone*, New York: McGraw-Hill, pp. 113–38.

Niepold, R. (2001) 'The UMTS related work of the European Commission, UMTS Task Force, UMTS Forum and GSM Association', in F. Hillebrand (ed.), *GSM and UMTS: The Creation of Global Mobile Communication*, New York: John Wiley, pp. 128–46.

Niosi, J. and Bellon, B. (1994) 'The global interdependence of national innovation systems: evidence, limits and implications', *Technology in Society*, 16: 173–97.

Noam, E., Groebel, J. and Gerbarg, D. (eds) (2004) *Internet Television*, Mahwah, NJ: Lawrence Erlbaum.

Noble, D.E. (1962) 'The history of land–mobile radio communications,' *Proceedings of the Institute of Radio Engineers*, 50: 1405–14.

Noguchi, Y. (2005) 'Gone in 60 seconds; mobile-phone TV demands quick shows', *Washington Post*, 30 January, AO1.

Nokia (2000) *WAP*, White paper, http://nds2.ir.nokia.com/downloads/aboutnokia/press/pdf/dec001.pdf (accessed 16 August 2005).

—— (2004a) 'Experience mobile multimedia with the widescreen Nokia 7710', press release, 2 November, www.nokia.com (accessed 9 January 2006).

—— (2004b) 'Nokia and Six Apart announce mobile web logging for Content Sharing', press release, 9 August, www.nokia.com (accessed 1 May 2005).

—— (2004c) 'Nokia Lifeblog provides the richest mobile sharing experience', 11 February, www.nokia.com (accessed 1 May 2005).

—— (2005a) 'Consumers also want to watch TV programs on their mobiles', press release, 30 August, http://www.mobiletv.nokia.com/news/showPressReleases/?id=53 (accessed 12 December 2005).

—— (2005b) 'Mobile TV Forum . . . broadcast network operator benefits', http://www.mobiletv.nokia.com/overview/bno/ (accessed 12 December 2005).

—— (2005c) 'Mobile TV Forum . . . broadcaster benefits', http://www.mobiletv.nokia.com/overview/broadcasters/ (accessed 12 December 2005).

—— (2005d) 'Mobile TV Forum . . . mobile network operator benefits', http://www.mobiletv.nokia.com/overview/mno/ (accessed 12 December 2005).

Nolan, J. (2004) 'The technology of difference: ASCII, hegemony, and the Internet', in P. Trifonas (ed.), *Communities of Difference: Language, Culture, and the Media*, New York: Palgrave Macmillan.

Noonan, T. (2000) *Blind Citizens Australia Submission to the Human Rights and Equal Opportunity Inquiry into Electronic Commerce*, http://www.hreoc.gov.au/disability_rights/inquiries/ecom_subs/bca1.htm (accessed 12 July 2005).

Nye, D.E. (1994) *American Technological Sublime*, Cambridge, MA: MIT Press.

Nyíri, K. (2002) *Mobile Democracy: Essays on Society, Self and Politics*, Vienna: Passagen Verlag.

—— (ed.) (2003a) *Mobile Communication: Essays on Cognition and Community*, Vienna: Passagen Verlag.

—— (2003b) *Mobile Learning: Essays on Philosophy, Psychology and Education*, Vienna: Passagen Verlag.

—— (ed.) (2005) *A Sense of Place: The Global and the Local in Mobile Communication*, Vienna: Passagen Verlag.

Office of Telecommunications (Oftel) (1999) *Competition in the Mobile Market: A Consultative Document Issued by the Director General of Telecommunications*, February, London: Oftel, http://www.ofcom.org.uk/static/archive/oftel/publications/1999/consumer/cmm 0299.htm#Annex%20A (accessed 27 October 2005).

Ohmori, S., Wakana, H. and Kawase, S. (1998) *Mobile Satellite Communications*, Boston: Artech House.

Okada, T. (2005) 'Youth culture and the shaping of Japanese mobile media: personalization and the *keitai* Internet as multimedia', in M. Ito, D. Okabe and M. Matsuda (eds), *Personal, Portable, Pedestrian: Mobile Phones in Japanese Life*, Cambridge, MA: MIT Press, pp. 41–60.

Orange (2005) 'Our brand', http://www.orange.com/English/aboutorange/ourbrand.asp

O'Sullivan, K. (2005) 'Reclaim our streets', 13 May, *Mirror.co.uk*.

Owen, B.M. (1999) *The Internet Challenge to Television*, Cambridge, MA: Harvard University Press.

Palmberg, C. (2002) 'Technological systems and competent procurers – the transformation of Nokia and the Finnish telecom industry revisited?', *Telecommunications Policy*, 26: 129–48.

Pandya, N. (2001) 'Company vitæ', *Guardian*, 2 June, http://www.guardian.co.uk (accessed 27 September 2005).

Parreñas, Rachel Salazar (2001) *Servants of Globalization: Women, Migration and Domestic Work*, Stanford: Stanford University Press.

Pelton, J.N. (1995) *Wireless and Satellite Telecommunications: The Technology, the Market & the Regulations*, Upper Saddle River, NJ: Prentice Hall.

Pempel, T.J. (1978) 'Land mobile communications in Japan: technical developments and issues of international trade', in R. Bowers, A. M. Lee and C. Hershey (eds), *Communications for a Mobile Society: An Assessment of New Technology*, Beverley Hills, CA: Sage.

Perrone, Jane (2002) 'Weblogs get upwardly mobile', *Guardian*, 12 December, www.guardian.co.uk (accessed 1 May 2005).

—— (2002) *The Work of Culture*, Manila: De La Salle University Press.

—— (2003) *Science, Technology and the Culture of Everyday Life in the Philippines*, Manila: Ateneo de Manila University.

Pertierra, R. (2005a) 'Mobile phones, identity and discursive intimacy', *Human Technology*, 1: 23–44.

—— (2005b) 'Without a room of your own? Buy a cell phone', in A. Lin (ed.), *Proceedings of International Conference on Mobile Communication and Asian Modernities, 7–8 June, City University of Hong Kong, Kowloon*. Hong Kong: City University of Hong Kong, pp. 157–70.

Pertierra, R. and Koskinen, I. (eds) (2006) *The Social Construction and Usage of Communication Technologies: European and Asian Experiences*, Singapore: Singapore University Press.

Pertierra, R., Ugarte, E.F., Pingol, A., Hernandez, J. and Dacanay, N.L. (2002) *Txt-ing Selves: Cellphones and Philippine Modernity*, Manila: De La Salle University Press, http://www.finlandembassy.ph/texting1.htm (accessed 22 July 2005).

Plant, S. (2002) *On the Mobile: The Effects of Mobile Telephones on Social and Individual Life*, Motorola, www.motorola.com/mot/doc/0/234_MotDoc.pdf (accessed 30 December 2005).

Popovic, M. (2002) 'About hiptop nation', http://hiptop.bedope.com/about.html (accessed 9 January 2006).

Powell, S. (1992) 'Mobile Cathy rarely home, never out of touch', *Sydney Morning Herald*, 3.

Power, M. and Power, D. (2004) 'Everyone here speaks TXT: deaf people using SMS in Australia and the rest of the world', *Journal of Deaf Studies and Deaf Education*, 9: 333–43.

Rachman, T. (2003) 'Cell phone messages uncover cheating Italians', *Chicago Sun-Times*, 29 September, 4.

Rafael, Vicente L. (2003) 'The cell phone and the crowd: messianic politics in the contemporary Philippines', *Public Culture*, 15: 399–425.

Rakow, L.F. (1993) *Gender on the Line: Women, the Telephone, and Community Life*, Chicago: University of Illinois Press.

Ramirez, A. (1992) 'Eavesdroppers troll for salable chat, but it's a big pond', *New York Times*, 27 September, final edition, 6.

Ramos, L. (2003) 'Text 'n' pay', *CMPnet.Asia*, 1 May, http://www.cmpnetasia.com/PrintArticle.cfm?Artid=19607 (accessed 25 May 2005).

Rees-Mogg, W. (1993) 'The paparazzi are preferable – press controls', *The Times*, 11 January.

Rheingold, H. (1993) *The Virtual Community: Homesteading on the Electronic Frontier*, Reading, MA: Addison-Wesley.

—— (2002) *Smart Mobs: The Next Social Revolution*, Cambridge, MA: Perseus.

—— (n.d.) 'Smart Mobs – book summary', http://www.smartmobs.com/book/book_summ.html (accessed 12 January 2006).

Richards, J., Wilson, S. and Woodhead, L. (1999) *Diana: The Making of a Media Saint*, London and New York: I.B. Tauris.

Rivière, C. (2005) 'Mobile camera phones: a new form of "being together" in daily interpersonal communication', in R. Ling and P.E. Pederson (eds), *Mobile Communications: Re-negotiation of the Social Sphere*, London: Springer, pp. 167–85.

Roberts, J. (2004) *The Modern Firm: Organizational Design for Performance and Growth*, Oxford: Oxford University Press.

Robertson, R. (1991) 'Testimonial to Alex and the mobile phone', *Australian Financial Review*, 26 November, 51.

Robinson, J. (2005a) 'In the digital future, less means More4', *Guardian Unlimited*, 9 October, www.guardian.co.uk (accessed 3 December 2005).

—— (2005b) 'TV's nice and cosy, but could soon die', *Guardian Unlimited*, 18 September, www.guardian.co.uk (accessed 3 December 2005).

Roe, P. (ed.) (1993) *Telephones and Hearing Aids*, proceedings of the COST 219 seminar, The Hague, March 17 1993, XIII/61/94-EN.

Rojek, C. (2001) *Celebrity*, London: Reaktion.

Ronel, A (1989) *The Phone Book: Technology, Schizophrenia, Electric Speech*, Lincoln: University of Nebraska Press.

Roper, S. and Grimes, S. (2005) 'Wireless valley, silicon wadi and digital island – Helsinki, Tel Aviv and Dublin and the ICT global production network', *Geoforum*, 36: 297–313.

Rosenbrock, K. and Andersen, N.P.S. (2001) 'The Third Generation Partnership Project (3GPP)', in F. Hillebrand (ed.), *GSM and UMTS: The Creation of Global Mobile Communication*, New York: John Wiley, pp. 221–61.

Ross, K. and Nightingale, V. (2003) *Media and Audiences: New Perspectives*, Maidenhead: Open University Press.

Royce, R. (2005) 'I have been betrayed Victoria . . .', *Daily Mail*, 28 April.

Sadowski, B.M., Dittrich, K. and Duysters, G.M. (2003) 'Collaborative strategies in the event of technological discontinuities: the case of Nokia in the mobile telecommunications industry', *Small Business Economics*, 21: 173–86.

Sandhana, L. (2003) 'Blind "see with sound" ' *BBC News*, http://news.bbc.co.uk/2/hi/science/nature/3171226.stm (accessed 1 August 2005).

Sandman, P.M. (1989) 'Hazard versus outrage in the public perception of risk', in V.T. Covello, D.B. McCallum and M.T. Pavlova (eds), *Effective Risk Communication*, New York: Plenum, pp. 45–9.

—— (1995) *Responding to Community Outrage: Strategies for Effective Risk Communication*, Fairfax, VA: American Industrial Hygiene Association.

Sarikakis, K. and Thussu, D. (eds) (2005) *Ideologies of the Internet*, Cresskill, NJ: Hampton Press

Sawhney, H. (2004) 'Mobile communication: new technologies and old archetypes', paper delivered at Mobile Communication and Social Change conference, Seoul, South Korea, October 18–19.

—— (2005) 'Wi-Fi networks and the reorganisation of wireline–wireless relationship', in R. Ling and P.E. Pederson (eds), *Mobile Communications: Re-negotiation of the Social Sphere*, London: Springer, pp. 45–61.

Scifo, B. (2005) 'The domestication of the camera phone and MMS communications: the experience of young Italians', in K. Nyíri (ed.), *A Sense of Place: The Global and the Local in Mobile Communication*, Vienna: Passagen Verlag, pp. 363–73.

Sconce, J. (2000) *Haunted Media: Electronic Presence from Telegraphy to Television*, Durham, NC: Duke University Press.

Seelman, K.D. (2002) 'Science and technology policy: is disability the missing factor?', in G.L. Albrecht, K.D. Seelman and M. Bury (eds), *Handbook of Disability Studies*, London and Thousand Oaks, CA: Sage, pp. 663–92.

—— (2005) 'Universal design and orphan technology: do we need both?', *Disability Studies Quarterly*, 25.3, http://www.dsq-sds.org/_articles_html/2005/summer/seelman.asp.

Segerstad, Y.H. (2005) 'Language use in Swedish mobile text messaging', in R. Ling and P.E. Pederson (eds), *Mobile Communications: Re-negotiation of the Social Sphere*, London: Springer, pp. 313–33.

Seiter, E. (1999) *Television and New Media Audiences*, Oxford and New York: Clarendon Press.

Shaw, W. (2006) 'One day in July', *Observer*, 1 January, http://www.observer.co.uk (accessed 8 January 2006).

Shipley, T. and Gill, J. (2000) *Call Barred? Inclusive Design of Wireless Systems*, London: Royal National Institute of the Blind, http://www.tiresias.org/phoneability/wireless.htm (accessed 1 August 2005).

Sieber, A. and Weck, C. (2004) 'What's the difference between DVB-H and DAB – in the mobile environment', *EBU Technical Review*, 299, http://www.ebu.ch/en/technical/trev/trev_299-weck.pdf.

Smith, G.D. (1985) *The Anatomy of a Business Strategy: Bell, Western Electric, and the Origins of the American Telephone Industry*, Baltimore: Johns Hopkins University Press.

Snyder, S.L., Brueggemann, B.J. and Garland-Thomson, R. (eds) (2002) *Disability Studies: Enabling the Humanities*, New York: Modern Language Association of America.

Solymar, L. (1999) *Getting the Message: A History of Communications*, Oxford: Oxford University Press.

Sommerer, C. and Mignonneau, L. (eds) (1998) *Art@science*, Vienna and New York: Springer.

Sontag, S. (1977) *On Photography*, New York: Farrar, Strauss and Giroux.

—— (2003) *Regarding the Pain of Others*, New York: Farrar, Strauss and Giroux.

—— (2004) 'Regarding the torture of others', *New York Times Magazine*, 23 May, 24–5.

Spurgeon C. and Keane, M. (2005) 'Advertising industries and China's creative vision', paper presented to the 14th AMIC Annual Conference, Media and Society in Asia: Transformations and Transitions, 18–21 July, 2005, Beijing, PRC.

Steinbock, D. (2001a) 'Assessing Finland's wireless valley: can the pioneering continue?', *Telecommunications Policy*, 25: 71–100.

—— (2001b) *The Nokia Revolution*, New York: American Management Association.

—— (2003) *Wireless Horizon: Strategy and Competition in the Worldwide Mobile Marketplace*, New York: American Management Association.

—— (2005) *Mobile Marketing: The Making of Mobile Services Worldwide*, London: Kogan Page.

Stewart Report, *see* Independent Expert Group on Mobile Phones.

Stiker, H.-J. (1999) *A History of Disability*, trans. W. Sayers, Ann Arbor: University of Michigan Press.

Storey, R. (1996) 'Mobile video phone – seeing is believing', *Sydney Morning Herald*, 'Computers', 25 June, 3.

Strom, G. (2002) 'The telephone comes to a Filipino village', in J.E. Katz and M. Aakhus (eds), *Perpetual Contact: Mobile Communication, Private Talk, Public Performance*, Cambridge: Cambridge University Press, pp. 274–83.

Sturgis, P. and Allum, N. (2004) 'Science in society: re-evaluating the deficit model of public attitudes', *Public Understanding of Science*, 13: 55–74.

Suchman, L. (2002) 'Practice-based design of information systems: notes from the hyper-developed world', *The Information Society*, 18: 1–6.

Sullivan, R. (2000) 'Ring leader', *Vogue*, April.

Sun (1996) '5 bugged calls; who is the Di Spy? The most sensational royal video you'll ever see', *Sun*, 8 October.

―― (1997) 'Camilla: the people speak; Sun says', *Sun*, 7 August.

Sunday Times (2005) 'Wozat Warney?' *Sunday Times*, 3 July, 3.

Sussman, G. (2003) 'Introduction: the struggle for and within public television', *Television & New Media*, 4: 111–15.

Syvertsen, T. (2003) 'Challenges to public television in the era of convergence and commercialization', *Television & New Media*, 4: 155–75.

Tabbi, J. (1995) *Postmodern Sublime: Technology and American Writing from Mailer to Cyberpunk*, Ithaca, NY: Cornell University Press, 1995.

Taylor, A. and Harper, R. (2002) 'Age-old practices in the "new world": a study of gift-giving between teenage mobile phone users', Paper presented at Changing Our World, Changing Ourselves, the SIGCHI Conference on Human Factors in Computing Systems, Minneapolis

―― (2003) 'The gift of gab? A design oriented sociology of young people's use of mobiles', *Journal of Computer Supported Cooperative Work*, 12: 267–96.

Taylor, A.S. and Vincent, J. (2005) 'A SMS history', in L. Hamill and A. Lasen (eds), *Mobile World: Past, Present and Future*, London: Springer-Verlag, pp. 75–91.

Taylor, B.C., Demont-Heinrich, C., Broadfoot, K.J., Dodge, J. and Jian, G. (2002) 'New media and the circuit of cyber-culture: conceptualizing Napster', *Journal of Broadcasting & Electronic Media*, 46: 607–29.

Taylor, R. (2005) 'Prescott and the boys in the hoods', *Guardian*, 12 May, http://www.guardian.co.uk (accessed 1 December 2005).

Telecommunications Access Program (TAP) (2002) 'Wireless telephones and TTYs', Washington, DC: TAP, Gallaudet University, http://tap.gallaudet.edu/WirelessPhoneTTY0902.htm (accessed 12 May 2005).

Telecoms InfoTechnology Forum (2004) *Hong Kong as Asia's Wireless Development Center*, Telecoms InfoTechnology Forum, Telecommunications Research Project, University of Hong Kong, http://www.trp.hku.hk/tif/papers/2004/mar/briefing_040325.pdf (accessed 25 May 2005).

Temko, N. (2005) 'Schools face call to jam mobiles', *Guardian*, 26 June, http://guardian.co.uk (accessed 1 September 2005).

Thompson, K. (1998) *Moral Panics*, London: Routledge.

3G newsroom (2004) 'Hybrid approach to 3G location services', http://www.3gnewsroom.com/3g_news/mar_04/news_4316.shtml (accessed 15 November).

Thurlbeck, N. (2004) 'World exclusive: Beckham's secret affair', *News of the World*, 4 April.

Timms, D. (2004a) 'Beckham drafts in new PR chief', *MediaGuardian*, 11 June, http://media.guardian.co.uk (accessed 14 October 2005).

―― (2004b) 'Beckham interview hits ratings high', *MediaGuardian*, 16 April, http://media.guardian.co.uk (accessed 14 October 2005).

―― (2004c) 'Fresh fears over mobile security', *MediaGuardian*, 14 April, http://media.guardian.co.uk (accessed 14 October 2005).

―― (2005a) 'Endemol targets mobile market', *MediaGuardian*, 19 October, http://media.guardian.co.uk (accessed 12 December 2005).

—— (2005b) 'Mobile TV and the bigger picture', *MediaGuardian*, 31 October, http://media.guardian.co.uk (accessed 12 December 2005).

—— (2005c) 'Orange adds cricket to its mobile TV services', *MediaGuardian*, 4 October, http://media.guardian.co.uk (accessed 12 December 2005).

—— (2005d) 'Television will not be revolutionised', *MediaGuardian*, 13 October, http://media.guardian.co.uk (accessed 12 December 2005).

—— (2005e) 'Warnie eyes Hollywood', *Herald Sun* (Melbourne), 15 June.

Totally Frank (2005) 'Mobile episodes', http://www.channel4.com/entertainment/tv/microsites/T/totally_frank/mobile.html (accessed 8 December 2005).

Toyne, P. (1994) 'The potential impacts of future telecommunications developments on Aboriginal people in Australia', in *Planning for an Information Society Project: Population Group Discussion Papers and Policy Issue Discussion Papers*, Melbourne: Telecom Australia, pp. 6–16.

Tracey, M. (1998) *The Decline and Fall of Public Service Broadcasting*, Oxford: Oxford University Press.

Trosby, F. (2004) 'SMS, the strange duckling of GSM', *Telektronikk*, 3: 187–94.

Tryhorn, C. (2005) 'Mobile TV may prove expensive flop, says report', *MediaGuardian*, 9 November, http://media.guardian.co.uk (accessed 12 December 2005).

TTY Forum (2002), 'TTY Forum consensus statement for the FCC', TTY Forum, sponsored by Alliance for Telecommunications Industry Solutions, 27 June, http://www.atis.org/atis/tty/ttyforum.htm (accessed 20 June 2005).

Turner, G. (2004) *Understanding Celebrity*, London: Sage.

Tuttlebee, W., Babb, D., Irvine, J., Martinez, G. and Worrall, K. (2003) 'Broadcasting and mobile telecommunications: internetworking not convergence', *EBU Review*, 293, http://www.ebu.ch/en/technical/trev/trev_293-tuttlebee.pdf.

UMTS Forum (2003) *The Social Shaping of UMTS: Preparing the 3G User*, UMTS Forum, http:/www.umts-forum.org/servlet/dycon/ztumts/umts/Live/en/umts/Resources_Reports_26_index (accessed 17 July 2005).

—— (2005a) 'About the Forum', http://www.umts-forum.org/servlet/dycon/ztumts/umts/Live/en/umts/About_index (accessed 5 November 2005).

—— (2005b) *3G/UMTS: Towards Mobile Broadband and Personal Internet*, UTMS Forum, October, http://www.umts-forum.org/servlet/dycon/ztumts/umts/Live/en/umts/MultiMedia_PDFs_Papers_Towards-Mobile-Broadband-Oct05.pdf (accessed 5 January 2006).

Ungar, S. (2001) 'Moral panic versus the risk society: the implications of the changing sites of social anxiety', *British Journal of Sociology*, 52: 271–92.

Ure, J. (2003a) 'Mobile commerce in Hong Kong', http://www.trp.hku.hk/papers/2003/mobile_mkt.pdf (accessed 25 May 2005).

—— (2003b) 'Perspectives on mobile cellular telecommunications', Paper presented at the Digital News, Social Change and Globalization Conference, Hong Kong Baptist University, 11–12 December, http://www.trp.hku.hk/papers/2003/HKBU-Mobile.pdf (accessed 25 May 2005).

Victorian, T. (1998) 'Update on digital cellular telephone interference and hearing aid compatibility', *Hearing Journal*, 51: 53–60.

—— (2004) 'Hearing aid compatibility: technical update', *Audiology Online*, 12 June, http://www.audiologyonline.com/articles/pf_arc_disp.asp?id=1263 (accessed 25 July 2005).

Victorian, T. and Preves, D. (2004) 'Progress achieved in setting standards for hearing aid/ digital cell phone compatibility', *Hearing Journal*, 57: 25–9.

Vincent, J. (2004) 'Incorporating social shaping into technology planning for 3G/UMTS 2004', proceedings of IEE Fifth International Conference on Mobile Communication Technologies, http://www.surrey.ac.uk/dwrc/Publications/IncorporatingSocialShaping.PDF (accessed 5 January 2006).

Vodafone (2005) 'About Vodafone – history', www.vodafone.com (accessed 25 October 2005).

Vodafone New Zealand (2001) 'Txt messaging provides a world of mobility for the deaf', media release, http://www.vodafone.co.nz/aboutus/media_releases/12.4_20010921.jsp (accessed 31 May 2005).

Vodafone UK (2002) 'Valentine with Vodafone – passion, text fashion', media release, 13 February, www.vodafone.com (accessed 27 September 2005).

The vOICe (2005) 'The vOICe MIDlet for mobile camera phones', http://www.seeingwithsound.com/ (accessed 24 June 2005).

Von Tetzchner, S. (ed.) (1991) *Issues in Telecommunication and Disability*, COST 219, CEC-DGXIII (EUR 13845 EN), Brussels: COST 219.

Waag Society for Old and New Media (2005) 'Frequency 1550', http://freq1550.waag.org (accessed 18 October 2005).

Wajcman, J. (2004) *Technofeminism*, Cambridge: Polity.

Walker, M. and Wright, T. (2001) 'Security', in F. Hillebrand (ed.), *GSM and UMTS: The Creation of Global Mobile Communication*, New York: John Wiley, pp. 385–406.

Wang, J. (2005) 'Youth culture, music and cell phone branding in China', *Global Media and Communication*, 1: 185–201.

Warschauer, M. (2003) *Technology and Social Inclusion: Rethinking the Digital Divide*, Cambridge, MA: MIT Press.

Waters, P. (2004) 'Mobile competition: How many is too many?', ITU Telecom Asia 2004, *ITU Daily*, 10 September, http://www.itudaily.com/new/printarticle.asp?articleid=4091001 (accessed 25 May 2005).

Webb, C. (1998) 'Mobiles to break the sight barrier', *Sun-Herald*, 19 July.

Wetherall, J. and Stukoff, M.N. (2005) 'Mobile-phony', http://mobilebox.typepad.com/photos/blubox/mobilephone.html (accessed 5 January 2006).

Whitaker, J. (1996) 'Charles & Diana', *Mirror*, 13 July.

Wikipedia (2005a) 'Global positioning system', *Wikipedia*, 5 November, http://en.wikipedia.org/w/index.php?title=Global_Positioning_System&oldid=27447944 (accessed 1 November 2005).

—— (2005b) 'iPod', *Wikipedia*, 10 December, http://en.wikipedia.org/w/index.php?title=IPod&oldid=30770660 (accessed 10 December 2005).

—— (2005c) 'Pay as you go (phone)', *Wikipedia*, 1 September, http://en.wikipedia.org/w/index.php?title=Pay_as_you_go_%28phone%29&direction=next-&oldid=22170935 (accessed 25 October 2005).

—— (2005d) 'Vodafone Ireland', *Wikipedia*, 26 July, http://en.wikipedia.org/w/index.php?title=Vodafone_Ireland&oldid=19663880 (accessed 25 October 2005).

—— (2006a) 'Celebrity sex tape', *Wikipedia*, 6 January, http://en.wikipedia.org/w/index.php?title=Celebrity_sex_tape&oldid=34122586 (accessed 9 January 2006).

—— (2006b) 'Kludge', *Wikipedia*, 1 January, http://en.wikipedia.org/w/index.php?title=Kludge&oldid=33488866 (accessed 9 January 2006).

—— (2006c) '1 night in Paris', *Wikipedia*, 7 January, http://en.wikipedia.org/w/index.php?title=1_Night_in_Paris&oldid=34225002 (accessed 7 January 2006).

—— (2006d) 'Paris Hilton', *Wikipedia*, 7 January, http://en.wikipedia.org/w/index.php?title=Paris_Hilton&oldid=34215242 (accessed 7 January 2006).

Wilde, S. (2005) 'The Top 10 Shane Warne moments', *The Sunday Times*, Sport, 15 May.

Wilhelm, A., Takhteyev, Y., Sarvas, R., Van House, N. and Davis, M. (2004) 'Photo annotation on a camera phone', paper presented at *CHI2004*, 24–29 April, Vienna, Austria.

Wilson, T. (2003) *The Playful Audience: From Talk Show Viewers to Internet Users*, Cresskill, NJ: Hampton Press, 2003.

Winston, B. (1998) *Media Technology and Society: A History: From the Telegraph to the Internet*, London: Routledge.

Wintour, P. and Norton-Taylor, R. (1993) 'Clarke refuses Royal bugging inquiry', *The Guardian*, 14 May, 2.

Wisniewski, S. (2005) *Wireless and Cellular Networks*, Upper Saddle River, NJ: Pearson/Prentice Hall.

Wood, A. (1997) 'Students hung up on latest school accessory', *Sydney Morning Herald*, 30 January.

Woolford, K. (2003) 'Reckless Eyes', *Playing Field: Streaming Media Art*, http://www.playingfield.net/kirk.htm (accessed 12 May 2005).

Woolgar, S. (2005) 'Mobiles back to front: uncertainty and danger in the theory–technology relation', in R. Ling and P.E. Pederson (eds), *Mobile Communications: Re-negotiation of the Social Sphere*, London: Springer, pp. 23–44.

World Wide Web Consortium (W3C) (1998) *WAP Forum – W3C Cooperation White Paper*, W3C Note 30 October 1998, http://www.w3.org/TR/NOTE-WAP (accessed 16 August 2005).

Worthington, T. (2005) 'Website design', http://www.tomw.net.au/2005/wd/mobile.html#wap (accessed 16 August 2005).

Wray, R. (2005) 'Phone operator 3 plans to sell advertising on mobiles', *Guardian*, www.guardian.co.uk 19 October.

Wurtzel, J. (2002), 'Deaf go mobile phone crazy', *BBC News*, 8 February, http://news.bbc.co.uk/1/hi/sci/tech/1808872.stm (accessed 1 August 2005).

Young, J.S. and Simon, W.L. (2005) *iCon Steve Jobs: The Greatest Second Act in the History of Business*, New York: John Wiley.

Young, W.R. (1979) 'Advanced mobile phone service: introduction, background, and objectives', *Bell System Technical Journal*, 48: 1–14.

Yu, L. and Tng, T.H. (2003) 'Culture and design for mobile phones for China', in J.E. Katz (ed.), *Machines That Become Us: The Social Context of Personal Communication Technology*, New Brunswick, NJ: Transaction Publishers, pp. 187–200.

Yung, V. (2005) 'The construction of symbolic values of the mobile phone in the Hong Kong Chinese print media', in R. Ling and P.E. Pederson (eds), *Mobile Communications: Re-negotiation of the Social Sphere*, London: Springer, pp. 351–66.

Zimonjic, P. and Hastings, C. (2005) 'Tortured for £75: a victim of the new form of "happy slapping" ', 29 May, *Telegraph.co.uk*, http://telegraph.co.uk (accessed 15 October 2005).

Index

Related titles from Routledge

Language and Creativity
The Art of Common Talk
Ronald Carter

'Ronald Carter has always recognized that casual spontaneous conversation is extraordinarily rich and creative in the way its speakers use the resources of their language. Thanks to the CANCODE corpus he has been able to document this creativity with dialogue taken from real life...The book affords major insights not only into "common talk" but through and beyond this into the nature of language in general'. – *Michael Halliday, University of Sydney, Australia*

Do we just use language? Or do we create it?
Who says only a genius can be creative?
What do our everyday conversations tell us about ourselves?

Creativity in language has conventionally been regarded as the preserve of institutionalised discourses such as literature and advertising, and individual gifted minds. *Language and Creativity* explores the idea that creativity, far from being a property of exceptional people, is an exceptional property of all people.

In this ground-breaking book, Ronald Carter builds on previous theories of creativity, and offers a radical contribution to linguistic, literary and cultural theory. A must for anyone interested in the creativity of our everyday speech.

ISBN10: 0–415–23448–4 (hbk)
ISBN10: 0–415–23449–2 (pbk)

ISBN13: 978–0–415–23448–1 (hbk)
ISBN13: 978–0–415–23449–8 (pbk)

Available at all good bookshops
For ordering and further information please visit:
www.routledge.com

Related titles from Routledge

Everyday Life and Cultural Theory:
An Introduction
Ben Highmore

Everyday Life and Cultural Theory provides a unique critical and historical introduction to theories of everyday life. Ben Highmore traces the development of conceptions of everyday life, from the cultural sociology of Georg Simmel, through the Mass-Observation project of the 1930s to contemporary theorists such as Michel de Certeau.

Individual chapters examine:

- Modernity and everyday life
- Georg Simmel and fragments of everyday life
- Surrealism and the marvellous in the everyday
- Walter Benjamin's trash aesthetics
- Mass-Observation and the science of everyday life
- Henri Lefebvre's dialectics of everyday life
- Michel de Certeau's poetics of everyday life
- Everyday life and the future of cultural studies.

ISBN10: 0–415–22302–4 (hbk)
ISBN10: 0–415–22303–2 (pbk)

ISBN13: 978–0–415–22302–7 (hbk)
ISBN13: 978–0–415–22303–4 (pbk)

Available at all good bookshops
For ordering and further information please visit:
www.routledge.com